Also by Chalmers Johnson

Peasant Nationalism and Communist Power:
The Emergence of Revolutionary China, 1937–1945

Revolution and the Social System

An Instance of Treason:
Ozaki Hotsumi and the Sorge Spy Ring

Revolutionary Change

Change in Communist Systems
(editor and contributor)

Conspiracy at Matsukawa

Ideology and Politics in Contemporary China
(editor)

Autopsy on People's War

Japan's Public Policy Companies

MITI and the Japanese Miracle:
The Growth of Industrial Policy, 1925–1975

The Industrial Policy Debate
(editor and contributor)

Politics and Productivity:
How Japan's Development Strategy Works
(with Laura Tyson and John Zysman)

Japan: Who Governs?
The Rise of the Developmental State

BLOWBACK

BLOWBACK

THE COSTS AND CONSEQUENCES OF AMERICAN EMPIRE

CHALMERS JOHNSON

Metropolitan Books

Henry Holt and Company ▪ New York

Metropolitan Books
Henry Holt and Company, LLC
Publishers since 1866
115 West 18th Street
New York, New York 10011

Metropolitan Books™ is an imprint of
Henry Holt and Company, LLC.

Library of Congress Cataloging-in-Publication Data
Johnson, Chalmers A.
Blowback : the costs and consequences of American empire /
Chalmers Johnson.
p.   cm.
Includes bibliographical references and index.
ISBN 0-8050-6238-6
1. United States—Foreign relations—1989–   2. United States—
Military policy.   3. United States—Foreign relations—Asia.
4. Asia—Foreign relations—United States.   5. Intervention
(International law).   6. Imperialism—United States—History—
20th century.   I. Title.
E840 .J63 2000
327.73—dc21   99-047713

First Edition 2000

Designed by Michelle McMillian

Printed in the United States of America

1   3   5   7   9   10   8   6   4   2

CONTENTS

PROLOGUE:
A SPEAR-CARRIER FOR EMPIRE

Instead of demobilizing after the Cold War, the United States imprudently committed itself to maintaining a global empire. This book is an account of the resentments our policies have built up and of the kinds of economic and political retribution that, particularly in Asia, may be their harvest in the twenty-first century. But before I turn to the sometimes sorry details of the American empire, the reader may want to know a bit about who I am. For how I came to the views presented in this book may help explain why I am putting them forward now, a decade after the end of the Cold War.

Fifty years ago, on the eve of the Korean War, I was an undergraduate at the University of California, Berkeley, majoring in economics. I had given no thought at all to East Asia, but like most Americans I regarded the Communist revolution in China as a dangerous, deeply disturbing development in our country's growing confrontation with what we then called the "Communist bloc." Military conscription was in effect, and any young man had to go into the army—the shortest but most dangerous, unpleasant, and unrewarding way to fulfill one's obligatory service—or join the navy or air force for a longer but less physically demanding hitch.

I chose the navy—or rather I simply drifted into it. My father had served in the navy. In World War I, he went to Europe as an ordinary seaman on the old *St. Louis*. In the summer of 1943, during World War II, his ship was sunk by a long-range Japanese torpedo at Iron Bottom Bay, Guadalcanal. He survived and was in the reserves when, in 1950, as the Korean War began, he was "activated" and sent to Japan for a last fling at naval service. Two older cousins of mine fought in the navy at Leyte Gulf, and the idea that men from my family would do their military duty in the navy was more or less taken for granted.

As an undergraduate, I joined the Naval Air Reserve at Oakland Naval Air Station. I was an aviation machinist's mate third class and flew around in the back of old Grumman Avenger torpedo bombers. Unlike my father's unit, my reserve squadron was never activated during the Korean War. Having spent two summers in training and after receiving a bachelor's degree in 1953, I emerged as a newly minted ensign.

What happened next changed my life, but was also a typical occurrence of the Cold War years. When we received our assignments to the fleet, I was dismayed to discover that I was assigned to a ship that did not even have a name—the U.S.S. *LST-883*, part of the amphibious forces based in Japan. No glamorous aircraft carriers in the Mediterranean for me; I was off to a rust bucket in the Gray Line. A chief petty officer who had been an instructor of mine said to me in his gruff way, "Johnson, you don't know it, but you lucked out. Those guys going to carriers will just be errand boys, but you're going to a ship with only six officers. You'll be given important things to do fast and you won't have to waste a lot of time heel clicking or boot licking." As it turned out, he was absolutely right.

One night in the late summer of 1953, I found myself climbing the sheer ladder of an LST moored to a buoy in the harbor of the former Japanese naval base at Yokosuka, then, as today, the headquarters of the U.S. Seventh Fleet. Used to land tanks directly onto a beachhead during an amphibious assault, LSTs are diesel-powered, flat-bottomed ships with bow doors. Lacking any sort of keel, they roll all the time, even at anchor, and are no place for anyone given to motion sickness. I came aboard the *Hachi-hachi-san* (883, in Japanese) as the communications officer and left two years later as the operations officer.

Although we helped marine and army units practice amphibious landings in Korea and Japan, and twice crossed the Pacific at a top speed of ten knots, our diesel engines broke down regularly. The 883 spent fairly long periods being repaired at either the Yokosuka or Sasebo naval bases. Except for a few weekends in Tijuana, this was my first extended stay outside the United States, and I was enchanted by Japan. So I began to read voraciously in its history and literature. I spent Christmas 1953 in Kyoto among the old temples of Higashiyama; then, in that impoverished postwar land, they were still covered with weeds and in states of serious neglect. I began to study the language with an old Japanese naval officer who did not really believe a foreigner could learn it but was happy to be paid for giving lessons anyway.

War-defeated Japan in the 1950s was as different from the Japan of today as the Depression-era United States was from the world's present-day "lone superpower." Those of us drawn to Japan then could not imagine that two decades later it would be the first "miracle" economy of East Asia. What attracted us were aspects of an artistic and philosophic culture of great power that offered truly fresh insights to a foreigner from the United States. Even though the American occupation had ended a year earlier, I took it for granted that "United Nations Forces" deserved to ride in heated railroad cars while citizens of Japan shivered in ice-cold, often windowless ones at the end of the train. Nor did it seem at all unusual to me that some Yokosuka entrepreneurs had had the good sense to provide an upscale whorehouse for the exclusive use of American naval officers.

I took it for granted as well that the United States had no choice but to confront the evils of Communist totalitarianism politically, militarily, economically, and ideologically; and I assumed that the Cold War in East Asia was not essentially different from the Cold War in Europe. Admittedly, the French, British, and Dutch had been ridiculously slow to give up their Asian colonies, but American support for the European imperialists was just an unfortunate side effect of a necessary, global anti-Communist effort. I had no doubt that the Japanese-American Security

Treaty was a legitimate undertaking meant to shield Japan from revolutionary events elsewhere in Asia and to give it time to evolve into a true democracy.

In 1955, released to inactive duty in the naval reserve, I enrolled as a graduate student at Berkeley. In no rush to find a career, I wanted to put my experiences in Japan into perspective, something the G.I. Bill made possible. Although I returned to Berkeley to study modern Japan, I came under the spell of the university's preeminent historian of China, Joseph R. Levenson. Perhaps more than any other scholar of the time, he succeeded in intellectualizing Chinese history, drawing those of us who heard his lectures into the myriad complexities of Chinese civilization.

With my G.I. Bill benefits running out, I took up Chinese studies seriously, in part because that was where the money was. Some leading intellectual institutions of the time—notably the government's foreign policy and intelligence agencies and the Ford Foundation—were then paying handsomely to attract graduate students into the study of China and, of course, Chinese communism. I saw these fellowships not as inducements to study the enemy in the service of the state but as a wonderful opportunity. I had no hint that, as a student of Asia, I would become as much a spear-carrier for empire as I had been in the navy.

My faculty adviser, political scientist Robert Scalapino, had recently acquired from Ken'ichi Hatano microfilmed files of the Japanese wartime Asia Development Board (Koain), one of the main organs through which Japan had exploited conquered China. Hatano, a former Koain official, had in 1944 moved his office files to his home, thereby saving them from the firebombing of Tokyo. Since I was a graduate student in need of work who could read Japanese, Scalapino hired me to index these once highly classified documents. Buried in them, I discovered a remarkable tale of how after 1937, Japan's armies, bogged down in the interior of China, had resorted to "burn all, loot all, kill all" campaigns against the Chinese peasantry, and so had helped give birth to the most monumental and catastrophic revolutionary movement of our time. To sit alone in the university library at night and see in these dry accounts

Japanese army officers sent back to Tokyo, how the then-minuscule Chinese Communist Party began organizing the peasants who had survived Japanese brutality, was revelatory—and exciting. I knew that I was witnessing, years late, a story still remarkably relevant to postwar Asia, racked with similar revolts against foreign armies of occupation.

Sometime in the late 1950s, I mentioned to Professor Levenson that on-the-spot Western observers of the Chinese Communist movement from 1937 to 1945 had almost uniformly reported on the party's remarkable popularity among ordinary Chinese. Levenson replied that they had all paid a price for such reportage, for every one of them had subsequently been tarred as a leftist and possible traitor by Senator Joseph McCarthy or other red hunters of the time. The firsthand testimony of Edgar Snow, Evans Carlson, Agnes Smedley, Nym Wales, George Taylor, and others was still considered valueless in the America of the late 1950s, coming as it did from those believed, at best, to be ideologically predisposed to accept the Chinese Communists as mere "agrarian reformers."

Having by now read a range of Imperial Japanese Army documents on China, I responded that I could supply secret assessments of the popularity of the Chinese Communist movement in the crucial period of 1937 to 1941 from an unimpeachably anti-Communist source—namely, the Japanese high command in China. Levenson pointed out that such a topic would make a good doctoral dissertation, and so, in 1962, my dissertation was published under the title *Peasant Nationalism and Communist Power: The Emergence of Revolutionary China, 1937–1945.*[1] The book had a significant impact on the study of modern China. The Japanese invaders, I argued, had created conditions of such savagery, particularly in North China, that the peasant masses who survived their depredations naturally gravitated toward the only group that offered them hope and resistance—the Chinese Communist Party. China illustrated what was soon to become a major political lesson of twentieth-century Asia: only in those circumstances in which the most patriotic act is to join the Communist Party does a Communist movement become a mass movement.

On a personal level, *Peasant Nationalism* allowed me to avoid the two worst rites of passage of academic life—getting a job and then tenure. My own university hired me. I was lucky and I worked hard, but I was also in the right place at the right time. Between research stints in Japan and Hong Kong, I made my one and only visit to Saigon, in 1962. I was appalled by our government's policy of "sink or swim with Ngo Dinh Diem." Knowing what I did about guerrilla war, revolutionary politics, and foreign armies, I thought it a mistake for us to involve ourselves further in what was visibly a Vietnamese civil war.[2] But once we did so in the mid-sixties, I was sufficiently aware of Mao Zedong's attempts to export "people's war" to believe that the United States could not afford to lose in Vietnam. In that, too, I was distinctly a man of my times.

It proved to be a disastrously wrong position. The problem was that I knew too much about the international Communist movement and not enough about the Untied States government and its Department of Defense. I was also in those years irritated by campus antiwar protesters, who seemed to me self-indulgent as well as sanctimonious and who had so clearly not done their homework. One day at the height of the protests, I went to the university library to check out what was then available to students on Vietnamese communism, the history of communism in East Asia, and the international Communist movement. I was surprised to find that all the major books were there on the shelves, untouched. The conclusion seemed obvious to me then: these students knew nothing about communism and had no interest in remedying that lack. They were defining the Vietnamese Communists largely out of their own romantic desires to oppose Washington's policies. As it turned out, however, they understood far better than I did the impulses of a Robert McNamara, a McGeorge Bundy, or a Walt Rostow. They grasped something essential about the nature of America's imperial role in the world that I had failed to perceive. In retrospect, I wish I had stood with the antiwar protest movement. For all its naïveté and unruliness, it was right and American policy wrong.

During a year of China-watching (as it was then called) from Hong

Kong, I began to have inklings of the Cultural Revolution to come, and in 1966, I wrote a long piece on how China's People's Liberation Army was being transformed into the personal political instrument of Mao Zedong.[3] As we would later learn, Mao was indeed in the process of allying himself with the army—in order to attack the Communist Party itself, the very organization he had begun building into a mass movement in those years of Japanese occupation. But none of us studying China then came close to imagining what the Cultural Revolution would be like or what kind of a disaster it would become, all because Mao Zedong wanted revenge on some of his fellow revolutionaries. Before the savagery ended with Mao's death in 1976, the so-called Cultural Revolution came to resemble Stalin's purges of the late 1930s. It destroyed the last shreds of Chinese idealism about the promise of communism.

The Cultural Revolution isolated China from the First, Second, and Third Worlds. It became a pariah state, unable even to forge a united front with the Soviet Union to support the Vietnamese Communists. China and Russia came perilously close to war. The only stable person left among the top Chinese leadership, Premier Zhou Enlai, sought to avoid a preemptive Soviet strike against China's fledgling nuclear weapons program by opening relations with the devil himself—the United States. President Nixon and his national security adviser, Henry Kissinger, jumped at the opportunity, and Sino-American rapprochement unfolded—against a backdrop of the war in Vietnam, Watergate, and China's purge of anyone not totally committed to the cult of Mao. Nixon's visit to China in 1972 renewed popular interest in an etherealized China of acupuncture, the Great Wall, ancient cultural artifacts, and pandas—just as the real land was being run into the ground by its most despicable twentieth-century regime.

Like other foreign specialists in Chinese politics, I was active in trying to understand what was going on, writing papers and attending conferences where Chinese matters were discussed. In 1967, at age thirty-six, I was appointed chairman of Berkeley's Center for Chinese

Studies. Perhaps the most important action I took in my five years at the center was to hire, as our librarian, John Service, one of America's great State Department China hands of the 1940s, who had been savaged by Senator Joseph McCarthy and whose career in the Foreign Service had been ruined. When, after Kissinger's initial visit, Zhou Enlai told American reporters that Service was one of only three Americans the Chinese would welcome back (the other two were Professors John Fairbank and Owen Lattimore), we at the center hastily helped arrange for his trip. I can vividly remember him calling me on the day in July 1971 when it was announced that President Nixon had accepted an invitation from Mao Zedong to visit China. As much as he hated Nixon, he told me, he had to give him credit as virtually the only conceivable president who could have brought off such a breakthrough.

American university campuses in the late sixties and early seventies were not ideal places for anyone who doubted that Mao Zedong was a true scourge of bureaucracy or who questioned whether there was any wisdom at all in his "Little Red Book" of sayings. Campus Maoism was everywhere, fueled by the general euphoria over China that Nixon and Kissinger had unleashed. (Let us not forget that even seasoned journalists like James Reston and Harrison Salisbury of the *New York Times* went a little gaga over the China they thought they saw.)

It was clear to me, however, that the Chinese "revolution" had degenerated into a Herodian horror show, destructive to the lives of all honest Chinese—fascinating to monitor, perhaps, but no longer of great significance to the global balance of power. In Japan, on the other hand, something interesting *was* going on to which no one in America seemed to be paying serious attention. In the summer of 1972, I returned to a Japan well on its way toward becoming the most advanced industrial nation on earth. The contrast with my earliest naval experiences there or with the Japan of 1961, when my wife and I had set up a household in a Tokyo suburb, was stark indeed. Japan's economic "miracle" (a term used by Westerners to denote something attractive but from their point of view unexpected) was everywhere becoming obvious. Its economy had been growing for fifteen years at an annual rate of around 10 percent, and the results were starting to come in. Japan was producing a line of automobiles that American and East Asian consumers were beginning to buy in large numbers, thanks to their low price, reliability, fuel efficiency, built-in air-conditioning, and compact size. In design, its cameras, consumer electronics, and ships, among many other products, rivaled in simplicity and elegance the traditional designs of its houses and ceramics.

To a China specialist disillusioned by the savageries of the Cultural Revolution, Japan looked like a unique case of successful socialism in one country. A state bureaucracy guided the economy, setting social goals but avoiding the misallocation of resources, loss of incentives, and extreme rigidity that were hallmark features of the Soviet and Chinese economies. How had it done this? Americans were largely uninterested in answering such a question, even though Japan's trade surpluses were starting to irritate their government. Americans were not even curious about the new institutional structures that Japan had forged to engineer high-speed economic growth, structures that would prevent any quick or easy solution to the trade imbalance. We still saw Japan as a "little brother," learning from and emulating its postwar mentor. The idea that Japan could be experimenting with a different form of capitalism was, if even imaginable, certainly heresy. That they were beating us in manufacturing and marketing certain major products had to mean they were cheating.

Americans defined Japan as a democracy organized around a free-market economy, just as the United States itself was said to be. In his memoirs, Edwin O. Reischauer—the best-known American specialist on Japanese history and ambassador to Japan during the 1960s, at the height of that country's "income-doubling plan"—hardly bothered to mention the economy. The truly amazing thing about such American myopia and condescension was that it would last well into the late 1990s, when it would suddenly turn into contempt for Japan precisely because it had a different kind of capitalism.

In the summer of 1972, one of my mentors and a preeminent political scientist, Professor Junnosuke Masumi, urged me to consider the then-emerging economic miracle. American scholars like me, he pointed out, tended to focus on left-wing and protest politics in Japan; virtually none of us had devoted any attention to its ruling elites. There were only a few studies in English of the Liberal Democratic Party, which had been continuously in power since the country had regained its independence in 1952, and nothing at all on the vast bureaucratic state apparatus that supported and guided the economy in much the same way the Department of Defense supported and guided the military-industrial-university complex in the United States.

We talked specifically about the Ministry of International Trade and Industry (MITI). Among knowledgeable Japanese in the Tokyo of that moment, it was the openly acknowledged author of the economic miracle. Much as Professor Levenson had suggested that I look into Japanese-occupied China to find the roots of the Chinese Communist Party's success, so Professor Masumi suggested that I look into the roots of MITI to find the basis for his country's "successful socialism." I spent the next decade on this project, writing a history of an economic ministry that I thought might interest a few public policy specialists who did not read Japanese, as well as the usual group of Japanologists. I did not realize then that my research would inadvertently lead me to see clearly for the first time the shape of the empire that I had so long uncritically supported.

I have already indicated the main intellectual debts I owe. For help in conceptualizing and writing this particular book, I would like to acknowledge the following people, who gave me ideas, told me I was wrong, or otherwise provided inspiration: Sumi Adachi, Kozy Amemiya, Ron Bevacqua, Steven C. Clemons, Bruce Cumings, Jim Fallows, Patrick Lloyd Hatcher, George Hicks, Jim Impoco, Sam Jameson, Andrew Janos, Barry Keehn, Andrew MacIntyre, Gavan McCormack, Yoshihiko Nakamoto, Masahide Ota, Murray Sayle, Tim Shorrock, Patrick Smith, Odete Sousa, Koji Taira, Norman Thorpe, Chikako Yoshida, and Eiji Yutani. The monthly papers and conference presentations of members of the Japan Policy Research Institute over the past six years have also contributed greatly to my thinking. Sandra Dijkstra, my agent, was instrumental in causing me to write this book. At Metropolitan Books, Tom

Engelhardt was the best editor an author could imagine, meticulous in challenging and sharpening my ideas and my writing; publisher Sara Bershtel encouraged me with her unflagging commitment to the book. Sheila K. Johnson has been my constant companion in trying to understand the world we live in.

Cardiff, California
July 1999

BLOWBACK

BLOWBACK

Northern Italian communities had, for years, complained about low-flying American military aircraft. In February 1998, the inevitable happened. A Marine Corps EA-6B Prowler with a crew of four, one of scores of advanced American jet fighters and bombers stationed at places like Aviano, Cervia, Brindisi, and Sigonella, sliced through a ski-lift cable near the resort town of Cavalese and plunged twenty people riding in a single gondola to their deaths on the snowy slopes several hundred feet below. Although marine pilots are required to maintain an altitude of at least one thousand feet (two thousand, according to the Italian government), the plane had cut the cable at a height of 360 feet. It was traveling at 621 miles per hour when 517 miles per hour was considered the upper limit. The pilot had been performing low-level acrobatics while his copilot took pictures on videotape (which he later destroyed).

In response to outrage in Italy and calls for vigorous prosecution of those responsible, the marine pilots argued that their charts were inaccurate, that their altimeter had not worked, and that they had not consulted U.S. Air Force units permanently based in the area about local hazards. A court-martial held not in Italy but in Camp Lejeune, North Carolina, exonerated everyone involved, calling it a "training accident." Soon after, President Bill Clinton apologized and promised financial compensation to the victims, but on May 14, 1999, Congress dropped the provision for aid to the families because of opposition in the House of Representatives and from the Pentagon.[1]

This was hardly the only such incident in which American service personnel victimized foreign civilians in the post–Cold War world. From Germany and Turkey to Okinawa and South Korea, similar incidents have been common—as has been their usual denouement. The United States government never holds politicians or higher-ranking military officers responsible and seldom finds that more should be done beyond offering pro forma apologies and perhaps financial compensation of some, often minimal sort.

On rare occasions, as with the Italian cable cutting, when such a local tragedy rises to the level of global news, what often seems strangest to Americans is the level of national outrage elsewhere over what the U.S. media portray as, at worst, an apparently isolated incident, however tragic to those involved. Certainly, the one subject beyond discussion at such moments is the fact that, a decade after the end of the Cold War, hundreds of thousands of American troops, supplied with the world's most advanced weaponry, sometimes including nuclear arms, are stationed on over sixty-one base complexes in nineteen countries worldwide, using the Department of Defense's narrowest definition of a "major installation"; if one included every kind of installation that houses representatives of the American military, the number would rise to over eight hundred.[2] There are, of course, no Italian air bases on American soil. Such a thought would be ridiculous. Nor, for that matter, are there German, Indonesian, Russian, Greek, or Japanese troops stationed on Italian soil. Italy is, moreover, a close ally of the United States, and no conceivable enemy nation endangers its shores.

All this is almost too obvious to state—and so is almost never said. It is simply not a matter for discussion, much less of debate in the land of the last imperial power. Perhaps similar thinking is second nature to any imperium. Perhaps the Romans did not find it strange to have their troops in Gaul, nor the British in South Africa. But what is unspoken is no less real, nor does it lack consequences just because it is not part of any ongoing domestic discussion.

I believe it is past time for such a discussion to begin, for Americans to consider why we have created an empire—a word from which we shy away—and what the consequences of our imperial stance may be for the rest of the world and for ourselves. Not so long ago, the way we garrisoned the world could be discussed far more openly and comfortably because the explanation seemed to lie at hand—in the very existence of the Soviet Union and of communism. Had the Italian disaster occurred two decades earlier, it would have seemed no less a tragedy, but many Americans would have argued that, given the Cold War, such incidents were an unavoidable cost of protecting democracies like Italy against the menace of Soviet totalitarianism. With the disappearance of any military threat faintly comparable to that posed by the former Soviet Union, such "costs" have become easily avoidable. American military forces could have been withdrawn from Italy, as well as from other foreign bases, long ago. That they were not and that Washington instead is doing everything in its considerable powers to perpetuate Cold War structures, even without the Cold War's justification, places such overseas deployments in a new light. They have become striking evidence, for those who care to look, of an imperial project that the Cold War obscured. The by-products of this project are likely to build up reservoirs of resentment against all Americans—tourists, students, and businessmen, as well as members of the armed forces—that can have lethal results.

For any empire, including an unacknowledged one, there is a kind of balance sheet that builds up over time. Military crimes, accidents, and atrocities make up only one category on the debit side of the balance sheet that the United States has been accumulating, especially since the Cold War ended. To take an example of quite a different kind of debit, consider South Korea, a longtime ally. On Christmas Eve 1997, it declared itself financially bankrupt and put its economy under the guidance of the International Monetary Fund, which is basically an institutional surrogate of the United States government. Most Americans were surprised by the economic disasters that overtook Thailand, South Korea, Malaysia, and Indonesia in 1997 and that then spread around the world, crippling the Russian and Brazilian economies. They could hardly imagine that the U.S. government might have had a hand in causing them, even though various American pundits and economists expressed open delight in these disasters, which threw millions of people, who had previously had hopes of achieving economic prosperity and security, into the most abysmal poverty. At worst, Americans took the economic meltdown of places like Indonesia and Brazil to mean that beneficial American-supported policies of "globalization" were working—that we were effectively helping restructure various economies around the world so that they would look and work more like ours.

Above all, the economic crisis of 1997 was taken as evidence that our main doctrinal competitors—the high-growth capitalist economies of East Asia—were hardly either as competitive or as successful as they imagined. In a New Year's commentary, the columnist Charles Krauthammer mused, "Our success is the success of the American capitalist model, which lies closer to the free market vision of Adam Smith than any other. Much closer, certainly, than Asia's paternalistic crony capitalism that so seduced critics of the American system during Asia's now-burst bubble."[3]

As the global crisis deepened, the thing our government most seemed to fear was that contracts to buy our weapons might now not be honored. That winter, Secretary of Defense William Cohen made special trips to Jakarta, Bangkok, and Seoul to cajole the governments of those countries to use increasingly scarce foreign exchange funds to pay for the American fighter jets, missiles, warships, and other hardware the Pentagon had sold them before the economic collapse. He also stopped in Tokyo to urge on a worried Japanese government a big sale not yet agreed to. He wanted Japan to invest in the theater missile defense system, or TMD, antimissile missiles that the Pentagon has been trying to get the Japanese to buy for a decade. No one knew then or knows now whether the TMD will even work—in fifteen years of intercept attempts only a few missiles in essentially doctored tests have hit their targets—but it is unquestionably expensive, and arms sales, both domestic and foreign, have become one of the Pentagon's most important missions.

I believe the profligate waste of our resources on irrelevant weapons systems and the Asian economic meltdown, as well as the continuous trail of military "accidents" and of terrorist attacks on American installations and embassies, are all portents of a twenty-first-century crisis in America's informal empire, an empire based on the projection of military power to every corner of the world and on the use of American capital and markets to force global economic integration on our terms, at whatever costs to others. To predict the future is an undertaking no thoughtful person would rush to embrace. What form our imperial crisis is likely to take years or even decades from now is, of course, impossible to know. But history indicates that, sooner or later, empires do reach such moments, and it seems reasonable to assume that we will not miraculously escape that fate.

What we have freed ourselves of, however, is any genuine consciousness of how we might look to others on this globe. Most Americans are probably unaware of how Washington exercises its global hegemony, since so much of this activity takes place either in relative secrecy or under comforting rubrics. Many may, as a start, find it hard to believe that our place in the world even adds up to an empire. But only when we come to see our country as both profiting from and trapped within the structures of an empire of its own making will it be possible for us to explain many elements of the world that otherwise perplex us. Without good explanations, we cannot possibly produce policies that will bring us sustained peace and prosperity in a post–Cold War world. What has gone wrong in Japan after half a century of government-guided growth under U.S. protection? Why should the emergence of a strong China be to anyone's disadvantage? Why do American policies toward human rights, weapons proliferation, terrorism, drug cartels, and the environment strike so many foreigners as the essence of hypocrisy? Should American-owned and -managed multinational firms be instruments, beneficiaries, or adversaries of United States foreign policy? Is the free flow of capital really as valuable as free trade in commodities and manufactured goods? These kinds of questions can only be answered once we begin to grasp what the United States really is.

If Washington is the headquarters of a global military-economic dominion, the answers will be very different than if we think of the United States as simply one among many sovereign nations. There is a logic to empire that differs from the logic of a nation, and acts committed in service to an empire but never acknowledged as such have a tendency to haunt the future.

The term "blowback," which officials of the Central Intelligence Agency first invented for their own internal use, is starting to circulate among students of international relations. It refers to the unintended consequences of policies that were kept secret from the American people. What the daily press reports as the malign acts of "terrorists" or "drug lords" or "rogue states" or "illegal arms merchants" often turn out to be blowback from earlier American operations.

It is now widely recognized, for example, that the 1988 bombing of Pan Am flight 103 over Lockerbie, Scotland, which resulted in the deaths of 259 passengers and 11 people on the ground, was retaliation for a 1986 Reagan administration aerial raid on Libya that killed President Muammar Khadaffi's stepdaughter. Some in the United States have suspected that other events can also be explained as blowback from imperial acts. For example, the epidemic of cocaine and heroin use that has afflicted American cities during the past two decades was probably fueled in part by Central and South American military officers or corrupt politicians whom the CIA or the Pentagon once trained or supported and then installed in key government positions. For example, in Nicaragua in the 1980s, the U.S. government organized a massive campaign against the socialist-oriented Sandinista government. American agents then looked the other way when the Contras, the military insurgents they had trained, made deals to sell cocaine in American cities in order to buy arms and supplies.[4]

If drug blowback is hard to trace to its source, bomb attacks, whether on U.S. embassies in Africa, the World Trade Center in New York City, or an apartment complex in Saudi Arabia that housed U.S. servicemen, are another matter. One man's terrorist is, of course, another man's freedom fighter, and what U.S. officials denounce as unprovoked terrorist attacks on its innocent citizens are often meant as retaliation for previous American imperial actions. Terrorists attack innocent and undefended American targets precisely because American soldiers and sailors firing cruise missiles from ships at sea or sitting in B-52 bombers at extremely high altitudes or supporting brutal and repressive regimes from Washington seem invulnerable. As members of the Defense Science Board wrote in a 1997 report to the undersecretary of defense for acquisition and technology, "Historical data show a strong correlation between U.S. involvement in international situations and an increase in terrorist attacks against the United States. In addition, the military asymmetry that denies nation states the ability to engage in overt attacks against the United States drives the use of transnational actors [that is, terrorists from one country attacking in another]."[5]

The most direct and obvious form of blowback often occurs when the victims fight back after a secret American bombing, or a U.S.-sponsored campaign of state terrorism, or a CIA-engineered overthrow of a foreign political leader. All around the world today, it is possible to see the groundwork being laid for future forms of blowback. For example, it is estimated that from the Gulf War of 1991 through 1998, the U.S.-sponsored blockade of Saddam Hussein's Iraq has helped contribute to the deaths of an estimated half million Iraqi civilians due to disease, malnutrition, and inadequate medical care. President Clinton's national security adviser, Sandy Berger, takes pride in the thought that this blockade has been "unprecedented for its severity in the whole of world history." By 1999, it had still not brought down Saddam Hussein, the single-minded goal of American policy in the area, but it had ensured that surviving Iraqis were likely to hold a grudge against the American government and its citizens. At the same time, the slipping of "CIA paramilitary covert operators" onto the United Nations teams of postwar weapons inspectors in Iraq, who were charged with uncovering Saddam

Hussein's efforts to develop weapons of mass destruction, has ensured that one of the most promising experiments in nonproliferation controls has been tainted forever.[6]

Blowback itself can lead to more blowback, in a spiral of destructive behavior. A good illustration of this lies in the government's reaction to the August 7, 1998, bombings of American embassy buildings in Nairobi and Dar es Salaam, with the loss of 12 American and 212 Kenyan and Tanzanian lives and some 4,500 injured. The U.S. government promptly placed the blame on Osama bin Laden, a Saudi who had long denounced his country's rulers and their American allies. On August 20, the United States retaliated by firing nearly eighty cruise missiles (at a cost of $750,000 each) into a pharmaceutical plant in Khartoum, Sudan, and an old mujahideen camp site in Afghanistan. (One missile went four hundred miles off course and landed in Pakistan.) Both missile targets had been identified by American intelligence as enterprises or training areas associated with bin Laden or his followers. It was soon revealed, however, that the intelligence on both places had been faulty and that neither target could be connected with those who were suspected of attacking the embassies. On September 2, 1998, the U.S. secretary of defense said that he had been unaware that the plant in Khartoum made medicines, not nerve gas, when he recommended that it be attacked. He also admitted that the plant's connection to bin Laden was, at best, "indirect."[7] Nonetheless, President Clinton continued to insist that he had repelled an "imminent threat to our national security," and Secretary of State Madeleine Albright called Sudan a "viper's nest of terrorists."

Government spokesmen continue to justify these attacks as "deterring" terrorism, even if the targets proved to be irrelevant to any damage done to facilities of the United States. In this way, future blowback possibilities are seeded into the world. The same spokesmen ignore the fact that the alleged mastermind of the embassy bombings, bin Laden, is a former protégé of the United States. When America was organizing Afghan rebels against the USSR in the 1980s, he played an important role in driving the Soviet Union from Afghanistan and only turned against the United States in 1991 because he regarded the stationing of American troops in his native Saudi Arabia during and after the Persian Gulf War as a violation of his religious beliefs. Thus, the attacks on our embassies in Africa, if they were indeed his work, are an instance of blowback rather than unprovoked terrorism. Instead of bombing sites in Sudan and Afghanistan in response, the United States might better have considered reducing or removing our large-scale and provocative military presence in Saudi Arabia.

There are more effective—and certainly less destructive—ways of dealing with the threat of "terrorism" than instant military retaliation. In 1994, patient and firm negotiations finally resulted in the Sudan's turning over the terrorist known as Carlos to the French government for trial; and in September 1998, Libya finally agreed to surrender to a Dutch court the two men charged with bombing the Pan Am airliner over Lockerbie, Scotland. The latter agreement came about through a multilateral reliance on international law and an economic embargo of Libya and so avoided the spiral of blowback and retaliation that is undoubtedly not yet at an end in the case of bin Laden.

Needless to say, blowback is not exclusively a problem faced by Americans. One has only to look at Russia and its former satellites today to see exactly how devastating imperial blowback can be. The hostage crisis of 1996–97 at the Japanese embassy in Lima, in which a handful of Peruvian revolutionaries took virtually the entire diplomatic corps hostage, was probably blowback from Japan's support for the antiguerrilla policies of President Alberto Fujimori and for the operations of Japanese multinational corporations in Peru. Israel's greatest single political problem is the daily threat of blowback from the Palestinian people and their Islamic allies because of Israeli policies of displacing Palestinians from their lands and repressing those that remain under their jurisdiction. The United States, however, is the world's most prominent target for blowback, being the world's lone imperial power, the primary source of the sort of secret and semisecret operations that shore up repressive regimes, and by far the largest seller of weapons generally.

It is typical of an imperial people to have a short memory for its less pleasant imperial acts, but for those on the receiving end, memory can be long indeed. Among the enduring sources of blowback, for instance, are the genocidal cruelties some nations have perpetrated during wartime. Japan to this day is trying to come to grips with the consequences of its actions in China during World War II. Japanese reactionaries are still reluctant to face atrocities committed in China and Korea: the rape of Nanking, conscription of conquered women to serve as prostitutes for frontline troops, and gruesome medical experimentation on prisoners of war are but the better known of these. But given the passage of time and some payment of compensation, many Chinese would probably accept a sincere apology for these events. However, Japanese armies also terrorized and radicalized an essentially conservative peasant population and thereby helped bring the Chinese Communist Party to power, leading to thirty million deaths during the Great Leap Forward and savaging Chinese civilization during the Cultural Revolution. There are many educated Chinese who can never forgive Japan for contributing to this outcome.

Today, we know of several similar cases. In pursuing the war in Vietnam in the early 1970s, President Richard Nixon and his national security adviser Henry Kissinger ordered more bombs dropped on rural Cambodia than had been dropped on Japan during all of World War II, killing at least three-quarters of a million Cambodian peasants and helping legitimize the murderous Khmer Rouge movement under Pol Pot. In his subsequent pursuit of revenge and ideological purity Pol Pot ensured that another million and a half Cambodians, this time mainly urban dwellers, were murdered.

Americans generally think of Pol Pot as some kind of unique, self-generated monster and his "killing fields" as an inexplicable atavism totally divorced from civilization. But without the United States government's Vietnam-era savagery, he could never have come to power in a culture like Cambodia's, just as Mao's uneducated peasant radicals would never have gained legitimacy in a normal Chinese context without the disruption and depravity of the Japanese war. Significantly, in its calls for an international tribunal to try the remaining leaders of the

Khmer Rouge for war crimes, the United States has demanded that such a court restrict its efforts to the period from 1975 to 1979—that is, after the years of carpet bombing were over and before the U.S. government began to collaborate with the Khmer Rouge against the Vietnamese Communists, who invaded Cambodia in 1978, drove the Khmer Rouge from power, and were trying to bring some stability to the country.

Even an empire cannot control the long-term effects of its policies. That is the essence of blowback. Take the civil war in Afghanistan in the 1980s, in which Soviet forces directly intervened on the government side and the CIA armed and supported any and all groups willing to face the Soviet armies. Over the years the fighting turned Kabul, once a major center of Islamic culture, into a facsimile of Hiroshima after the bomb. American policies helped ensure that the Soviet Union would suffer the same kind of debilitating defeat in Afghanistan as the United States had in Vietnam. In fact, the defeat so destabilized the Soviet regime that at the end of the 1980s it collapsed. But in Afghanistan the United States also helped bring to power the Taliban, a fundamentalist Islamic movement whose policies toward women, education, justice, and economic well-being resemble not so much those of Ayatollah Khomeini's Iran as those of Pol Pot's Cambodia. A group of these mujahideen, who only a few years earlier the United States had armed with ground-to-air Stinger missiles, grew bitter over American acts and policies in the Gulf War and vis-à-vis Israel. In 1993, they bombed the World Trade Center in New York and assassinated several CIA employees as they waited at a traffic light in Langley, Virginia. Four years later, on November 12, 1997, after the Virginia killer had been convicted by an American court, unknown assailants shot and killed four American accountants, unrelated in any way to the CIA, in their car in Karachi, Pakistan, in retaliation.

It is likely that U.S. covert policies have helped create similar conditions in the Congo, Guatemala, and Turkey, and that we are simply waiting for the blowback to occur. Guatemala is a particularly striking example of American imperial policies in its own "backyard." In 1954, the Eisenhower administration planned and the CIA organized and funded a military coup that overthrew a Guatemalan president whose modest land reform policies were considered a threat to American corporations. Blowback from this led to a Marxist guerrilla insurgency in the 1980s and so to CIA- and Pentagon-supported genocide against Mayan peasants. In the spring of 1999, a report on the Guatemalan civil war from the U.N.-sponsored Commission for Historical Clarification made clear that "the American training of the officer corps in counter-insurgency techniques" was a "key factor" in the "genocide. . . . Entire Mayan villages were attacked and burned and their inhabitants were slaughtered in an effort to deny the guerrillas protection."[8] According to the commission, between 1981 and 1983 the military government of Guatemala—financed and supported by the U.S. government—destroyed some four hundred Mayan villages in a campaign of genocide in which approximately two hundred thousand peasants were killed. José Pertierra, an attorney representing Jennifer Harbury, an American lawyer who spent years trying to find out what happened to her "disappeared" Guatemalan husband and supporter of the guerrillas, Efraín Bámaca Velásquez, writes that the Guatemalan military officer who arrested, tortured, and murdered Bámaca was a CIA "asset" and was paid $44,000 for the information he obtained from him.[9]

Visiting Guatemala in March 1999, soon after the report's release, President Clinton said, "It is important that I state clearly that support for military forces and intelligence units which engaged in violence and widespread repression was wrong, and the United States must not repeat that mistake. . . . The United States will no longer take part in campaigns of repression."[10] But on virtually the day that the president was swearing off "dirty tricks" in other people's countries, his government was reasserting its support for Turkey in its war of repression against its Kurdish minority.

The Kurds constitute fifteen million people in a Turkish population estimated at fifty-eight million. Another five million Kurds live largely within reach of Turkey's borders in Iraq, Iran, and Syria. The Turks have discriminated against the Kurds for the past seventy years and have conducted an intense genocidal campaign against them since 1992, in the process destroying some three thousand Kurdish villages and hamlets in the backward southeastern part of the country. Former American ambassador to Croatia Peter W. Galbraith comments that "Turkey routinely jails Kurdish politicians for activities that would be protected speech in democratic countries."[11] The Europeans have so far barred Turkey from the European Union because of its treatment of the Kurds. Because of its strategic location on the border of the former Soviet Union, however, Turkey was a valued American ally and NATO member during the Cold War, and the United States maintains the relationship unchanged even though the USSR has disappeared.

After Israel and Egypt, Turkey is the third-highest recipient of American military assistance. Between 1991 and 1995, the United States supplied four-fifths of Turkey's military imports, which were among the largest in the world. The U.S. government, in turn, depends on the NATO base at Incirlik, Turkey, to carry out Operation Provide Comfort, set up after the Gulf War to supply and protect Iraqi Kurds from repression by Saddam Hussein—at the same time that the United States acquiesces in Turkish mistreatment of its far larger Kurdish population. One obvious reason is that communities like Stratford and Bridgeport, Connecticut, where Black Hawk and Comanche helicopters are made, depend for their economic health on continued large-scale arms sales to countries like Turkey. At the time of the Gulf War, a senior adviser to the Turkish prime minister said to John Shattuck, assistant secretary of state for human rights, "If you want to stop human rights abuses do two things—stop IMF credits and cut off aid from the Pentagon. But don't sell the weapons and give aid and then complain about the Kurdish issue. Don't tell us about human rights while you're selling these weapons."[12]

The capture in February 1999 of the Kurdish guerrilla leader Abdullah Ocalan exposed the nature of American involvement with Turkey, in this case via a CIA gambit that holds promise as a rich source of future blowback. The CIA term for this policy is "disruption," by which it means the harassment of terrorists around the world. The point is to flush them out of hiding so that cooperative police forces or secret services can then arrest and imprison them. According to John Diamond of the Associated Press, "The CIA keeps its role secret, and the foreign countries that actually crack down on the suspects carefully hide the U.S. role, lest they stir up trouble for themselves." There are no safeguards at all against misidentifying "suspects," and "the CIA sends no formal notice to Congress." Disruption is said to be a preemptive, offensive form of counterterrorism. Richard Clarke, President Clinton's antiterrorism czar, likes it because he can avoid "the cumbersome Congressional reporting requirements that go with CIA-directed covert operations" and because "human rights organizations would have no way of identifying a CIA role." The CIA has carried out disruption operations in at least ten countries since September 1998. In the case of Ocalan's capture, the United States "provided Turkey with critical information about Ocalan's whereabouts." This was the first time some of the details of a "disruption" campaign were made public.[13]

In many other countries there are milder or subtler versions of these kinds of covert manipulations that may lead to future blowback. To take but one example, the U.S. State Department recently published volume 22 of *Foreign Relations of the United States, 1961–1963*, the official chronicle of American foreign policy, in this case devoted to relations between the United States, China, Korea, and Japan thirty-five or more years ago. Nonetheless, the government refused to declassify some 13.5 percent of the documents that should have been included in the section on Japan, particularly materials relating to military operations and U.S. bases in that country. For the first time, the Advisory Committee on Historical Diplomatic Documentation, charged by law with supervising the editing and publication of this venerable series, wrote in the Preface that volume 22 "does not constitute a 'thorough, accurate, and reliable documentary record of major United States foreign policy decisions.'" The State Department, surely under instructions from the CIA and the Department of Defense, took the unusual step of holding back key documents—undoubtedly involving among other matters secret CIA payments to the conservative, long-ruling Liberal Democratic Party and its leading politicians, as well as the presence of nuclear arms at American bases in Japan, fearing that their publication might result in the kind of blowback of which a poor Third World country like Guatemala would be incapable, but which Japan might well undertake.

In a sense, blowback is simply another way of saying that a nation reaps what it sows. Although people usually know what they have sown, our national experience of blowback is seldom imagined in such terms because so much of what the managers of the American empire have sown has been kept secret. As a concept, blowback is obviously most easy to grasp in its most straightforward manifestation. The unintended consequences of American policies and acts in country X are a bomb at an American embassy in country Y or a dead American in country Z. Certainly any number of Americans have been killed in that fashion, from Catholic nuns in El Salvador to tourists in Uganda who just happened to wander into hidden imperial scenarios about which they knew nothing. But blowback, as demonstrated in this book, is hardly restricted to such reasonably straightforward examples.

From the hollowing out of key American industries due to Japan's export-led economic policies to refugee flows across our southern borders from countries where U.S.-supported repression has created genocidal conditions or where U.S.-supported economic policies have led to unbearable misery, blowback can hit in less obvious and more subtle ways and over long periods of time. It can also manifest itself domestically in ways that are often not evident, even to those who created or carried out the initial imperial policies.

Because we live in an increasingly interconnected international system, we are all, in a sense, living in a blowback world. Although the term originally applied only to the unintended consequences for *Americans* of American policies, there is every reason to widen its meaning. Whether, for example, any unintended consequences of the American policies that fostered and then heightened the economic collapse of Indonesia in 1997 ever blow back to the United States, the unintended consequences for Indonesians have been staggering levels of suffering, poverty, and loss of hope. Similarly, the unintended consequences of American-supported coups and bombing in Cambodia in the early 1970s were unimaginable chaos, disruption, and death for Cambodians later in the decade.

Our role in the military coup in Chile in 1973, for example, produced little blowback onto the United States itself but had lethal consequences for liberals, socialists, and innocent bystanders in Chile and elsewhere. On the nature of American policies in Chile, journalist Jon Lee Anderson reports, "The plan, according to declassified United States government documents, was to make Chile ungovernable under [elected socialist president Salvador] Allende, provoke social chaos, and bring about a military coup. . . . A CIA cable outlined the objectives clearly to the station chief in Santiago: 'It is firm and continuing policy that Allende be overthrown by a coup. . . . We are to continue to generate maximum pressure toward this end utilizing every appropriate resource. It is imperative that these actions be implemented clandestinely and securely so that United States Government and American hand be well hidden.' "[14]

No ordinary citizen of the United States knew anything about these machinations. The coup d'état took place on September 11, 1973, resulting in the suicide of Allende and the seizure of power by General Augusto Pinochet, whose military and civilian supporters in their seventeen years in power tortured, killed, or "disappeared" some four thousand people. Pinochet was an active collaborator in Operation Condor, a joint mission with the Argentine militarists to murder exiled dissidents in the United States, Spain, Italy, and elsewhere. This is why, when Pinochet traveled to England in the autumn of 1998 for medical treatment, Spain tried to extradite him to stand trial for genocide, torture, and state terrorism against Spanish citizens. On October 16, 1998, the British police arrested Pinochet in London and held him pending his possible extradition.

Although few Americans were affected by this covert operation, people around the world now know of the American involvement and were deeply cynical when Secretary of State Madeleine Albright opposed Pinochet's extradition, claiming that countries like Chile undertaking a "transition to democracy" must be allowed to guarantee immunity from prosecution to past human rights offenders in order to "move forward."[15] America's "dirty hands" make even the most well-intentioned statement about human rights or terrorism seem hypocritical in such circumstances. Even when blowback mostly strikes other peoples, it has its corrosive effects on the United States by debasing political discourse and making citizens feel duped if they should happen to take seriously what their political leaders say. This is an inevitable consequence not just of blowback but of empire itself.

What, then, of the very idea of an American empire or, for that matter, American imperialism? "Hegemony," "empire," and "imperialism" have often been used as epithets or fighting words. They lie at the heart of Marx's and, especially, Lenin's condemnation of capitalism. During the Cold War, Communists asserted that imperialism was one of the "contradictions" of capitalism and hence a root cause of class struggle, revolution, and war. However, the terms also evoke images of the Roman and British empires, as well as of the Pax Romana and the Pax Britannica that were said to have accompanied them. Imperialism is further associated with the racism and exploitation that accompanied European, American, and Japanese colonialism in the nineteenth and twentieth centuries and with the violent reactions to it that dominated the non-Western world in the wake of the Second World War.

In speaking of an "American empire," however, I am not using the concept in these traditional senses. I am not talking about the United States' former colony in the Philippines, or about such dependent territories as Puerto Rico; nor when I use the term "imperialism" in this book do I mean the extension of one state's legal dominion over another; nor do I even want to imply that imperialism must have primarily economic causes. The more modern empires I have in mind normally lie concealed beneath some ideological or juridical concept—commonwealth, alliance, free world, the West, the Communist bloc—that disguises the actual relationships among its members.

According to Milovan Djilas, Stalin pithily described the origin of such new empires in a conversation he had with Marshal Tito of Yugoslavia in the Kremlin in April 1945 in this way: "This war is not as in the past.

Whoever occupies a territory also imposes on it his own social system. Everyone imposes his own social system as far as his army has power to do so. It cannot be otherwise."[16] Imposing one's own social system is precisely what the former Soviet Union proceeded to do in the territories it occupied in Eastern Europe and what the United States did in the territories it occupied in East Asia, particularly Japan and South Korea. Over the forty years of the Cold War these original "satellites" became the cores of Soviet and American new-style empires, only one of which—the American empire—still remains today. The nature of that remaining empire and how it has changed over time is the subject of this book.

In 1917, the Soviet Union inherited an older czarist empire in Europe and central Asia, a multinational union of peoples based on conquest and a particular civilization, similar to the former Hapsburg and Ottoman Empires. This imperial past undoubtedly colored the nature of the Soviet Union then taking shape, but in talking about the Cold War Soviet empire, I am referring mainly to the seven "people's democracies" in Eastern Europe that formed the heart of the Communist camp until its collapse in 1989: East Germany, Poland, Czechoslovakia, Hungary, Romania, Albania, and Bulgaria. Its American equivalent was not NATO—Western Europe's American-inspired and American-supported defensive reaction to the massive armies and armaments the Soviet Union had mobilized to defeat the Third Reich—but the system of satellites the United States created in East Asia. These included at one time regimes in Japan, South Korea, Thailand, South Vietnam, Laos, Cambodia, the Philippines, and Taiwan.

Over time, and with the development of a nuclear arms race between the United States and the USSR, the two empires based on satellite regimes created after World War II expanded into much more extensive alignments based on ideology, economic interactions, technology transfers, mutual benefit, and military cooperation. For the Soviet Union this was the world that for a brief moment during the 1950s stretched from Moscow to Hanoi in the east and to Havana in the west and that even included, at least formally, China. For the United States it came to include most of the rest of the world—places where the United States assumed responsibility for maintaining some ill-defined "favorable" military environment (what the Pentagon now likes to call "stability") and where we insisted on free access for our multinational corporations and financiers (what our economists now call "globalization").

There was, I believe, far more symmetry between the postwar policies of the Soviet Union and the United States than most Americans are willing to recognize. The USSR in Eastern Europe and the United States in East Asia created their satellite systems for essentially the same reasons. In the course of the Cold War, the USSR intervened militarily to hold its empire together in Hungary and Czechoslovakia. The United States intervened militarily to hold its empire together in Korea and Vietnam (where it killed a great many more people in losing than the USSR did in its two successful interventions).

The richest prize in the Soviet empire was East Germany; the richest prize in the American empire is still Japan. Today, much like East Germany before the Berlin Wall came down, Japan remains a rigged economy brought into being and maintained thanks to the Cold War. Its people seem increasingly tired of the American troops stationed on their soil for the last half century and of the gray, single-party regimes that presided in Tokyo for almost all of those years. East Germany's dreary leaders Walter Ulbricht and Erich Honecker can appear almost dynamic when compared to the prime ministers Japan's Liberal Democratic Party has put in office since 1955.

Just as the two satraps of the German Democratic Republic faithfully followed every order they ever received from Moscow, each and every Japanese prime minister, as soon as he comes into office, gets on an airplane and reports to Washington. And as in the former East Germany, so Japanese voters long ago discovered that as long as they continue to be allied with the United States, nothing they do ever seems to change their political system. Many ordinary Japanese have learned to avoid politics like the plague, participating only in local elections, where a surprising number vote Communist both to register a protest and because the party is competent and honest. In Japan, political idealists tend to become nihilists, not unlike their German brethren before 1989.

The Soviet Union started setting up its satellites largely because it could not compete with the largesse of the United States' Marshall Plan for the rebuilding of war-torn Europe. (This, of course, reflected a major outcome of World War II: much of the Soviet Union had been reduced to rubble, while the United States emerged unscathed.) The USSR quickly recognized that in the conflict between democracy and totalitarianism developing in postwar Europe, it was on the less popular side. In Eastern Europe it could not bring its supporters to power through the ballot box, and so it ruthlessly ousted local democrats. In a Czech coup in February 1948 and elsewhere it imported Stalinism, claiming it was merely a version of socialism.

The Soviet Union had a defensive need to secure its Western approaches. By contrast, after Japan's defeat no regime in East Asia was capable of threatening the United States itself, least of all a China devastated by war and revolution. We therefore built our system of satellites for more genuinely imperialist reasons, although the government argued that our efforts were necessary due to the natural aggression of Sino-Soviet communism and the possibility that the fall of any country, however minor, to communism would lead other countries to topple like a set of "dominoes," until the chain reaction might reach the heartland of capitalism itself.

The American decision to create satellites in East Asia followed in part from the Communist revolution in China, which meant that American plans for a new postwar international order in East Asia based on an alliance with China, its wartime ally, were no longer viable. Although unwilling to go to war against the popular forces of Chinese communism to prop up the failing Nationalist leader Chiang Kai-shek, we reversed our policies for occupied Japan, giving up on further efforts to democratize the country and committing ourselves instead to its swift economic rehabilitation. Japan, the former implacable enemy, replaced China as America's primary East Asian ally. The U.S. government now devoted its energies to defending Japan and building it up as an East Asian alternative to the Chinese revolution. Even though we did not try to "roll back" that revolution, President Truman's decision in 1950 to order the Seventh Fleet to defend Taiwan and police the Taiwan Strait, and General Douglas MacArthur's decision to march north to the Chinese border during the Korean War, nonetheless ensured Chinese hostility for at least two decades.

Needless to say, the United States did not consult the defeated Japanese people about these decisions or about the decision to cultivate the remnants of that country's unquestionably anti-Communist wartime establishment. Our reliance in some cases on literal war criminals—for example, Nobusuke Kishi, former minister of munitions in Tojo's wartime cabinet, who became the country's prime minister in 1957—and on a CIA-financed single-party regime were the mirror image of Soviet policies in the former German Democratic Republic. Such policies actually led to an anti-American revolt in 1960. In the largest mass demonstrations in postwar Japanese history, protesters surrounded the parliament building and demanded that lawmakers not ratify a renewal of the Japanese-American Security Treaty. The situation became so tense that President Dwight D. Eisenhower was forced to cancel a proposed visit. (The first sitting American president ever to visit Tokyo would be Gerald Ford.) Using its rigged majority, the conservative party forced through ratification, keeping American troops in Japan, and the political system never again fully regained the trust of the public. For thirty years, the Liberal Democratic Party successfully prevented any alteration in political power and dutifully legitimated Japan's status as a satellite of the United States. Unfortunately, it did little else, leaving the actual governance of the country to the state bureaucracy, ensuring that any impulses the citizenry might have had toward self-government would atrophy. By the 1990s Japan was the world's second-richest country, but with a government remarkably similar to that of the former East Germany.

In order to support Britain, France, and Holland in the face of fears that the rest of Europe might "go Communist," the United States abandoned its wartime promises to help liberate those nations' colonies. Instead, the United States came to support or replace the former imperialists in wars intended to secure their prewar possessions. This meant that in East Asia, except in our own colony, the Philippines, we wound up on the wrong side of history. (Even in the Philippines, which we granted formal independence on July 4, 1946, we kept enormous military base complexes until the Filipinos expelled us in 1992.)

Unlike in Europe, the main Cold War conflicts in East and Southeast Asia were not between democracy and totalitarianism but between European colonialism and national independence movements. The reluctance of the main European powers to give up their colonies led to wars of national liberation in Indochina against the French, in Malaya against the British, and in Indonesia against the Dutch, in all of which the United States supported the side of imperialism. The Dutch were finally driven from Indonesia; the British, after a decade-long war, finally acquiesced in Malaya's independence, followed by its becoming two independent countries, Malaysia and Singapore. After the French were defeated militarily in Vietnam, the United States fought an incredibly bloody and prolonged conflict before it, too, was forced to abandon its imperial role there. The United States also supported a long counterinsurgency struggle in the Philippines against a guerrilla movement that considered the postindependence Filipino government a creature of the Americans. Only after our defeat in Vietnam did we begin to adjust to the idea that East Asia was different from Europe. Nixon's opening to China was the first sign that some understanding of East Asian history was finally starting to penetrate Washington minds.

The problem for the United States was that national Communist parties had filled a leadership vacuum in colonial East Asia. To prevent much of that region, possibly even Japan, from coming under the influence of nationalistic Communist parties, the U.S. government from time to time used the sort of brutal methods to which the USSR had resorted in Eastern Europe to hang on to its sphere of influence. The clearest example of this was the role it played in South Korea after 1945, a history that has been almost totally suppressed in the United States.

South Korea has been occupied by American forces virtually continuously since the end of World War II. It was the scene of the most important armed conflict of the early Cold War years, the place where the United States and China fought each other to a standstill and froze relations with each other for two decades. Thanks to the United States and the Soviet Union, which in 1945 divided the country for their own convenience, a half century later Korea remains the last place on earth whose borders are determined by where the armies of World War II stopped. South Korea's rise during the 1960s as a "miracle economy" and its spectacular financial collapse of 1997 were directly related to its status as a satellite of the United States.

South Korea was the first place in the postwar world where the Americans set up a dictatorial government. With the exception of its authoritarian president, Syngman Rhee, it consisted largely of former Korean collaborators with the Japanese colonialists. Despite opposition from the Korean people, America's need for a staunchly anti-Communist regime took precedence, given the occupation of North Korea by the USSR. In 1960, after Koreans searching for democracy overthrew Rhee, the U.S. government threw its support behind Park Chung-hee, the first of three army generals who would rule from 1961 to 1993. The Americans tolerated a coup d'état by General Chun Doo-hwan in 1979 and covertly supported his orders that led to the killing of several hundred, maybe several thousand, Korean civilians at Kwangju in 1980 (probably far more people than the Chinese Communists killed in and around Tiananmen Square in 1989). In order to keep South Korea firmly under its control, during the 1980s the Americans sent as successive ambassadors two senior officials of the Central Intelligence Agency, James Lilly and Donald Gregg. Nowhere else did the United States so openly turn over diplomatic relations to representatives of its main clandestine services organization.

South Korea is today probably closer to a genuine parliamentary democracy than any country in East Asia, but no thanks to the American State Department, the Pentagon, or the CIA. It was the Korean people themselves, particularly the students of the country's leading universities, who through demonstrations and street confrontations in 1987 finally brought a measure of democracy to their country. After the democratically elected government of Kim Young-sam took office in 1993, President Kim felt sufficiently secure to put the two surviving dictators,

Chun and Roh Tae Woo, on trial. They were convicted of state terrorism, sedition, and corruption. The American press gave the trials only
the most minimal coverage, while the U.S. government ignored them as
a purely internal Korean affair.

The rule of Syngman Rhee and the U.S.-backed generals was merely
the first instance in East Asia of the American sponsorship of dictators. The list is long, but it deserves reiteration simply because many
in the United States fail to remember (if they ever knew) what East
Asians cannot help but regard as a major part of our postwar legacy. U.S.-
sponsored Asian dictators include:

- Chiang Kai-shek and his son Chiang Ching-kuo in Taiwan. (Taiwan
  started to democratize only in the 1980s after the Carter administration had broken relations with it.)

- Ferdinand Marcos in the Philippines (brought down by Corazon
  Aquino and her People Power movement after Presidents Ronald
  Reagan and George Bush had hailed him as a democrat).

- Ngo Dinh Diem (assassinated on American orders), General Nguyen
  Khanh, General Nguyen Cao Ky, and General Nguyen Van Thieu in
  Vietnam.

- General Lon Nol in Cambodia.

- Marshals Pibul Songgram, Sarit Thanarat, Praphas Charusathien, and
  Thanom Kittikachorn in Thailand (where they were essentially care-
  takers for the huge American air bases at Udorn, Takli, Korat, and
  Ubon).

- General Suharto in Indonesia (brought to power with the help of
  the Central Intelligence Agency and overthrown with the help of the
  Pentagon's Defense Intelligence Agency).

Several others had careers too brief or obscure to remember clearly
(for example, General Phoumi Nosavan in Laos). These men belong to

the same category of petty tyrants that the former Soviet Union used to staff its satellites in Eastern Europe from 1948 to 1989 (although the Russians usually chose obedient members of the local Communist Party apparatus over militarists).

The U.S. government used economics, as well as authoritarian regimes, as a tool of empire building. Our most effective, nonmilitary policies in East Asia were to trade access to our markets for East Asian toleration of the indefinite billeting of our soldiers, aircraft, and ships in their countries. Admittedly, following the Vietnam War, the United States briefly toyed with the idea of letting its empire in East Asia go. President Jimmy Carter explored withdrawing our troops from South Korea, particularly since North and South Korea were at that point nearly indistinguishable in terms of human rights abuses and Stalinist-style development policies. But he was forestalled in 1979 by the assassination of the South Korean dictator, General Park Chung-hee, and by his inability politically to cast off one satellite just as another one, Iran, was in open rebellion against the United States. When, in the final days of the Carter administration, the Soviet Union invaded Afghanistan in order to prop up its own puppets there, any talk of giving up our empire evaporated.

During the 1980s, the last decade of the Cold War, the parallelism between the policies of the United States and the USSR continued but with a new geographical focus. Both sought to shore up or establish puppet regimes in territories that were on their borders or in adjacent regions that had long been claimed as spheres of influence. The USSR was preoccupied with Afghanistan; the United States, with Central America. Both superpowers utilized the rhetoric of the Cold War to justify their aggressive actions against much smaller states—anticapitalism for the USSR in Afghanistan, anticommunism for the United States in Guatemala, El Salvador, Nicaragua, Panama, and the island of Grenada—even though capitalism in Afghanistan and communism in Central America were both essentially absurd ideas. Propaganda apparatuses in the United States and the USSR effectively disguised from their own peoples the true roots of revolt in both regions—a religious revival in

Afghanistan, opposition to oligarchies that had long fronted for American corporations in Central America.

President Reagan and his CIA director, William Casey, claimed they were trying to halt the erosion of the "free world" in the wake of the Vietnam War. Whether this was truly their strategy or merely political rhetoric has never been clear, but what could not be clearer was that, in 1981, the United States launched Vietnam-style operations in Central America and put large sums of money, often covertly raised, into supporting an insurgency against a Sandinista government in Nicaragua sympathetic to Castro's Cuba. At the same time, superpower détente, arms control talks, and Sino-American rapprochement virtually eliminated any real threat of war between hostile camps in Europe or East Asia. While the American demonization of Castro's Cuba ratcheted upward and the government argued vociferously that Cuban-inspired insurgencies were the hemisphere's greatest threat, the Cold War was already essentially over. The superpowers continued it only as propaganda cover for their respective neighborhood imperialisms.

It is not necessary to detail here the many American covert operations in Latin America. Americans supported a series of activities that ranged from the widespread use of paramilitary death squads in countries like El Salvador to military-directed genocidal campaigns in Guatemala, seriously compromising American rhetoric about human rights for the rest of the century. Similar largely covert operations continued throughout the 1980s and probably still continue. Although the CIA has done everything in its power to hide the American hand in these imperial policing actions, a pattern has developed in the revelation of American-sponsored atrocities and their ensuing blowback. An American regional newspaper—the *Baltimore Sun* in the case of Honduran death squads, the *San Jose Mercury News* in the case of the cocaine trade of our Nicaraguan counterrevolutionaries, the "Contras"—publishes a report based on the research of its staff reporters. The report offers evidence that an agency of the United States condoned war crimes against civilians in Central America and lied to Congress when asked about it or turned a deaf ear to evidence that "assets" under our control were engaged in activities such as drug smuggling that were extremely deleterious to the welfare of Americans. The establishment press—the *Washington Post*, the *New York Times*, or the *Los Angeles Times*—then accuses the regional paper of sloppy journalism; the publisher of the regional paper apologizes and fires the reporters who filed the story.

Meanwhile, the CIA orders its inspector general to investigate the charges. He duly releases a report saying that not a shred of evidence can be found in the official files to support the story. Months or even years later, a research organization, such as the National Security Archive at George Washington University, discovers that there was a second internal report by the inspector general. The second report still disputes the newspaper account but also acknowledges that the substance of its charges was accurate. As the CIA's internal response to the *Baltimore Sun's* report put it in the gingerly and euphemistic language of imperialism, "CIA reporting to Congress in the early 1980s underestimated Honduran involvement in abuses."[17]

The United States now faces an agenda of problems that simply would not exist except for the imperial commitments and activities, open and covert, that accompanied the Cold War. The most common government argument for such continued imperialist activism in the wake of that half-century-long superpower confrontation is still a version of the old "domino theory," discredited during the Vietnam War: America's armed forces and covert warriors—for the sake of the world's good—have no choice but to hold off "instability" wherever it may threaten. The Department of Defense's East Asia Strategy Report of 1998 explains the one hundred thousand troops "forward deployed" in Okinawa and South Korea as necessary to maintain "stability" in the region. But instability, a nebulous concept at best, is the normal state of affairs in an international system of sovereign states. Instability as such does not threaten the security of the United States, particularly when there is no superpower rival eager to exploit it.

Actual military intervention in brutal civil wars or civil strife in places like Somalia, Haiti, Bosnia, and Kosovo has been justified as "deterrence by example." Even though the United States may have no obvious or vital interest in the outcome of ethnic, religious, or internecine struggles in such places, advocates of military activism argue that it is a good thing for us to intervene because it shows allies and adversaries alike that we will not be "bullied" or "blackmailed." Such interventions, it is thought, will cause others to respect our power and authority—and hesitate to plunge into similar bloody strife in their own areas. But deterrence by example does not work. As foreign policy analyst Barbara Conry puts it, "The aborted U.S. intervention in Haiti . . . is not going to lead to a rash of military dictatorships any more than strong American responses to Manuel Noriega and Saddam Hussein deterred Serbian president Slobodan Milosevic from pursuing his aims in Bosnia."[18]

Not only are such military interventions often ineffective, but the use of military force in the name of democracy or human rights regularly makes a mockery of these very principles. More serious yet, an injudicious intervention can create threats where none existed before, as was the case in Truman's intervention in the Chinese civil war and in General MacArthur's menacing of China's borders during the Korean War.

Thirty years ago the international relations theorist Ronald Steel noted, "Unlike Rome, we have not exploited our empire. On the contrary, our empire has exploited us, making enormous drains on our resources and energies."[19] Our economic relations with our East Asian satellites have, for example, hollowed out our domestic manufacturing industries and led us into a reliance on finance capitalism, whose appearance has in the past been a sign of a hitherto healthy economy entering decline. An analogous situation literally wrecked the former USSR. While fighting a losing war in Afghanistan and competing with the United States to develop ever more advanced "strategic weaponry," it could no longer withstand pent-up desires in Eastern Europe for independence.

The historian Paul Kennedy has dubbed this condition "imperial overstretch." In an analysis of the United States in his book *The Rise and Fall of the Great Powers*, he wrote that it too cannot avoid confronting the two great tests which challenge the *longevity* of every major power that occupies the "number one" position in world affairs: whether, in the military/strategic realm, it can preserve a reasonable balance between the nation's perceived defense requirements and the means it possesses to maintain these commitments; and whether, as an intimately related point, it can preserve the technological and economic bases of its power from relative erosion in the face of the ever-shifting patterns of global production. This test of American abilities will be the greater because it, like Imperial Spain around 1600 or the British Empire around 1900, is the inheritor of a vast array of strategical commitments which had been made decades earlier, when the nation's political, economic, and military capacity to influence world affairs seemed so much more assured.[20]

I do not believe that America's "vast array of strategical commitments" were made in past decades largely as the result of attempts to exploit other nations for economic gain or simply to dominate them politically and militarily. Although the United States has in the past engaged in imperialist exploitation of other nations, particularly in Latin America, it has also tried in various ways to liquidate many such commitments. The roots of American "imperial overstretch" today are not the same as those of past empires. Instead they more closely resemble those that brought down the Soviet Union.

Many Americans do not care to see their country's acts, policies, or situations compared with the Soviet Union's; some condemn such a comparison because it commits the alleged fallacy of "moral equivalence." They insist that America's values and institutions are vastly more humane than those of Stalin's Russia. I agree. Throughout the years of the Cold War, the United States remained a functioning democracy, with rights for its citizens unimaginable in the Soviet context (even if its more recent maintenance of the world's largest prison population suggests that it should be cautious in criticizing other nations' systems of criminal justice). Comparisons between the United States and the former Soviet Union are useful, however, because those two hegemons developed in tandem, challenging each other militarily, economically, and ideologically. In the long run, it may turn out that, like two scorpions in a bottle, they succeeded in stinging each other to death. The roots of both modern empires lay in World War II and in their subsequent contest to control the forces that the war unleashed. A stress on the costs of the Cold War to the United States also draws attention to the legacies of that struggle. America's role as the planet's "lone superpower"—as leader of the peace-loving nations and patron of such institutions as the United Nations, the World Bank, and the World Trade Organization—is made much more difficult by the nature of the harvest we continue to reap for imprudent, often secret operations undertaken in the past.

The most important of our Cold War legacies may be in East Asia. The wealth of that region today has fundamentally altered the world balance of power. Starting with Japan, many East Asian countries adapted to the bipolar confrontation of the Cold War years and took advantage of its conditions to engineer their own self-sustaining economic growth. Even though the high-speed economic growth of some countries in the area stalled or even collapsed with the economic crisis of 1997, that in no way alters the basic shift in manufacturing's global center of gravity to East Asia.

The American political and intellectual establishments remain mystified by and hostile to the economic achievements of Asians, just as the Soviet establishment remained mystified by and hostile to the economic achievements of Anglo-American and Western European capitalism. It is time to realize, however, that the real dangers to America today come not from the newly rich people of East Asia but from our own ideological rigidity, our deep-seated belief in our own propaganda. As sociologists Giovanni Arrighi and Beverly Silver warn, "There are no credible aggressive new powers that can provoke the breakdown of the U.S.-centered world system, but the United States has even greater capabilities than Britain did a century ago to convert its declining hegemony into an exploitative domination. If the system eventually breaks down, it will be primarily because of U.S. resistance to adjustment and accommodation. And conversely, U.S. adjustment and accommodation to the rising economic power of the East Asian region is an essential condition for a non-catastrophic transition to a new world order."[21]

The United States today desperately needs a new analysis of its role in a post–Cold War world and of the sorts of policies that might prevent another major war, like its last three, in East Asia. Some of the significant changes to come in East Asia are already visible: China's increasing attempt to emulate high-growth economies elsewhere in Asia; the reunification of Korea; Japan's need to overcome its political paralysis; America's confusion over how to adjust to a self-confident China and to a more independent Japan; the growing importance of Southeast Asia as a new economic center of gravity. American policy making needs to be taken away from military planners and military-minded civilians, including those in the White House, who today dominate Washington policy making toward the area. American ambassadors and diplomats in Asia should have at least an elementary knowledge of East Asian history, languages, and aspirations. The United States desperately needs options for dealing with crises other than relying on the carrier task force, cruise missiles, and the unfettered flow of capital, just as it needs to overcome the complacency and arrogance that characterize American official attitudes toward Asia today.

Terrorism by definition strikes at the innocent in order to draw attention to the sins of the invulnerable. The innocent of the twenty-first century are going to harvest unexpected blowback disasters from the imperialist escapades of recent decades. Although most Americans may be largely ignorant of what was, and still is, being done in their names, all are likely to pay a steep price—individually and collectively—for their nation's continued efforts to dominate the global scene. Before the damage of heedless triumphalist acts and the triumphalist rhetoric and propaganda that goes with them becomes irreversible, it is important to open a new discussion of our global role during and after the Cold War. There is no place more appropriate to begin a reconsideration of America's imperial policies than with American behavior in East Asia.

2

OKINAWA:
ASIA'S LAST COLONY

At about eight P.M. on September 4, 1995, two American marines and a sailor seized a twelve-year-old Okinawan girl on her way home from shopping, bound and gagged her, drove her in a rented car to a remote location, and raped her. Marine Pfc. Rodrico Harp and Seaman Marcus Gill confessed that they violently beat her and that Marine Pfc. Kendrick Ledet bound her mouth, eyes, hands, and legs with duct tape. Described in court by an acquaintance as a "tank," Gill was six feet tall and weighed 270 pounds. He confessed to raping the girl, while the other two claimed that they had merely abducted and beaten her. According to an Associated Press account of the trial, "The court interpreter broke down upon hearing [Gill's] account of lewd jokes he and his companions made about their unconscious and bleeding victim."[1] Police introduced into the trial proceedings a plastic bag found in a trash can that contained three sets of bloodstained men's underwear, a school notebook, and duct tape.

The three accused rapists—Gill, twenty-two, of Woodville, Texas; Harp, twenty-one, of Griffin, Georgia; and Ledet, twenty, of Waycross, Georgia—were in no way unusual for U.S. servicemen stationed on the island of Okinawa. Harp was the father of a nine-month-old daughter and a graduate of an ROTC program in Griffin. Ledet had been a Boy

Scout and church usher. Gill had taken advanced-placement English and had won a football scholarship. All were based at Camp Hansen. Gill told the court that the three men had embarked on the rape "just for fun" and had picked the girl out at random as she was leaving a stationery store.

A few weeks later, from his headquarters at Pearl Harbor, Hawaii, the commander of all U.S. forces in the Pacific, Admiral Richard C. Macke, remarked to the press, "I think that [the rape] was absolutely stupid. For the price they paid to rent the car, they could have had a girl."[2] Although Macke was permitted to retire following this lighthearted comment, there was no Congressional or official inquiry into his leadership of the Pacific Command and no review of why a decade after the end of the Cold War the United States still had one hundred thousand troops based in Japan and South Korea. There was only endless public relations spin about how the gang rape of a child was a singular "tragedy," not a consequence of U.S. basing policy, and how East Asia "needs" its American peacekeepers.

Few Americans who have never served in the armed forces overseas have any conception of the nature or impact of an American base complex, with its massive military facilities, post exchanges, dependents' housing estates, swimming pools, and golf courses, and the associated bars, strip clubs, whorehouses, and venereal disease clinics that they attract in a land like Okinawa. They can extend for miles, dominating localities and in some cases whole nations. In South Korea, for example, huge military camptowns (*kijich'on*) have existed around all the American bases from the time of the Korean War. Katharine Moon writes, "They are like stage sets, in a sense, for the U.S. military presence in Korea, characterized by dimly lit alleys blinking with neon-lit bars boasting names like Lucky Club, Top Gun, or King Club. The alleys rock with loud country-western or disco music, drunken brawls, and American soldiers in fatigues and heavily made-up Korean women walking closely together with hands on each other's buttocks."[3] Until the withdrawal of U.S. forces from the Philippines in 1992, the town of Olongapo, adjacent to the U.S. naval base at Subic Bay, had no industry except for the "entertainment" business, which supported approximately 55,000 prostitutes and a total of 2,182 registered establishments offering "rest and recreation" to American servicemen.

At the height of the Cold War, the United States built a chain of military bases stretching from Korea and Japan through Taiwan, the Philippines, Thailand, and Australia to Saudi Arabia, Turkey, Greece, Italy, Spain, Portugal, Germany, England, and Iceland—in effect ringing the Soviet Union and China with literally thousands of overseas military installations. In Japan alone, immediately following the end of the Korean War, there were six hundred U.S. installations and approximately two hundred thousand troops. There are still today, ten years after the end of the Cold War, some eight hundred Department of Defense facilities located outside the United States, ranging from radio relay stations to major air bases. To those living around them (and often dependent upon them), the personnel based on them may feel less like "peacekeepers" than occupiers. This is certainly the case in Okinawa, a land whose people have in any case felt themselves under occupation by Japan since the seventeenth century and by the United States since 1945.

The island of Okinawa measures 454 square miles, almost exactly the size of Los Angeles and smaller than the island of Kauai in the Hawaiian chain. It now contains thirty-nine bases, ranging from Kadena Air Force Base, the largest airfield in East Asia, to the Sobe Communications Facility, known locally as the "elephant cage" because of its bizarre antennae, a center for communicating with submarines, intercepting other people's telephone conversations, and intelligence operations. In the 1960s, when Okinawa was directly administered by the Pentagon, there were 117 bases, and at the time of the rape there were 42. Though few of them are contiguous to each other, in total they take up an estimated 20 percent of the prime agricultural land in the central and southern parts of the main island of Okinawa. The United States also controls twenty-nine areas of the surrounding seas and fifteen air spaces over the Ryukyus. As a prefecture of Japan, Okinawa occupies only 0.6 percent of Japan's total land area, but about 75 percent of facilities exclusively used by the American armed forces stationed in Japan are concentrated there. With a population density amounting to 2,198 persons per square kilometer, it is one of the most densely populated areas in the world. Neither Japanese nor Okinawan courts or police have any jurisdiction over these American-occupied lands, seas, and air spaces.

It may be hard for Americans to imagine why a single rape case would cause such outrage among Okinawans or endanger an almost half-century-old Japanese-American security relationship. Part of the reason is because it is hard to grasp the particular imperial circumstances under which they live. A reader trying to imagine what follows would perhaps have to transpose the Okinawan situation to Greater Los Angeles, imagining the choicest fifth of it to be occupied in a similar way by an allied and "friendly" foreign military. In addition, the reader would have to understand that the very reason for the presence of those bases, weapons, and personnel, dinned into public consciousness for forty years—the enmity of an ominous neighboring superpower and its bloc of allies—had ceased to be relevant for a decade.

Certainly, from an Okinawan point of view, Admiral Macke's remark merely confirmed what they had already long experienced: that this was not an isolated incident committed by undisciplined enlisted men but part of a pattern ignored, if not condoned, at the highest levels of the American military hierarchy. But even more important, it posed in the starkest terms a question increasingly asked in the satellites of the informal American empire: Why absorb such costs? Why, in fact, are foreign troops based in countries like Japan more than half a century after the end of World War II and more than a decade after the disappearance of the Soviet Union as a military threat?

Okinawa is the largest island in the Ryukyu chain, which is located at the southernmost tip of Japan. Its capital, Naha, is considerably closer to Shanghai than to Tokyo, and the culture of the Ryukyu Islands reflects strong Chinese as well as Japanese influences. The Ryukyus were formerly an independent kingdom, annexed by Japan in the late nineteenth century, at about the same time the United States annexed the Hawaiian Islands.

The main island of Okinawa was the scene of the last great battle of World War II—also the last time the United States used military force victoriously in East Asia. (During the Korean War, General Douglas MacArthur's landing at Inchon was successful but led to his march north to the Yalu River, which precipitated Chinese intervention and the United States' ultimately having to settle for a divided Korea.) Some 14,005 Americans and 234,000 Japanese soldiers and civilians were killed in that brutal, three-month-long campaign, so bloody that it became the main American rationale for the atomic bombings of Hiroshima and Nagasaki. If using atomic weapons to end the war prevented more Okinawan-type carnage in an invasion of Japan's main islands, then, the Americans claimed, it was more than justified.

The monument the Okinawan government built to the war dead, unveiled on the fiftieth anniversary of the end of the war, is testimony to what the Okinawans call the "typhoon of steel." On dozens of stone tablets, it lists the names of all the people on all sides killed in the battle—Japanese and American soldiers and affiliated personnel (including the journalist Ernie Pyle), Okinawan and Japanese civilians, and Korean slave laborers. The battle lasted from April to June 1945 and totally devastated the island. In September 1945, the American armed forces occupied defeated Japan, promising to bring to those emperor-ruled islands an American-style series of democratic reforms. Okinawa, however, was separated off from Japan and ruled by the military in a purely autocratic manner.

From 1945 to 1972, American military officers governed Okinawa as their exclusive preserve. In 1952, retention of Okinawa proved to be the price the American government extracted from Japan in return for the signing of an early peace treaty and of the Japanese-American Security Treaty, which signaled the end of the occupation of Japan's main islands. Many Okinawans believe that Emperor Hirohito sacrificed them in 1945 in a meaningless battle meant to elicit better surrender terms from the Allies, and that Tokyo sacrificed them again in 1952 so that the rest of Japan could regain its independence and enjoy the beginnings of a return to economic prosperity. In this view, Japan felt relatively comfortable with the Japanese-American Security Treaty largely because most American military bases were consigned to a small southern island, where they and the problems that come with them could be ignored by the majority of Japanese. (There are still, it should be added, eight major American bases in Japan proper, located at Atsugi, Iwakuni, Misawa, Sagamihara, Sasebo, Yokosuka, Yokota, and Zama.)

America's two major wars against Asian communism—in Korea and Vietnam—could not have been fought without bases on Japanese territory. Those military outposts were critical staging and logistics areas for the projection of American power onto the Asian mainland, as well as secure sanctuaries, invulnerable to attack by North Korean, Chinese, Vietnamese, or Cambodian forces. Large American staffs involved in conducting those wars lived in security and comfort, and American troops often enjoyed "R & R" (rest and recreation) in Okinawa or Japan as well as in Thailand, Hong Kong, and the Philippines. In 1965, Admiral U. S. Grant Sharp, commander in chief of American forces in the Pacific, explicitly stated that the United States could not fight the Vietnam War without its Okinawan bases.

Had the Americans had to ask for Japanese permission to conduct wars from their territory, they would have been turned down. But when the Korean War broke out in 1950, the American military still occupied all of Japan, and throughout most of the Vietnam War they still governed Okinawa as if it were their private military colony. By the late 1960s, the Americans had built their complex of more than a hundred bases, much of it by forcibly seizing land from defenseless Okinawans who were without official citizenship, legal protections, or rights of any sort from any country. When, at the height of the Vietnam War, Okinawan protests against B-52s, bars, brothels, stores of nerve gas, and G.I.-committed crimes reached a combustible point, the Americans finally took the step of officially returning Okinawa to Japanese control. Nothing, however, changed in terms of the actual American presence— except that Americans now felt obliged to justify their behavior. This they proceeded to do, ushering in a period of extraordinary American hypocrisy, mendacity, and greed, which reached an apogee just when the end of the Cold War seemed to signal a possible end to the daily indignities inflicted on the 1.3 million people of the island.

Instead, during the Clinton administration the Americans simply began to invent new "threats" that required their presence and to offer heightened assurances of their goodwill and good-neighborliness. In a November 1995 speech to the National Press Club in Tokyo, then secretary of defense William Perry assured the Japanese, "The bases are here for your good more than ours," arguing that "without the troops, Japan would be vulnerable." On the rape, Perry added, "The American people share this pain with you."[4] General C. C. Krulak, commandant of the Marine Corps, wrote in reference to Okinawa that "a Marine installation is more than a collection of buildings and equipment; it is a community of good, decent and caring people, people with families and interests far beyond day-to-day military affairs; and people involved in the community. They are people who care about the lives of those beyond the fences of their installation."[5] Ambassador Walter Mondale, who helped engineer a deceitful scheme in which the American government publicly promised to give back the Marine Corps air station at Futenma to the Okinawans but privately required that Japan provide the United States with an equivalent base elsewhere in Okinawa, insisted to the press just before his return to the States that "we have tried in a very intensive way to be good neighbors to our friends in Okinawa."[6]

Certainly, Okinawan daily life in the 1990s was an improvement over the days when the territory was under exclusive American jurisdiction. Japan poured money into the island, understanding that the mainland's postwar economy had been built partly at the expense of the Okinawans and that a transfer of wealth was in order. Although Okinawa is still Japan's poorest prefecture, it had by the 1990s reached 70 percent of the national level of wealth. Since Japan is the world's richest large country in terms of per capita income, this meant that tiny Okinawa was now far richer than all of North Korea, to take but one example.

It is not absolute deprivation that maddens Okinawans but relative deprivation—the realization that American noise, traffic accidents, environmental degradation, and moral offenses should not *have* to be endured. As Etsuko Miyagi Utsumi, a leader of the women's coalition that came into being after the 1995 rape, puts it, "The Japanese government has so far been successful in making Okinawa, the most remote prefecture, serve as the 'garbage dump' of the Security Treaty."[7]

Sexual assault, for example, remains a fact of daily life. Shortly after the notorious rape that created a crisis in Japanese-American relations, the New York Times editorial page informed its readers that "American military behavior in Japan has generally been good since the occupation in 1945."[8] Given that in a period of only six months in 1949 journalist Frank Gibney reported G.I.s killing twenty-nine Okinawans and raping another eighteen and that in late 1958 a quarter to a third of the Third Marine Division in Okinawa was infected with venereal disease, one has to ask what the New York Times might consider bad behavior.[9]

Similarly, Air Force Lt. Gen. Richard Myers, commander of U.S. Forces in Japan, has maintained that the 1995 rape was an isolated incident, not characteristic behavior of "99.99 percent of U.S. Forces."[10] But General Myers is simply wrong. According to the conservative Japanese newspaper Nihon Keizai Shimbun, which studied bookings at the Okinawan Prefectural Police Headquarters, U.S. servicemen were implicated in 4,716 crimes between 1972 and 1995—just under a crime a day throughout the period of General Myers's command.[11]

Of course, most of these criminal acts were not sexual assaults. Russell Carollo and a team of reporters from the Dayton Daily News went through one hundred thousand court-martial records going back to 1988 to find out how many servicemen had been brought before military courts charged with rape and how they had been treated. They discovered that since 1988, navy and marine bases in Japan have had 169 courts-martial for sexual assaults, the highest number of all U.S. bases worldwide, 66 percent more cases than at the number-two location, San Diego, which has more than twice the personnel. Since the navy has a large Okinawa base at White Beach and another contingent at Kadena and the marines have twenty different bases spread all over the island, "Japan" here essentially meant Okinawa. As getting information on courts-martial required months of filing Freedom of Information Act requests, and the army released its records only after being sued by the *Dayton Daily News*, the statistics cited in their stories of October 1–5, 1995, do not even include army figures.[12]

While the incidence of reported rape in the United States is forty-one for every one hundred thousand people, at the military bases in Okinawa it is eighty-two per one hundred thousand. And that, of course, is counting only reported rapes. In Okinawan culture it is unbearably humiliating for an adult woman to bring a charge of rape (something that the Marine Corps has often relied on in covering up its record). Thus, the numbers undoubtedly significantly understate the actual occurrence of rape. Disturbingly, the *Dayton Daily News* articles revealed that the military had allowed hundreds of accused sex offenders in its ranks to go free despite courts-martial convictions. The *Nation* magazine, considering what the Dayton reporters uncovered, concluded, "Covering up sexual assault is Pentagon policy."[13]

But the Pentagon may finally have met its match in a group of women determined to publicize and bring to justice military rapists. The organization, Okinawa Women Act Against Military Violence, was founded by Suzuyo Takazato, a member of the Naha City Assembly, and Carolyn Francis, an American Methodist missionary in Okinawa. They had attended the Fourth U.N. Forum on Women in Beijing in September 1995, and with colleagues they presented a revealing report on and chronology of what Okinawan women had experienced during the military occupation of their country. Returning to Okinawa to news of the gang rape of the twelve-year-old girl, they spearheaded a mobilization of Okinawans and their government that led to the largest protest demonstration in Okinawa's history. A rally of eighty-five thousand people on October 21, 1995, demanded that the American and Japanese governments pay some attention to their grievances. The Okinawan Women repeatedly (and without irony, despite her husband's seeming indifference to the victims of sex crimes by American servicemen) quoted from the speech of Hillary Rodham Clinton, honorary chairwoman of the U.S. delegation to the Beijing women's forum, that "women's rights are human rights" and that military rape is a war crime.

The rape took place on September 4; by September 8, the Okinawan police had identified the perpetrators on the basis of rental-car records and had issued warrants for their arrest, but the military did not turn them over to local authorities until September 29. It was widely reported that the three had the run of their base and were spending their time "eating hamburgers."[14] This is a matter not of simple delays but of "extraterritoriality," one of the historically most offensive aspects of Western (and Japanese) imperialism in East Asia. From the time the United States got it written into its treaty with China following the Opium War of 1839–42 (yes, it was an American invention), "extra'lity," as it was informally called, meant that if a European, American, or Japanese committed a crime in China (or today in Japan or Korea if he or she is a member of, married to, or the child of a member of the American armed forces), that foreigner would be turned over to his or her own consular officials, rather than being tried under the laws of the country in which the crime occurred.

It is not an exaggeration to say that the Chinese revolution was in part fought to be rid of this demeaning provision, which lasted in China until 1943. The Western insistence on extraterritoriality reflected the belief that Asian law was barbaric and that no "civilized" person should be subjected to it. In actuality, all sorts of Chinese criminals took advantage of it, claiming Christian conversion or other ruses to ingratiate themselves with one or another imperialist power in order to place themselves beyond the reach of local laws.

Article 17, section 5, of the Japan-U.S. Status of Forces Agreement (SOFA) stipulated: "When U.S. servicemen and their families commit crimes, they shall be detained by U.S. authorities until Japanese law enforcement agencies file complaints with the prosecutors' office based on clear suspicion." While not quite full-blown extraterritoriality, it gave U.S. authorities the right to refuse Japanese investigators' requests to hand over suspects attached to the military. Delays built into the system were often used as opportunities to transfer American suspects back to the United States, where they were beyond the reach of Japanese authorities.

Under the pressure of escalating protests in Okinawa and mainland Japan following news of the rape, the United States and Japan signed a "side letter" to SOFA allowing G.I.s suspected of rape or murder to be placed in Japanese custody before being indicted if Japanese investigators request it. This represented a distinct break in American global policies. In Korea, suspects still get handed over to local authorities only after being convicted by a U.S. military court. Similarly, in Italy, the American fliers charged in 1998 with flying so low that their jet cut a ski-lift cable, plunging twenty skiers to their deaths, were returned to the States for a military trial where, to the outrage of Italians, they were exonerated of responsibility. It is, of course, unimaginable that Americans would accept such special treatment for foreign military personnel visiting or training in our country. And that is precisely what breeds such a deep sense of injustice among Okinawans.

Certainly, the initial American response to the rape caused the greatest crisis in Japanese-American relations since a tumultuous struggle against the renewal of the security treaty in 1960. No one should be surprised to discover, however, that the sexual offenses that had plagued Okinawans did not abate. Only three months later, in December 1995, the U.S. military released a composite sketch of an American suspected of raping a woman at knifepoint near Futenma Marine Corps Air Station. Ben Takara, an Okinawan poet and chemistry teacher at Futenma Senior High School, told *Newsweek*, "We once surveyed our girl students, asking if they had had any scary experiences with U.S. soldiers on their way to school or back home. One-third to one-half of the students answered yes. . . . The rape case . . . was just the tip of the iceberg. I must say that the Japan-U.S. security treaty has not protected the safety of Okinawans."[15]

Many of the acts that so disrupt Okinawan life are less sensational than rape but no less disturbing to the people of that island. Traffic accidents are an example. On a Sunday in early January 1996, four months after the rape that had allegedly caused the U.S. military to tighten up discipline, a female marine from the air base at Futenma drove off the road and onto a sidewalk at high speed in Chatan, near Kadena Air

Force Base, killing Rojita Kinjo, thirty-six, and her daughters, Mitsuko, ten, and Mariko, one. Lance Corporal Lori Padilla, twenty, the driver, pleaded guilty to a charge of professional negligence leading to death. It may be that she was confused by driving on the left side of the road, as is the custom in Japan. She received a two-year prison sentence.

Five months later, the remaining Kinjo family sued Padilla and the two marine co-owners of the car in the Naha District Court for sixty-two million yen (about $580,000) as a solatium to compensate them for the emotional losses due to the deaths of their relatives. The payment of a solatium in the case of accidents of all kinds is an essential and long-accepted part of Japanese culture. None of the defendants appeared at the trial, one having already left for the United States (the average tour of duty for American service personnel in Okinawa is only six months). In December, the court ordered Padilla and her two codefendants to pay the sum requested, but the second codefendant had by then also left Japan and was untraceable. Padilla had neither savings nor insurance. Ultimately the U.S. military paid the family twenty-five million yen (40 percent of the total) but extracted from them, in return, a statement that this was a gift from the U.S. government and that the family in accepting it gave up any further claims against the United States. At this point, the Japanese government paid the remaining thirty-seven million yen to the victims' family.

It was noted that at the time of the accident the driver was neither arrested nor checked to see if she was drunk but was instead transported to a military hospital. This was, of course, only one of just over a thousand auto accidents each year in Okinawa involving U.S. service personnel (slightly under two thousand for Japan as a whole), and it was quite typical in that American drivers normally do not have insurance (or at least not enough) and have often left Japan by the time Okinawan victims catch up to them in court.

Not until after the rape incident of September 1995, as part of an effort to reduce the American "footprint" in Okinawa (as Secretary of Defense Perry called it) and fifty-one years after their arrival in Okinawa, did American military cars and trucks begin to carry license plates. Prior to that Okinawans usually had no way of identifying a vehicle that collided with theirs or injured them. It took the "sacrifice of a schoolgirl," noted the *Okinawa Times*, to achieve any progress at all in making "good neighbors" out of the Americans.[16] There are still about fifteen thousand licensed drivers at Kadena Air Force Base and another twenty-five thousand affiliated with the marines on Okinawa, including service personnel and Department of Defense civilians, teachers, and dependents, who also pay specially reduced automobile taxes. By one estimate, were they to pay at Japanese rates, the incomes of the Okinawan prefectural government and the Tokyo municipal government would increase by ¥250 million and ¥200 million respectively.

In February 1996, a month after the Padilla case, a nineteen-year-old on a motor scooter was struck and killed by a car driven by a U.S. Navy chief petty officer. The young man's father, Daisuke Ebihara, a mainland schoolteacher, described the callous attitudes of U.S. military representatives to a reporter for the *Japan Times*. "Nobody . . . attended the funeral or sent a telegram or wreath of condolence. And a Japanese working for the U.S. military phoned my wife and urged us not to engage a lawyer, saying it would be cheaper. Even before I got to the hospital, they were telling me 'we will decide how much compensation you get.' "[17] An American spokesman, Major Kevin Krejcarek, admitted that the U.S. forces had not properly understood how to handle the custom of a solatium in Japanese culture. This prompted Dr. Robert Orr of Nippon Motorola and the American Chamber of Commerce in Japan to comment that there is something wrong when a military that has occupied Okinawa for half a century has never heard of such a basic aspect of local judicial custom.

On October 7, 1998, the inevitable again happened. A twenty-two-year-old marine corporal, drunk and driving at high speed, knocked an eighteen-year-old high school student, Yuki Uema, off her motorbike. He fled, only to be apprehended by an alert guard at his base who noticed the heavy damage to the front of his car. Possibly because the marine failed to help his victim, she died a week later, without regaining consciousness. U.S. forces then refused to hand over the suspect to the local police for a week, on the grounds that under the Status of Forces Agreement, the United States did not have to give up suspects except in "heinous crimes" until a Japanese court indicted them. The American ambassador and the Japanese prime minister were quick this time to express their condolences and to offer money as compensation; they recognized that much—from large-scale arms sales to the Japanese place in U.S. global strategy—might be at stake. A Japanese court sentenced the hit-and-run marine to twenty months in prison, and in March 1999, the Marine Corps started sending patrols of off-duty marines to the bar districts around Futenma, Kadena, Camp Foster, and Camp Hansen in a limited attempt to curb drunkenness and lawlessness among service personnel and their dependents.

Even if they avoid being raped or run down, no Okinawans can escape the endless noise the Americans make. A teacher in Ginowan City typically reports, "My class lasts for fifty minutes. It is interrupted at least three times by the incredible noise of planes landing and departing. My students cannot hear me, so we just wait patiently."[18] There are 52,000 takeoffs and landings each year at Futenma Marine Corps Air Station alone, or 142 a day. The military airfield is in the center of and entirely surrounded by Ginowan's neighborhoods. The middle of a densely populated city is hardly an appropriate place to locate an airport, let alone a military one, and genuinely thoughtful neighbors would have moved it long ago. Even the marines know this. In March 1997, the corps grounded its helicopters for a day just so the students of Ginowan's high schools could take their college entrance exams in peace. " 'Not in my backyard' politics have motivated Okinawans for a long time," asserts Joseph Nye, a Harvard political scientist and former assistant secretary of defense for international security affairs whom the Pentagon employed to study potential new "threats" to national security that might justify its expensive presence in other people's countries.[19] But Nye, while suggesting the United States keep one hundred thousand troops in Japan and South Korea until at least the year 2015, like so many American officials and policy advisers, never once visited Okinawa to see what that "backyard" was really like.

47

While the major cause of noise pollution in Okinawa is military aircraft, there are some other unusual sources. From 1973 to 1997, the 12th Marine Regiment passed its time in Okinawa by periodically firing 155 mm. howitzer shells over Highway 104 where it enters Kin village (which also happens to be where the rape took place). Every time the marines decided to fire their guns, the highway had to be closed. In 1993, for example, the marines poured 5,606 rounds into Mount Onna on the other side of the highway, causing great environmental damage, including repeated forest fires. Unsurprisingly, they also left numerous unexploded shells on its gently inclined slopes. Requests to stop lest the tourist industry, which is by far Okinawa's most important current source of income, be damaged were simply ignored.

Only after the rape did the local marine commander suspend the firing for three months, as a gesture of contrition. In response to continuing protests, the Japanese government finally found mainland sites for marine artillery practice. In so doing, it allocated ¥238 million to help relocate mainland families likely to be disturbed by one of the new firing ranges near Sendai in Miyagi Prefecture, which led the mayor of Kin to ask bitterly, "If the government can provide such compensation on the mainland, why the hell not in Okinawa?"[20]

Noise-pollution suits are starting to prove expensive for the Japanese government. In 1982, some 906 residents of Kadena and Chatan villages filed a noise-pollution suit against Kadena Air Force Base and asked the court to halt night flights. Sixteen years later the Naha branch of the Fukuoka High Court ordered the central government to pay compensation of ¥1,373 million to those plaintiffs still alive. The court did not, however, order a suspension of flights between seven P.M. and seven A.M., on the grounds that nothing in the security treaty or in domestic law allows Japan to interfere with the operations at Kadena Air Force Base. The U.S. military likes to say that the noise from its aircraft is the "sound of freedom," but many Okinawans have been so deafened that they can no longer hear it.

Closely related to noise pollution is damage to the environment. This includes serious soil erosion from artillery firing and damage to coral reefs by ships and amphibious landing practice (despite a U.S. commitment to an international initiative to save the globe's dying coral reefs). Runoff jet fuel and other toxic substances permeate the soil and water supplies in certain areas of the island and have generally neither been controlled nor cleaned up. As the U.S. Congress's General Accounting Office reported in 1998, "Marine Corps Bases, Japan, and other Okinawa-based U.S. forces were informed by a letter dated August 25, 1997, from the Government of Japan's Naha Defense Facilities Administration Bureau that the toxic substances mercury and polychlorinated biphenyls were found on the Onna communications site. The United States had closed the base and returned the land to Japan in November 1995. . . . The letter indicated that the presence of these substances has prevented the land from being returned to its owners and thus being available for reuse. The letter concludes by requesting that the United States conduct a survey, identify any contamination that may exist, and clean up bases scheduled for closure in the future."[21] The government, while proclaiming itself devoted to protecting the environment, has also claimed that the security treaty explicitly exempts the United States from any responsibility for environmental cleanup.

The most spectacular documented environmental outrage to date has been a barrage of some 1,520 "depleted uranium" shells fired in December 1995 and January 1996 into Torishima Island, located about a hundred kilometers west of the main island of Okinawa. These 25 mm. armor-piercing shells, each of which contained 147 grams of uranium, were first used by the United States in the Gulf War. It is suspected that the uranium oxide produced when this kind of projectile hits its target (along with other gases released when the Americans demolished Saddam Hussein's armories) may have been a cause of so-called Gulf War syndrome.[22] For over a year the Americans failed to inform Japanese officials about this open violation of Pentagon regulations specifying that such ammunition should be used only at specific firing ranges on the U.S. mainland. No one, in fact, would ever have known, had the *Washington*

Times not broken the story.[23] Clearly fearing its culpability, however, the military had already sent troops into Torishima in March and April 1996 but had recovered only 192 of the shells.

The use of any weapon laced with uranium in any capacity in the only nation on earth to have experienced atomic warfare firsthand—and especially given that the "hands" that destroyed Hiroshima and Nagasaki were American—was hardly likely to engender good publicity, to say the least. When the story broke, in fact, a deeply embarrassed Prime Minister Hashimoto had to reveal that he had learned about the depleted uranium shells still on Torishima from the Americans (who undoubtedly knew that the story would soon break) and had done nothing. When the unauthorized use of such ammunition in Okinawa was exposed, the assistant secretary of defense for public affairs assured the media, "There is no danger to the human body or to the environment. The level of radiation [emitted by depleted uranium bullets] is just about half that of a TV set in the 1950s."[24] But a TV set emits ultraviolet rays, not gamma or X-rays, and ultraviolet rays do not cause cancer—as the Japanese media were quick to point out. Depleted uranium bullets, on the other hand, gasify into uranium oxide upon hitting a target, such as a tank or the ground. This gas is then carried as particles in the air or dust into the lungs, bloodstream, kidneys, and bone marrow, leading to possible leukemia and tumors.

Each mini-crisis like this is in itself a mini-example of blowback, as American imperial policies and attitudes, long established, manifest themselves in particular incidents. Each of these further undermines not only long-term American policy in Asia but, far more important, long-term attitudes of the Japanese toward Americans in general. The Americans have a record of degrading some of the most exquisite subtropical terrain in the Pacific and also of depriving the Okinawan people of the livelihoods they might have reasonably expected if the bases were not located in their midst. It is a common bit of American folklore that such bases are valuable to local economies, whose peoples have vested interests in them. In the case of Okinawa, this could not be further from the truth. Its major industry today is tourism. The presence of so many sprawling, disconnected American installations, as well as over fifty thousand Americans who do not pay taxes and have no stake in Okinawa's future, does nothing to enhance the islands' attraction to Japanese and Taiwanese tourists.

As the economist and editor of the *Ryukyuanist*, Koji Taira, observes, "According to the best estimates, the incomes generated directly or indirectly by the bases are only 5 percent of the gross domestic product of Okinawa. This is far too small a contribution for an establishment sitting on 20 percent of Okinawa's land. Given the choice locations of the bases, if these areas were used as part of the civilian market economy, they should yield more than 20 percent of Okinawa's GDP [gross domestic product]. In effect, the U.S. and Japan are forcing on Okinawa's economy a deadweight loss of 15 percent of its GDP every year. In a democracy, such an abuse of the state's taxing power should never be tolerated."[25] According to the *Nikkei Weekly*, a Japanese business newspaper, the aggregate income from the bases, including off-base consumption by American military personnel, the salaries of the approximately eight thousand Okinawans working on the bases, and rents paid to Okinawan landowners by the Japanese government for the land on which the bases sit, totaled ¥162 billion in fiscal year 1994, or 4.9 percent of gross prefectural income.[26]

Most of the acreage on the mainland used for American bases is owned by the Japanese government and housed Imperial Japanese military installations up until 1945. In Okinawa, virtually all the land occupied by bases was seized from private owners either at the time of the Battle of Okinawa or during the 1950s. As former governor of Okinawa Prefecture, Masahide Ota, an authority on the island's postwar history, testified in a base lands case before the Fukuoka High Court on December 22, 1995: "Just after the Battle of Okinawa, while forcibly confining survivors in concentration camps, they [the American military] immediately enclosed all the land and picked up land for military use to the extent they wanted for ensuring U.S. military purposes. It was done as if drawing lines on a blank map. When residents were allowed to come home from the camps, they found their hometowns had disappeared behind barbed wire."[27]

This process of seizure at bayonet point followed by the burning and bulldozing of houses and cultivated fields continued throughout the 1950s. Okinawan objections to American arbitrariness and unwillingness to pay appropriate compensation led to the first demonstrations against the U.S. presence and to the election in 1956 of a Communist mayor of Naha. The Americans thereupon rescinded the law under which the mayor had been elected, stripped him of office, and used the Central Intelligence Agency to funnel money to his conservative opponents.

The protest movement that lasted from 1952 to 1957 was the first of three major waves of protest focusing on bringing democracy to Okinawa. Its issues were the right to freedom of speech for Okinawans, unionization, proper compensation for expropriated lands, and popular election of a chief executive. The second wave crested at the end of the 1960s; its issues were the use of B-52s based in Okinawa to bomb Vietnam and the impact of the segregated military whorehouses that served the black and white G.I.s, near Kadena Air Force Base. This movement resulted in the reversion of Okinawa to Japanese sovereignty. The third wave, which arose in the wake of the 1995 rape case, still continues. Although none of these can claim to have produced victory—which by definition will not be achieved until the last base has been shut down—they have given Okinawa a special political culture. Unlike the main islands, where after the war the Allied occupation bestowed democracy and a "peace constitution" on the people from above, Okinawa is the only Japanese community whose residents have fought for what democracy they enjoy.

In the 1950s, one of the least-known American tactics for seizing land while controlling the rebellious sentiments of expropriated farmers was to offer them land in Bolivia and aid in emigrating. On arrival in Bolivia, however, the Okinawan farmers discovered that the land was nearly unusable jungle and the Americans had no intention of delivering any of the promised financial assistance. As neither American nor Japanese citizens, they had no place to turn for help and so were at the mercy of the terrain, the climate, and their Bolivian neighbors. Most of the early settlers died of disease or fled to Bolivian towns, to Peru or Brazil. The few who survived at Colonia Okinawa, as it was called, north of Santa Cruz, Bolivia, are today, after almost unbelievably difficult lives, comparatively successful farmers. However, of some 3,218 identified emigrants whom the Americans shipped to Bolivia between 1954 and 1964, only 806 (including their offspring) reside there today.[28]

Most of the land that the Americans occupy in Okinawa is still legally owned by 31,521 individuals or families who are forced by various laws to lease it to the Japanese government, which, in turn, subleases it to the Americans without charge. These leases must periodically be renewed. In 1991, newly elected Governor Ota exercised the power given to him under the forced leasing laws to renew some 2,636 leases that had expired. This was, he has explained, the "most difficult decision of my life"—the ruling Liberal Democratic Party had made economic support for Okinawa contingent on preservation of the bases.[29] In late 1995, with the movement inspired by the rape already growing, he refused to renew any more expired leases, forcing Prime Minister Hashimoto to play a politically unattractive role as lackey to the Pentagon. He had to renew the leases himself.

A sizable number of small landholders have become explicit and outspoken antiwar landlords, including some three thousand Okinawan and mainland intellectuals who have bought handkerchief-sized parcels of base land in order to protest the continued American presence. They are known as the one-*tsubo* landlords—a *tsubo* being a measure equal to 3.3 square meters—and have proved a severe thorn in Tokyo's side. In May 1997, as the leases of many of the one-*tsubo* landlords came up for renewal, it became clear that the prefectural government would not save Tokyo's face by forcibly renewing them. Prime Minister Hashimoto therefore introduced and guided through the Diet legislation that transferred all control over leases for base land to the central government. This law is almost surely unconstitutional on several grounds—

it deprives Japanese citizens of their property rights without due process of law and it applies to only one place, Okinawa, although Article 95 of the Constitution stipulates that no law can deal with a particular area without its people's consent.

The most famous of the Okinawan antiwar landlords is Shoichi Chibana. In 1945, his grandfather, armed only with a bamboo pole, attempted to protect his land from seizure and was shot to death. This land, in American hands ever since, is today on the site of the Sobe Communications Facility, one of numerous American installations in Okinawa for eavesdropping on the conversations of the surrounding nations, including Japan, and for communicating with U.S. submarines. In the spring of 1996, the lease on that land expired and Chibana refused to renew it. As a result, until the enactment of Hashimoto's law a year later, the Americans were illegally occupying Chibana's land. Much to the irritation of the American and Japanese governments, the Okinawan police forced the Americans to open their gates to Chibana and let him visit his land. On May 14, 1996, he and twenty-nine friends legally entered the Sobe Communications Facility, held a picnic on the lawn, sang Okinawan songs, and conducted a memorial service for his grandfather and father. The Japanese government will go to almost any lengths to avoid a repetition of this widely reported and photographed event.

One of the lengths to which it will go is to spend large amounts of public money to cover the costs of the bases, thereby turning the Pentagon into a central component of the Japan lobby in Washington, D.C. Japan is not obligated by any treaty to do this. The Status of Forces Agreement clearly states that "the United States will bear without cost to Japan all expenditures incident to the maintenance of the United States forces in Japan" except for the "construction of facilities." But in May 1978, Shin Kanemaru, then chief of the Japanese Defense Agency and one of the legendary power brokers of the Liberal Democratic Party, arranged for Japan to donate ¥6.2 billion toward support of the U.S. forces. Kanemaru dubbed this the *omoiyari yosan*, or "sympathy budget," because the American government had said to Tokyo that it was experiencing budgetary difficulties following the Vietnam War and could not cover all the costs of its bases in Japan. Initially the *omoiyari yosan* covered only the medical insurance of Japanese civilians working on the bases, but the Americans have asked for an increase in the sympathy budget every year since, and by 1997 it was ¥273.7 billion ($2.36 billion), more than forty-four times larger than the original sum.

Needless to say, the American press has barely reported these developments; and the Pentagon certainly never uses the term "sympathy budget," preferring instead the euphemism "host nation support." According to a 1998 Department of Defense report on allied nations' "contributions to the common defense," Japan's host nation support is the most generous of all. It supplied 78 percent of the costs of the 42,962 U.S. troops on its soil, while Germany paid only 27 percent of the costs of the 48,878 U.S. troops based there. Of the 1997 *omoiyari yosan*, a bit more than half, or ¥146.2 billion, went to pay the salaries of Japanese who provide some 1,472 separate services to the U.S. troops as translators, gardeners, waitresses, and manicurists, among other things; ¥95.3 billion went to improve American apartments, golf courses, and churches; and ¥31.9 billion, to pay the costs of the public utilities supplied to the bases.[30]

The overall Japanese government budget for the bases in fiscal year 1997 was ¥647 billion, including rents paid to landowners for use of their land, investments in countermeasures against noise pollution, and funds to "realign" bases in Okinawa in fulfillment of promises made by the Americans after the rape incident ("realignment" was the official Japanese-American euphemism for moving bases around *within* Okinawa but not actually changing them in any substantial ways). The total national budgetary support for U.S. forces is ¥28 billion more than the entire 1997 budget of Okinawa Prefecture, 2.2 times greater than Japan's expenditures for university subsidies, and 2.1 times the amount it spends for day-care centers. The United States has military bases in nineteen countries, but Japan is the only one that pays all the costs of local employees. Whatever economic interest some people in Okinawa might have in the presence of the facilities, one wonders why the rest of Japan puts up with this use of national tax moneys.

In May 1997, 296 Japanese citizens from twenty-nine prefectures filed suit in Osaka District Court arguing that the *omoiyari yosan* violates Article 9 of Japan's pacifist Constitution and asking that the amount of their national taxes spent for the bases be returned to them. This was the first suit to legally challenge the use of public money to maintain the American military, and its sponsors say that it was partly motivated by the 1995 rape incident. Given the length of time that Japan's ultra-conservative court system can take to resolve something it basically does not want to touch, it is extremely unlikely that this suit will ever be concluded. However, the global economic crisis that began in East Asia in 1997 may very well spell the end of the *omoiyari yosan* when it next comes up for reauthorization. Even Japan's obsequiously pro-American government may find it has better things on which to spend its money in the coming century.

Nonetheless, according to the *Pacific Stars and Stripes*, in 1998 the marines asked the Japanese to build them what would be, if completed, in 2003, the largest golf course on Okinawa. The new four-hundred-acre facility on virgin land at the Kadena Ammunition Storage Area would replace the 116-acre Awase Meadows Golf Course in urban Naha, which the Americans agreed to return to "civilian use" if Japan would supply them with equivalent facilities elsewhere on the island. The government has no desire to build the new golf course, noting that there is already an eighteen-hole course within Kadena Air Force Base. (Kadena also houses a twenty-six-lane bowling alley, two gymnasiums, two parks, two theaters, two libraries, three swimming pools, four tennis courts, seventeen baseball diamonds, four officers' and enlisted men's clubs, a riding academy, a ballet studio, and a dog obedience school.) But these are Air Force facilities, as Lt. Col. Billy Birdwell, deputy director of U.S. Forces Japan Public Affairs, explained: "We want the public to know that this is not going to be another golf course on Kadena Air Base. This will be a Marine facility, Marine managed."[31]

In 1996, General C. C. Krulak, the marine commandant, became so worried that the rape incident might force his troops to give up Okinawa's plush officers' clubs and golf courses that he proposed moving the 3rd Marine Division to Darwin, Australia. This idea fell through when it became clear that Australia would not pay the same lucrative benefits to keep the marines happy.

The prefecture of Okinawa is, in fact, forced to pay many other costs that are incidental to housing the bases. There are an estimated ten thousand children of mixed parentage—offspring of unknown or long-gone American fathers and Okinawan mothers—whom the prefecture is obliged to support and educate. During his 1998 visit to Washington, Governor Ota indicated to Kurt Campbell, deputy assistant secretary of defense for East Asia and the Pacific, that "we have a situation in Okinawa where children with dual citizenship and one parent who is American are not receiving an adequate education." He asked that they be allowed to attend schools on the bases free of charge. Campbell, who was three years old when the revision of the security treaty was signed in 1960, fobbed off the seventy-three-year-old Ota with a standard response that disguises the nature of the de facto American colonialism in Okinawa: he urged the governor to take up such issues with the government in Tokyo. Since Okinawa is part of Japan, the United States now pretends that its military bases are there as a result of Japan's allocation of base sites. This amounts to a permanent collusion of the United States and Japan against Okinawa.[32]

What does the U.S. government say it is doing in Okinawa fifty-five years after the end of World War II? Throughout the postwar period, the United States has vacillated between two basic arguments: the forces are there either in order to defend Japan or in order to contain Japan. Though one contradicts the other, each is alternately resurrected, depending on the current situation in East Asia, and used to justify policies that were first formulated to deal with conditions that existed in 1951, when the peace treaty and the security treaty were negotiated, and that ceased to exist at least two decades ago. Even in 1951, Japan was in no danger of being attacked by another nation and even less capable of attacking one of its neighbors.

According to Article 5 of the Japanese-American Security Treaty, the purpose of the treaty is to defend Japan. Needless to say, the document did not explain whom Japan was to be defended from or dwell on whether Japan needed America's help in defending itself. No attempt has been made to invade the main islands since a Mongol fleet dispatched by Kublai Khan was dispersed by a "divine wind" in A.D. 1281. After the Battle of Okinawa in 1945, the Americans essentially gave up on the idea of an invasion and turned instead to defeating Japan through the use of nuclear weapons, strategic bombing, and a blockade.

Since World War II, only the former Soviet Union could conceivably have mounted such an invasion, although there is no evidence that it ever seriously considered doing so. American and Japanese defense officials love to say that Okinawa's excessive burdens in the Cold War are a result of the island's "strategic location." But Okinawa was hardly well located to anchor a defense against the USSR, which in any case self-destructed a decade ago.

The Pentagon regularly suggests that Japan faces potential threats from North Korea and China. But North Korea is a failed Communist regime unable to feed its own people and still engaged in a barely repressed civil war with South Korea, which is twice as populous, infinitely richer, and fully capable of defending itself. The Japanese government has strongly expressed its own fears of a potential North Korean missile assault ever since Pyongyang in August 1998 fired a rocket over Japan in the process of launching a small satellite. The real threat, however, is that a suicidal North Korea—itself feeling threatened by the might of the United States—could deliver some kind of terror weapon (if it has one) to Japan by boat and detonate it there as a final, if futile, act of retaliation for Japan's brutal colonial rule of and postwar hostility toward it. This would be more than half a century late, the worst blowback nightmare and a horrific reminder that the acts of empire are seldom forgotten by those who have suffered them. To date, however, there is no evidence that North Korea is suicidally inclined. Public opinion in Japan, in fact, remains deeply suspicious of American claims that North

Korea is a threat. In 1994, when the possible existence of a North Korean nuclear arsenal first surfaced in the media, in a four-nation poll of attitudes, the Japanese named the United States as "the biggest threat to world peace," followed by Russia and only then by North Korea.[33]

The notion that the main thrust of the security treaty was to defend against Chinese expansionism, or to "contain" China, or to provide a platform from which the United States could intervene militarily in the Taiwan Strait to defend Taiwan, Japan's former colony, from attack by mainland China is a very embarrassing and dangerous one for Japan. In Japan's own peace treaty with China ending World War II, Japan clearly acknowledged Taiwan as a part of China. Chinese leaders regularly remind Japan that enlarging the scope of the security treaty to include Taiwan directly violates commitments Japan has long made to China.

The Japanese public (and even the conservative ruling party) do not in any case believe that their country is threatened by China. It is widely accepted that Taiwan's highly modern defense forces effectively deter any form of military takeover by the mainland. For the public, given what Japan did in China during World War II, a serious conflict with that nation over Taiwan is unthinkable. The Japanese also applaud the evolution of the previously revolutionary People's Republic from its emphasis on opposition to its former imperialist oppressors to domestic development through commerce with them. Japan's policy is to do everything in its power to adjust to the reemergence of China on the world stage. It also appreciates that China, while resurgent, still has only a gross domestic product of $560 billion, compared to Japan's $5 trillion and the United States' $7.2 trillion; a defense budget of $31.7 billion, compared to Japan's $47 billion and the United States' $263.9 billion; and perhaps as many as 149 strategic nuclear weapons, compared to the United States' 7,150.

In polls, the Japanese public has repeatedly expressed a greater concern about oscillations in U.S. policy toward China than about anything China has done or has the capability to do to Japan. Given the large military expeditionary forces the United States maintains in Japan, the real fear is that increased American belligerence toward China might invite Chinese retaliation against the bases in Japan. This is one reason why former Japanese prime minister Morihiro Hosokawa advocates maintaining the Japanese-American alliance while eliminating permanent U.S. forces from Japanese territory.[34]

The Japanese, too, have the ability to defend themselves from any likely nonnuclear threat to their security. With the second largest navy in the Pacific, more destroyers than the United States, and 120 F-15 fighter interceptors, Japan is quite capable of meeting any challenge that might arise, including one to its merchant fleet. Shunji Taoka, the military correspondent for the *Asahi* newspaper, argues that Japan has long been fully capable of supplying its own air, naval, and ground defenses and need rely on the United States only for its "nuclear umbrella." According to Taoka, if the United States withdrew its forces, Japan would not need to add anything further to its defense expenditures in order to maintain its security.[35]

If, then, American troops are not in Japan to defend Japan, could they be there to contain it? Is their role that of an "honorable watchdog" (*gobanken-sama*), as many conservative Japanese politicians have contended in the postwar years? The most famous expression of this came from Lt. Gen. Henry C. Stackpole, commander of the 3rd Marine Division in Okinawa, in a 1990 interview with the *Washington Post*.[36] His forces, he claimed, were like a "cap in the bottle," preventing the monster of revived Japanese militarism from jumping out and, as in the first half of the twentieth century, threatening other East Asian countries. Versions of this view are often seen in the American press; a typical example also from the *Post*: "Neighboring countries, with a particularly vivid memory of Japanese aggression during World War II, also worry that if the U.S. withdrew its troops, Japan would almost certainly build up its own military power."[37]

One problem with this theory is that the United States has long pushed Japan to build up exactly the military power it is supposed to be containing. The government sells more advanced weapons to Japan than to any other nation or territory except Saudi Arabia and Taiwan. It has allowed the licensing of the technology of General Dynamics' F-16 fighter plane (a derivative of which in Japan became the FS-X); it has sold Japan advanced Aegis ship missile-defense systems, ultrasophisticated AWACS command and control aircraft, Patriot missile-defense batteries, and with highly publicized threats about the dangers of the "rogue state" of North Korea has even gotten the Japanese to agree to help fund research for an antiballistic missile system. And that only scratches the surface of U.S. arms and technology transfers. In addition, administration and Pentagon officials have urged their Japanese equivalents to be strategically bolder in deploying Japanese defense forces in Asia—far bolder, in fact, than most Japanese would like their country to be.

The Pentagon is today the most important political force inside or outside Japan calling for a greatly expanded Japanese military role in world affairs. In a public-opinion poll conducted by the *Asahi* newspaper, 43 percent of the Japanese public opposed and only 37 percent approved the expanded Guidelines on U.S.-Japan Defense Cooperation that the two countries signed in 1997.[38] These commit Japan to supporting American troops in times of "emergency" with many forms of assistance—opening up Japan's civilian airports to American military operations, collaborating with American forces in removing mines, enforcing naval embargoes, and other types of direct military operations. These guidelines, as the *Asahi* newspaper declared editorially, have, in effect, rewritten the security treaty without consultations either with the Japanese Diet or Congress.[39] Such ongoing American policies undoubtedly serve to maintain American hegemony in the Pacific but bear no relation to a supposed "watchdog" role.

As former Okinawan governor Ota commented, "What's actually happening in Japan is that, with practically no public debate, hypothetical enemies are produced one after another, and potential threats are loudly proclaimed. People talk of the need to maintain an American military presence and to pass legislation to deal with national security emergencies, without making any move to accept bases in their own communities."[40] The Pentagon understands that it cannot come up with a credible threat to Japan or any other nation in East Asia that would demand the forward deployment of American troops. As mentioned in chapter 1, it has therefore decided to rely on something comparable to the old domino theory used to justify the war in Vietnam. According to that theory, nations all over Asia and elsewhere would "go Communist" if North Vietnam were allowed to win its civil war. With communism long gone as an enemy, the new, abstract danger is "instability." Grave dangers, it is said, will result from the "destabilizing" act of withdrawing American troops from Asia. This new, exceedingly vague doctrine indirectly acknowledges that the purpose of American forces in Japan is neither to defend nor to contain Japan but simply by their presence to prevent the assumed dangers of their absence. The Japanese are being propagandized to believe that in these unknown future conflicts they will have a huge if unspecified stake.

In 1995, this new domino-like theory was given a classic formulation in a series of essays by former assistant secretary of defense Joseph Nye. With very little in the way of specific scenarios or threats, he argued in *Foreign Affairs* magazine that "security is like oxygen: you tend not to notice it until you lose it."[41] In the *Washington Post*, he put it this way: "Our forward presence provides for the stability—the oxygen—that has helped provide for East Asian economic growth."[42] And in a Department of Defense publication, he offered, "Having United States forces in Asia also promotes democratic development in Asia, by providing a clear, readily observable example of the American military's apolitical role."[43]

Such formulations have since entered official Washington culture and are now served up as catechism. On March 24, 1997, for instance, Vice President Al Gore told American troops and their families at Yokota Air Force Base near Tokyo, "The peace and security of the Pacific region rest on your backs."[44] And the Pentagon has come to like this idea so much that it has announced its intention to keep troops in Korea indefinitely, even after North and South Korea have been unified. Secretary of Defense William Cohen has also defended the continued presence in Japan by insisting that any pullout would create a dangerous power "vacuum" that "might be filled in a way that would not enhance stability but detract from it."[45]

The most obvious problem with these propositions is that they have simply not proved true. When "instability" finally hit the region, the American forward bases offered no solace. The economic crisis that began in 1997 revealed that in East Asia, rather than security being like oxygen, it is money that you may not miss until it is pulled out. The presence of American military forces in the region did not prevent the instability—in some cases, chaos—that ensued in the wake of this crisis. In fact, the Pentagon only made matters worse by continuing to try to hawk massively expensive weapons systems to countries no longer able to afford them. As for the military's contributing to economic growth, former Japanese prime minister Morihiro Hosokawa has this sharp observation: "It was after U.S. forces withdrew from Indochina and Thailand in the 1970s that economic growth in Southeast Asia gained momentum and economic relations with the United States began to expand. The economy of the Philippines took off after the U.S. forces left there in the 1990s. These experiences show that there is little or no relation between foreign military presence and economic growth."[46]

That the forward deployment of American troops brings "stability" to East Asia is, of course, a false syllogism and, as military strategist Col. Harry Summers Jr. puts it, the equivalent of using elephant bane in New York City. Elephant bane is a chemical repellent spread by African farmers to keep elephants out of their gardens and orchards. Pentagon theorists, Colonel Summers suggests, are like the New Yorker who spreads elephant bane around his apartment and then extols its benefits because he encounters no elephants.[47] The strategy "works" because the threat is illusory. The real, long-term threat to stability in East Asia is the economic crisis caused by an American determination to perpetuate its system of satellites and its own regional hegemony long after it has lost whatever Cold War economic or political rationale it had.

Why is the United States really still in Okinawa? For its military personnel, the answer is obvious. They enjoy being based there for the same reasons that the former Soviet Union's troops enjoyed being based in East Germany. Life in one of their country's military colonies was for the officers and enlisted men and women of both armies better than anything most of them could possibly have experienced back home. As the unofficial guide to American military bases in Okinawa puts it, "If you prefer living with a view of beautiful Kin Bay from a lofty high-rise, [Camp] Courtney [headquarters of the 3rd Marine Division] provides hundreds of scenic dwellings in the form of nine-story apartment complexes." For the marine family's shopping needs, "At a construction cost of more than $11 million, the [Camp] Foster Exchange is the newest in the Pacific area. It offers all the conveniences of a modern shopping center. . . . When they're not at work, [Camp] Hansen Marines can take advantage of two of the most beautiful beaches on the island, Kin Red and Kin Blue."[48] All active-duty military personnel on Okinawa receive either rent- and utility-cost-free housing on base or enormous housing allowances ranging from $900 to $2,000 a month, depending on rank and family size. These benefits are supplemented by generous cost-of-living allowances—which for a captain or a major with one dependent is about $700 a month. This is not hardship living.

Okinawa is still essentially a military colony of the Pentagon's, a huge safe house where Green Berets and the Defense Intelligence Agency, not to mention the air force and Marine Corps, can do things they would not dare do in the United States. It is used to project American power throughout Asia in the service of a de facto U.S. grand strategy to perpetuate or increase American hegemonic power in this crucial region. The U.S. military is the author and prime beneficiary of this strategy, and it is in the driver's seat executing it. This becomes clear when we turn to some of its secret global (and especially Asian) activities that it is fully aware of—but that other parts of its government and its people are not.

3

STEALTH IMPERIALISM

Offering predictions about the future has never been one of the more reliable human activities, so to guess exactly how blowback may play itself out in the twenty-first century is, at best, a perilous undertaking. But one can certainly see that just as the North Koreans retain considerable bitterness toward their former Japanese overlords, so present American policy is seeding resentments that are bound to breed attempts at revenge.

To make this matter more complicated, much of what the U.S. military and intelligence communities do in Asia and globally is a lot less visible than in Okinawa. Largely by design, much of America's imperial politics takes place well below the sight lines of the American public. Throughout the world in the wake of the Cold War, official and unofficial U.S. representatives have been acting, often in covert ways, to prop up repressive regimes or their militaries and police forces, sometimes against significant segments of their own populaces. Such policies are likely to produce future instances of blowback whose origins, on arrival, will seem anything but self-evident to the American public.

Every now and then, however, America's responsibility for its imperial policies briefly comes into public view. One such moment occurred on July 17, 1998, in Rome, when, by a margin of 120 to 7, delegates from the nations of the world voted to establish an international criminal court to bring to justice soldiers and political leaders charged with war crimes, crimes against humanity, and genocide. This court will differ from the International Court of Justice in The Hague in that, unlike the older court, which can settle disputes only among nations, it will have jurisdiction over individuals. As a result, efforts like those to bring Bosnian and Rwandan war criminals to justice, which today need specially constituted U.N. tribunals, will be far easier. The new court will put on trial individuals who commit or order atrocities comparable to those of the Nazis during World War II, Pol Pot in Cambodia, Saddam Hussein in Iraq, the Serbs in Bosnia and Kosovo, the Hutus in Rwanda, or military governments like those of El Salvador, Argentina, Chile, Honduras, Guatemala, Burma, and Indonesia in the 1980s and 1990s.

Leading democracies of the world, including Britain, Canada, Holland, France, Japan, and Germany, supported the treaty. Only Algeria, China, Israel, Libya, Qatar, Yemen, and the United States voted against it. With his opening speech to the conference, American ambassador Bill Richardson managed to infuriate virtually every human rights group on earth and led many delegates to accuse the United States of "neocolonial aspirations." The United States, he said, would support only a court that received its cases solely from the U.N. Security Council, where a single American vote can veto any action.

American officials claim that they must protect their two hundred thousand troops permanently deployed in forty countries from "politically motivated charges." They maintain that, due to America's "special global responsibilities," no proceedings can be permitted to take place against its soldiers or clandestine agents unless the United States itself agrees to them. In essence, America's leaders believe that their "lone superpower" must be above the very concept of international law—unless defined and controlled by them.

The terms of the treaty setting up the court specifically include as war crimes rape, forced pregnancy, torture, and the forcible recruitment of children into the military. The United States objected to including these acts within the court's jurisdiction, claiming that the court should concern itself only with genocide. The French at first joined the United States in opposing the treaty because French troops had trained the Hutu-controlled Rwandan military, which in 1993 and 1994 helped organize the massacres of some eight hundred thousand people belonging to the Tutsi tribe. France feared that its officers and men could be charged with complicity in genocide. After a clause was added to the treaty allowing signatories to exempt themselves from the court's jurisdiction for its first seven years, France said that its fears had been assuaged and agreed to sign.

This escape clause was still not enough for the United States. Its representative held that because the "world's greatest military and economic power . . . is expected" to intervene in humanitarian catastrophes wherever they occur, this "unique position" makes its personnel especially vulnerable to the mandate of an international criminal court capable of arresting and trying individuals. He did not deal with the question of whether war crimes charges against Americans might on some occasions be warranted, nor did he, of course, raise the possibility that if his country intervened less often in the affairs of other states where none of its vital interests were involved, it might avoid the possibility of even a capricious indictment.

Secretary of Defense William Cohen attempted to intimidate delegates to the conference by threatening to withdraw American forces from the territories of those allies that did not support the United States' proposal for limiting the international criminal court's jurisdiction. In Washington, Jesse Helms, chairman of the Senate Foreign Relations Committee, at hearings on the new international criminal court treaty urged the president and Congress to announce that it would indeed make good on Cohen's threat—a suggestion that led some Japanese, among others, to speculate that ratifying the treaty might finally be a way to get the Americans out of their countries.

In his book *Death by Government*, the historian Rudolph Rummel estimates that during the twentieth century, 170 million civilians have been victims of war crimes, crimes against humanity, and genocide.[1] As Michael Scharf of the American Society of International Law notes, the pledge of "never again" by the two war crimes tribunals that the Allies set up in Nuremberg and Tokyo in the wake of World War II has in the intervening years become "again and again."[2]

At Nuremberg, the United States pioneered the idea of holding governmental leaders responsible for war crimes, and it is one of the few countries that has an assistant secretary of state for human rights. Its pundits and lawmakers endlessly criticize other nations for failing to meet American standards in the treatment of human beings under their jurisdiction. No country has been more active than the United States in publicizing the idea of "human rights," even if it has been notably silent in some cases, ignoring, implicitly condoning, or even endorsing acts of state terrorism by regimes with which it has been closely associated. (Examples would include the repression of the Kwangju rebels in South Korea in 1980; all of the right-wing death squads in Central America during the 1980s; the Shah's repression of dissidents in Iran when he was allied with the United States; the United States' support in bringing General Augusto Pinochet to power in Chile and its subsequent willingness to exonerate him from responsibility for the torture and killing of at least four thousand of his own citizens; and Turkey's genocide against its Kurdish population.) The American government displays one face to its own people (and its English-speaking allies) but another in areas where the support of repressive governments seems necessary to maintain American imperial dominance. Whenever this contradiction is revealed, as at Rome, Americans try to cover it up with rhetoric about the national burden of being the "indispensable nation," or what the Council on Foreign Relations calls the world's "reluctant sheriff."

Only seven months before the Rome vote, there was another moment when the nature of America's stealth imperialism was revealed. In December 1997, in Ottawa, 123 nations pledged to ban the use, production, or shipment of antipersonnel land mines. Retired American military leaders like General Norman Schwarzkopf, commanding general of allied forces in the Gulf War, have endorsed the ban, arguing that these primitive but lethal weapons have no role in modern warfare. The Clinton administration, however, bowed to military vested interests desperate to retain land mines in the American arsenal. Among other things, it insisted that land mines were needed to protect South Korea against the "North's overwhelming military advantage," itself a myth. The holdouts against this agreement were Afghanistan, China, Russia (which later reversed its position), Vietnam—and the United States. An American citizen, Jody Williams of Putney, Vermont, would later win the Nobel Peace Prize for her efforts in organizing nations and various lobbying groups like the Vietnam Veterans of America Foundation to work toward ending the use of this "garbage weapon"—a phrase from Robert Muller, another American and a Vietnam veteran wounded by a land mine, who set in motion the movement that resulted in the treaty.[3] The Clinton administration felt so embarrassed by its vote that in May 1998 it convened its own Conference on Global Humanitarian Demining at the State Department in a public relations attempt to improve its image. Only twenty-one countries attended.

There are today between sixty million and one hundred million deployed land mines in some sixty countries around the world (at least ten million in Cambodia alone and another nine million in Angola). They cost on average about three dollars apiece to produce. They kill some twenty-six thousand people a year, primarily civilians in developing countries, and they have been responsible for the deaths of more people than all the weapons of mass destruction combined.

Although the U.S. military claims that it has accounted for all the mines it has laid in Korea and that they cause no civilian casualties, this is simply untrue. There are, for example, still some twenty thousand to thirty thousand M14 antipersonnel mines in the ground in the Chungri mountain area of Yong-do, just off the seaport of Pusan in the extreme south of Korea. The U.S. forces laid the mines in 1956 to protect a missile unit it based there, and they were never removed when the unit was relocated. They have been blamed for many civilian injuries and deaths since the 1960s.[4]

The Australian government, which strongly backed the Ottawa treaty, estimates that it would take 1,100 years to clear the world's mines using current techniques, which depend on metal detection. Modern land mines actually contain little metal, and Australia is sponsoring research to locate buried mines through their "thermal footprints"—that is, by identifying irregularities in ground-surface temperatures created by the different properties of mines and the earth around them. It plans to incorporate this technology into unmanned aerial vehicles whose task will be to detect mines from the air and so lessen current risks to ground personnel in mine-clearing operations.[5] One might well ask why the Pentagon, with its $267.2 billion budget for the year 2000, has not provided serious funding for similar research.

Former marine Bobby Muller, who in 1969 was blown off a road in Vietnam by a mine and later crippled by gunfire, says that President Clinton told him he simply could not "risk a breach with the Pentagon establishment by daring to sign the treaty." Jody Williams put it more bluntly, saying that Clinton "did not have the courage to be the commander-in-chief of his military."[6] But these comments may miss the point. It is not just a matter of personal courage. The relationship between the civilian elite that runs this country and its powerful military has undergone a sea change since the 1950s. It is now increasingly likely that a congressman, a senator, a state department official, even a president will not have served in the military. The draft-deferment system during the Vietnam War signaled the early stages of this process, in which promising students and professionals—mainly middle- or upper-class young men—were kept out of Vietnam in the name of national security and the nation's welfare, while the poor and working-class largely fought the war. Both President Clinton and his secretary of defense William Cohen enjoyed student deferments during Vietnam (Cohen had a marital one as well), and neither served in the armed forces. In the wake of Vietnam, with the military transformed into a purely volunteer career choice, the gap between the experiences of the civilian and the military hierarchies has only widened—and with the threat of the former USSR ended, the fact is that the military has for the first time begun to slip beyond civilian control.

When it comes to an issue like land mines, a civilian president, even one with better command credentials than Clinton, can no longer afford to cross his military leaders. Similarly, it is hardly imaginable today that a president could support something like an international criminal court that offers the threat, no matter how distant, of putting American men in uniform (or their civilian surrogates around the world) at risk of indictment. George Washington's Farewell Address now reads more like a diagnosis than a warning: he counseled Americans to "avoid the necessity of those overgrown military establishments, which under any form of government are inauspicious to liberty, and which are to be regarded as particularly hostile to Republican Liberty."

When, in Rome, the U.S. representative expressed fears of "politically motivated charges" against Americans, he was actually worrying about, among other matters, situations in which Americans might use a brutal local military to undermine what it deemed an "unacceptable" regime, as has happened numerous times in the past—in Prime Minister Patrice Lumumba's Congo in 1961, in President Ngo Dinh Diem's South Vietnam in 1963, and in President Salvador Allende's Chile in 1973. Such activities have often been foreshadowed by the military "training" programs the United States has long conducted with the militaries of other nations around the world.

In 1987, in fact, the government created a new Special Operations Command headquartered in Tampa, Florida, and placed it under an equally new assistant secretary of defense for special operations and low-intensity conflict. The command's purpose was to consolidate and coordinate the activities of the forty-seven thousand "special forces" groups scattered across the military's complex organizational charts, including the army's Green Berets, Rangers, and covert Delta Force; the Navy's SEALS and covert Team 6; and the special operations and commando units of the air force and the Marine Corps. One of the sponsors of this new structure was William Cohen, then a Republican senator from Maine, whose "keen interest in special operations" *Washington Post* reporter Dana Priest has noted "dates back decades."[7] Some military professionals and observers discount special operations because they do not rely on traditional military subdivisions and because they cost so little money compared with carrier task forces or B-2 bombers. Their political clout, however, vastly exceeds their budgetary needs and they were in no way "downsized" after the end of the Cold War. These covert units work closely with the Central Intelligence Agency and the Pentagon's Defense Intelligence Agency (DIA). Programs like the CIA's efforts at an army base in Colorado and in Okinawa until 1968 to train some four hundred Tibetan exiles to fight the Chinese or the CIA's vast operations in supplying weapons to guerrillas harassing the Soviet forces in Afghanistan during the 1980s have now been turned over to the Special Operations Command.

In 1991, Congress inadvertently gave the military's special forces a green light to penetrate virtually every country on earth. It passed a law (Section 2011, Title 10) authorizing something called the Joint Combined Exchange Training (JCET) program. This allowed the Department of Defense to send special operations forces on overseas exercises with military units of other countries so long as the primary purpose of the mission was stated to be the training of our soldiers, not theirs. The law did not indicate what JCET exercises should train these troops to do, but one purpose was certainly to train them in espionage. They return from such exercises loaded with information about and photographs of the country they have visited, and with new knowledge of its military units, terrain, and potential adversaries. As of 1998 the Special Operations Command had established JCET missions in 110 countries.

The various special forces have interpreted this law as an informal invitation to train foreign military forces in numerous lethal skills, as well as to establish relationships with their officer corps aimed at bringing them on board as possible assets for future political operations. Most of this has been done without any oversight by Congress, the State Department, or ambassadors in the countries where JCET exercises have been conducted. As a series of exposé articles in the *Washington Post* indicated in 1998, most members of the foreign policy apparatus had never even heard of JCET, and the assistant secretary of defense in charge of these special operations was noticeably vague in his answers to congressional questions about the programs.[8]

It has only slowly come to light, for instance, that in JCET exercises Americans offered crucial training to the Turkish mountain commandos, who in their ongoing operations against their country's rebellious Kurdish population have killed at least twenty-two thousand people; that during 1998 multiple special forces operations were carried out in each of the nineteen countries of Latin America and in nine Caribbean nations; and that United States special forces units have given training in such skills as advanced sniper techniques, close-quarters combat, military operations in urban terrain, and psychological warfare operations to military units in Colombia, Rwanda, Surinam, Equatorial Guinea, Sri Lanka, Pakistan, and Papua New Guinea, among other nations. In each of these cases, they were acting in violation of U.S. human rights policies and sometimes of direct presidential or congressional prohibitions. (For example, special operations training continued in Colombia even after President Clinton had "decertified" that country for most military aid and assistance.)

The *Washington Post* obtained a copy of a 1990 Department of Defense manual entitled *Doctrine for Special Forces Operations*, which describes the main activity of special forces on JCET missions as giving instruction in FID, or "foreign internal defense." In other words, most of the training exercises are meant to prepare foreign militaries for actions against their own populaces or rebel forces in their countries. The manual defines FID as organizing, training, advising, and assisting a foreign military establishment in order to protect its society from "subversion, lawlessness, and insurgency." Brig. Gen. Robert W. Wagner of the U.S. Southern Command in Miami told Douglas Farah of the *Washington Post* that FID is the "heart" of special operations, and an officer of the U.S. Army's Special Forces Command assured Dana Priest that FID is "our bread and butter." FID is, of course, hardly what Congress specified in the law as the function of JCET, but congressional control over military activities is by now so minimal that the Pentagon pays little attention to specifications that are displeasing. Stripped of its euphemistic language, FID amounts to little more than instruction in state terrorism. Republican representative Christopher Smith, chairman of the House of Representatives Subcommittee on International Operations and Human

Rights, says, "Our joint exercises and training of military units—that have been charged over and over again with the gravest kind of crimes against humanity, including torture and murder—cry out for explanation." But the U.S. secretary of defense seems to be unconcerned. "In those areas where our forces conduct JCET," Secretary Cohen averred, "they encourage democratic values and regional stability."[9]

Just how JCET training contributes to "democratic values and stability" is nowhere better illustrated than by the case of Indonesia, a place Secretary Cohen has visited often to review the results of America's educational efforts. Indonesia is the world's fourth most populous country and the world's largest Islamic nation. During its early years, after fighting for its independence from the Netherlands, when its founder and leader was President Sukarno (like many Indonesians, including General Suharto, he has only one name), it was a champion of neutralism and a thorn in the side of American foreign policy. Many CIA covert operations were mounted against Indonesia in that period, including during the revolution of 1965, when Suharto came to power, ousted Sukarno, and in a bloody pogrom eliminated leftist forces throughout the islands. Suharto and the army ruled with a strong authoritarian hand until May 1998.

During this period and with considerable American and Japanese support, Suharto overcame starvation on the main island of Java and led the country into sustained economic growth. However, Indonesia was clobbered by the 1997 financial crisis that depressed its stock and currency values to as much as 80 percent below precrisis levels. Because of misguided policies by the United States and the International Monetary Fund, discussed later in this chapter and in chapter 9, the number of people in Indonesia living below the poverty line grew in a matter of months from twenty-seven million to over a hundred million (half the population), and thirty years of economic gains were wiped out. Hundreds of thousands of workers lost their jobs. The country remains destitute and threatened with possible disintegration, even though its political life has been invigorated by the return of democracy after thirty-two years of one-man rule. Thus far, the blowback from American policies in

Indonesia has affected primarily Indonesians and, in particular, the Chinese minority in the country, which is also the entrepreneurial elite. Americans have not been affected, but this is unlikely to last as Indonesia emerges from its present trauma and starts to assess what happened to it and who was responsible.

The bloody ouster of General Suharto as president of Indonesia and as one of America's favorite dictators in East Asia is a case study in the dangers of JCET programs. Between May 13 and May 15, 1998, nearly 1,200 people were killed in Jakarta in rioting that led to the resignation of General Suharto. It was subsequently revealed that during this "rioting" at least 168 women and girls, most of them of Chinese ancestry, had been raped by "organized groups of up to a dozen men" and that 20 had died during or after the assaults.[10] It was also revealed that groups of men had traveled the city in vehicles inciting the crowds to violence. Many Indonesians accused the army and its clandestine security forces—the elite commando regiment Kopassus, known as the "red berets"—of committing these acts. (The army later did publicly acknowledge that members of its special forces had been involved in the "disappearances" of opposition activists in the weeks before the riots.)

In his years of rule, General Suharto had long had a reputation for using Kopassus, run from 1995 on by his son-in-law Lt. Gen. Prabowo Soemitro Subianto, to abduct, torture, and kill dissidents and political rivals. In 1990, for instance, he declared the western area of the island of Sumatra around Aceh a "military operational zone" in order to suppress an Islamic secessionist movement. He then sent in Kopassus units. Hundreds, perhaps thousands of people in the area "disappeared" and are presumed to have been executed by Kopassus. In August 1998, after Suharto's ouster, General Wiranto (also just one name), commander in chief of the Indonesian armed forces, flew to Sumatra, inspected mass graves, apologized for "abuses committed by the military there," and ordered all combat troops pulled out of the province. Under Suharto's order, Kopassus had carried out similar campaigns in the past in East Timor and Irian Jaya (New Guinea).

In January 1998 some Kopassus battalions from western Sumatra and

New Guinea were transferred to Jakarta, where during the following three months at least fourteen activists against Suharto also "disappeared." After Suharto's fall, the army high command itself concluded that Kopassus was responsible for at least nine kidnappings in the capital. Five of the kidnappees are still unaccounted for and presumed dead. Singled out for immediate responsibility was one of General Prabowo's deputies, Colonel Chairawan, commander of the plainclothes Kopassus Group 4. Before his arrest, Chairawan, a figure well known to the American military, told *Nation* magazine correspondent Allan Nairn that his primary contact at the U.S. embassy was Colonel Charles McFetridge, the DIA attaché.[11] Nonetheless, the orders for these kidnappings and executions probably came from Suharto himself.

After the 1998 rioting and the mass exodus from Indonesia of those Chinese who could afford to emigrate, the elites of Indonesia, no longer as threatened by police-state methods as they were under Suharto, demanded an investigation. The successor government of President B. J. Habibie appointed an eighteen-member investigating team, including representatives of the government, private groups, the armed forces, and the Indonesian Commission on Human Rights. In its report of November 3, 1998, the team concluded that much of the violence had been organized and deliberately provoked by the armed forces, probably in order to create enough of the look of chaos to make a military coup seem a plausible and acceptable step. The Indonesian military had earlier claimed that it could find no evidence of any rapes at all during the disturbances, whereas the report confirmed that seventy-six women, virtually all of Chinese descent, had been raped or otherwise sexually assaulted. The initial Chinese community's claim of more than twice that number may actually be closer to the truth, since many women were understandably reluctant to reveal what had happened to them. The report also charged two generals, Lieutenant General Prabowo of Kopassus and Major General Syafrie Samsuddin, head of the Jakarta Military Command and a Prabowo aide, with responsibility for organizing the riots and killings. Officials of the Indonesian government, who had initially ordered the report, failed to show up for the meeting at which it was delivered.[12]

The Indonesian armed forces, known as ABRI, have long been the chosen instrument of American foreign policy in the area, bolstering Suharto's stoutly anti-Communist regime. In 1965, when General Suharto was in the process of coming to power, the United States provided ABRI with lists of suspected Communists, over half a million of whom were slaughtered. It also publicly endorsed ABRI's 1975 invasion of East Timor and the subsequent elimination of two hundred thousand East Timorese through what the State Department in its 1996 Human Rights Report calls "extrajudicial killings." From the time of the European voyages of "discovery," East Timor, an island in the Indonesian archipelago, was a colony of Portugal. When in the mid-1970s a revolution in Portugal precipitated the decision by Lisbon to liquidate the remnants of its empire, the heavily Catholic population of East Timor sought autonomy or independence. Indonesia instead annexed it. Rebellion and repression have been endemic there ever since. As an unexpected benefit of the end of the Suharto era, President Habibie offered East Timor the opportunity to affiliate with Indonesia or become independent. East Timor voted for independence, but army-incited murders and scorched-earth tactics have also plagued the territory.

When the 1997 financial crisis spread to Indonesia and it became apparent that the International Monetary Fund's bailout policies were likely to end the seventy-six-year-old Suharto's further usefulness to the United States, American policy remained focused on maintaining control inside Indonesia through its backing of the 465,000-man-strong ABRI. Indonesia totally lacks external enemies. Its armed forces are therefore devoted almost entirely to maintaining "internal security." During most of the Suharto years, the United States actively trained ABRI special forces in a variety of what the New York Times calls "specialized acts of warfare and counterinsurgency."[13] The CIA and the Defense Intelligence Agency have long maintained close ties with ABRI, which has often been implicated in cases of torture, kidnapping, and assassination. *Special Warfare*, the professional magazine of the John F. Kennedy Special Warfare School at Fort Bragg, North Carolina, calls Kopassus the "guarantor of national unity in the face of many threats and challenges."[14]

After November 12, 1991, when Indonesian troops killed 271 people allegedly demonstrating for independence in Dili, the capital of East Timor, Congress cut off financial support for further training, although it did not end arms sales to Indonesia. The Pentagon has nonetheless expanded its ABRI training programs under cover of JCET.[15] At least forty-one exercises involving fully armed U.S. combat troops—including Green Berets, Air Force commandos, and marines—transported to Indonesia from Okinawa have taken place since 1995. The American 1st Special Forces Group is permanently deployed at Torii, Okinawa.

The primary Indonesian beneficiary of this effort was evidently intended to be forty-seven-year-old Lieutenant General Prabowo, Suharto's son-in-law and business partner. Prabowo's wife, who is Suharto's second daughter, owned a sizable piece of Merrill Lynch, Indonesia. Prabowo, a graduate of elite military training courses at Fort Benning, Georgia, and Fort Bragg, North Carolina, spent ten years fighting guerrillas in East Timor, where he earned a reputation for cruelty and ruthlessness. In 1995, donning the red beret of Kopassus, he managed to enlarge the special forces corps from 3,500 to 6,000 troops. He worked closely with his American supporters; of the forty-one JCET training exercises conducted since Congress ordered all training stopped, at least twenty-four were with Kopassus. According to the *Nation* magazine's Indonesian correspondent Allan Nairn, one Kopassus unit received twenty-six days of American instruction in "military operations in urban terrain" after the economic crisis began.

When Secretary of Defense Cohen visited Jakarta in January 1998, he stated, "I am not going to give him [Suharto] guidance in terms of what he should or should not do in terms of maintaining control of his own country." However, Cohen also made a point of publicizing his visit to Kopassus headquarters, where he spent three hours with General Prabowo reviewing Kopassus units as they executed maneuvers. Indonesian officials said to Allan Nairn that they took the Cohen visit as a "green light" to use force to maintain the political status quo in the face of protests against the International Monetary Fund's hyperausterity measures.

There were good reasons why the United States would want to keep General Suharto in power. In the early years of his rule, Suharto contributed greatly to regional stability, while bringing at least a modicum of prosperity and optimism to the Indonesian people. The greatest single success of the green revolution occurred under Suharto's rule: in 1984, Indonesia achieved self-sufficiency in rice production. During Suharto's rule Indonesia's per capita income rose from around $75 in 1966 to almost $1,200 in 1996; former president Sukarno's belligerence toward Malaysia was ended; and Indonesian diplomats played an instrumental role in the creation in 1967 of ASEAN (the Association of Southeast Asian Nations), which has proved to be by far the most important regional organization in East Asia.

Like the government of another American-supported autocrat, Ferdinand Marcos of the Philippines, Suharto's government developed over time into a kleptocracy—firms still controlled by members of his family are said to be worth many billions of dollars; but unlike Marcos his achievements were formidable. He not only brought a measure of political stability and economic growth to Indonesia's diverse islands, he also restrained Islamic militancy, while allying himself with indigenous Chinese entrepreneurs. It can be argued that without his type of strong rule, Indonesia would have been rife with separatist movements (of the very sort now gaining strength) and the likelihood of conflicts with other ASEAN nations would have been far higher. The current decline of Indonesian economic and, possibly, political power certainly means that China is more likely to assert its political primacy in the region.

The U.S. government was aware of these dangers, and therefore when, in 1997, international financiers began to exploit the Indonesian currency and foreclose on their short-term loans, leading American officials loudly proclaimed their backing of Suharto, signaling their lack of desire to see him overthrown. This position was, however, undercut by a politically uncoordinated agent of American power, the International Monetary Fund (IMF), which agreed to lend huge amounts of money to Indonesia to help meet its debts, but only if it imposed economics-textbook prescriptions for reordering its economy.

The IMF, it must be noted, is staffed primarily with holders of Ph.D.s in economics from American universities, who are both illiterate about and contemptuous of cultures that do not conform to what they call the "American way of life." They offer only "one size (or, rather, one capitalism) fits all" remedies for ailing economic institutions. The IMF has applied these over the years to countries in Latin America, Russia, and East Asia without ever achieving a single notable success. Nonetheless, the IMF's officialdom assumed a triumphalist posture toward Suharto's government, denouncing its "crony capitalism" and using its failings to trumpet the benefits of Anglo-American neoclassical economics over an Asian model of economic development. They ignored the fact that Suharto, while enriching members of his own extended family and firms that cultivated their good graces, also granted ordinary Indonesians food and fuel subsidies. On May 4, 1998, the IMF ordered these subsidies stopped. This alone made political instability inevitable.

On May 8, the United States ordered JCET activities suspended in Indonesia after the *Nation*'s Allan Nairn, at this potentially embarrassing moment, exposed the nature of the Pentagon's covert assistance program for Kopassus. By mid-May 1998, U.S. officials had started to signal changes in their position and begun to leak to the press statements not for attribution indicating that the IMF's reform program would not work unless Suharto were replaced. Senators like John Kerry of Massachusetts and Paul Wellstone of Minnesota echoed this demand on Capitol Hill. All of this was taken in Indonesia by powerful ABRI generals as a signal that they should act to secure the country and their positions in it. At the same time, students of Jakarta's prestigious Trisakti University saw an opportunity to achieve a measure of democracy and took to the streets in orderly demonstrations, demanding an end to the privileges enjoyed by Suharto's relatives. Amid growing turbulence in Jakarta, President Suharto left Indonesia for a state visit to Egypt, and the country's top military officer, General Wiranto, left the capital on May 14 and flew to eastern Java for a divisional parade. In this context, Indonesia erupted.

Suharto was in Egypt when, on May 12, four students from Trisakti University were shot dead in the streets of Jakarta, even though the police were then armed only with blanks and rubber bullets. Eyewitnesses nonetheless saw snipers armed with rifles with telescopic sights and dressed in police uniforms fire on the students from a road overpass. The students were buried immediately without autopsies. As *Business Week* magazine reported, "On May 14, trucks loaded with muscular men raced to shopping centers and housing projects owned by ethnic Chinese. The men doused the shops and houses with gasoline and set off devastating fires. At least 182 women were raped or sexually tortured, some of them repeatedly, by men with crewcuts whom the victims believe to be soldiers."[16] At the Chinese-owned Lippo Karawaci Mall, security cameras tape-recorded six truckloads of men breaking into banks and cash dispensers, then inviting in thousands of looters. These actions were reported at more or less the same moment at forty different shopping malls across the city, resulting in 1,188 deaths, the looting and burning of 2,470 shops, and the destruction of 1,119 cars.

The Indonesian military high command and other top Indonesian officials would have liked the world to believe that this savagery was the result of visceral anti-Chinese feelings, "spontaneous outbursts of a crowd run amok," in the words of Maj. Gen. Syafrie Samsuddin, then military commander of Jakarta. Far too many American pundits also found this explanation convenient. For example, in the *New Republic*, Jonathan Paris, an international lawyer connected with the Council on Foreign Relations, typically attributed the "riots" to "racial hatred and economic jealousy."[17]

But there are obvious problems with this explanation. As George Hicks, an Australian economist who has written extensively on Indonesia, points out, it is unlikely that mobs could simultaneously attack forty different Chinese-owned shopping malls spread around more than twenty-five kilometers without planning and coordination, not to speak of "without a single culprit having to face any police or military units in a city of ten million normally crawling with heavily armed forces of law and order."[18] The Indonesian scholar Ariel Heryanto has observed that the events of May were not "racially motivated mass riots" but "racialized state terrorism." The evidence, he believes, indicates that "racism among members of civil society was not responsible for the recent riots, nor for most other major anti-Chinese riots in past decades."[19] Instead, he argues that these, like the massive anti-Chinese pogroms that accompanied Suharto's rise to power in 1965–66, were incited by the army. This time, as *Asiaweek* put it, General Prabowo believed "that he could take power in exactly the same way as his own father-in-law wrested power from Sukarno," by appearing to restore order in the face of uncontrolled ethnic rioting.[20]

Rather than a race riot, William McGurn, senior editor of the *Far Eastern Economic Review*, compares May 1998 in Jakarta to Kristallnacht, when in November 1938 Hitler sent Nazi thugs into the streets to attack Jewish stores and homes.[21] One of Hitler's intentions was to see how the rest of the world would respond, and he concluded, correctly as it turned out, that the democracies would not interfere with his genocidal plans for Europe's Jews. Many have noted that in the weeks before the Indonesian riots, hundreds of young men trained by Kopassus were brought into Jakarta from East Timor. The theory is that Prabowo, either on his own or on orders from Suharto, organized the chaos to create an excuse for a crackdown. It was, however, Prabowo's rival, General Wiranto, who proved to be the main beneficiary of the chaos. On May 21, Wiranto persuaded Suharto to resign in favor of his vice president, B. J. Habibie, and on May 28 he relieved General Prabowo of his command. According to Allan Nairn, during the week these events took place, General Wiranto rather than General Prabowo was observed "consulting nonstop with the U.S. Embassy."[22]

With Prabowo's fall, the Americans started to cover their tracks. In late July, John Shattuck, assistant secretary of state for human rights, finally seemed to notice the situation in Indonesia. Officials were, he now said, "watching very closely." Franklin Kramer, assistant secretary of defense for international security affairs, attempted to put a spin on events by praising the Indonesian military's "recent restraint in quelling unrest."[23] U.S. embassy officials in Jakarta expressed "shock and anger" at Prabowo; one nonetheless insisted that "even if U.S.-trained soldiers had committed some of the murders, the United States should continue to work with the military, to maintain influence over what happens next."[24] President Habibie pleaded with the White House for an invitation so he could "thank Clinton in person."[25] For what, one wonders?

Secretary of Defense Cohen led the first high-ranking American delegation to visit Indonesia after Suharto's resignation. He stated that the United States still hoped to "build upon a military relationship in the future," and he refused to comment on accounts of atrocities committed by military men, saying only, "I do know that the Indonesian government has a number of investigations under way in terms of any abuses of human rights." Two weeks later an Indonesian military tribunal found a first lieutenant and a second lieutenant guilty of "taking action outside of their orders" in the sniper killings of the four students, sentencing one to ten months, the other four months, in prison. Secretary of State Madeleine Albright, who attended an ASEAN meeting at the end of July, denounced the treatment of dissidents in China and Burma but said not a word about the rapes, murders, and disappearances of dissidents and ethnic Chinese in Indonesia.

It may seem that what happened in Indonesia was another successful American-choreographed replacement of a regime that had become "unacceptable"—especially since the army in which the United States had invested so much came out in an even more powerful position in the new, soon-to-be "democratic" Indonesia (even with the last-minute replacement of Prabowo by Wiranto). But the truth of the matter was that the IMF and the U.S. Department of Defense, having helped reverse a quarter century of economic progress, had probably made it impossible for any Indonesian government to recover from the disaster.

Indonesia's six million citizens of Chinese ancestry constituted only 3.5 percent of the population during Suharto's regime, but it was estimated that they contributed close to three-quarters of the country's wealth. In the wake of the riots, thousands of ethnic Chinese fled

Indonesia, taking some $85 billion in capital with them. This makes it virtually certain that Indonesian banks will sooner or later have to default on their loans from overseas lenders. Equally important, in 1997 China, Hong Kong, Taiwan, Malaysia, and Singapore were the largest investors in Indonesia, followed by Japan and South Korea. Money from overseas Chinese sources will no longer be readily forthcoming for Indonesia. Both mainland China and Taiwan denounced the riots. China also pointedly noted that it had tried to help Indonesia economically with cash, medical supplies, and a refusal to devalue its own currency in order to avoid competing with Indonesian exports. Indonesia has instead been turned into a ward of the IMF and the United States, although it is unlikely that the American public understands this or feels in any way responsible for the huge economic contraction under way there. But this is a blowback of monumental proportions.

The American government may be satisfied to see army rule in Indonesia, but the Indonesian people probably are not. The best thing that could happen to Indonesia would be for the Americans to get out of the way and let Japan assume some responsibility. Japan, like China, tried to do so in the autumn of 1997, but its efforts were blocked by the United States, which does not like rivals in providing "leadership" in Asia. Japan is nonetheless Indonesia's main economic partner, taking 40 percent of its exports and supplying 25 percent of its imports. Japan, still the world's second largest economy, has a huge stake in Indonesia's return to economic viability, and it has the financial clout to spur renewed growth.

If, instead, Indonesia is allowed to stagnate, living off food handouts from the Americans, it is quite possible to predict that Islam, which until now has shown its tolerant and broad-minded face throughout most of the country, will turn militant and implacable. This, in turn, would guarantee the end of American influence (much as it did in Khomeini's Iran) and it would greatly complicate Australia's foreign policy. It is a direction that some in the Indonesian army would welcome, despite their close friendships with American military officers developed over the years in JCET exercises.

Even should a U.S. president and Congress one day wake up to their constitutional duties and reassert authority over the Department of Defense, that still might not bring JCET and similar programs under control. The Pentagon's most recent route around accountability is "privatization" of its training activities. As investigative journalist Ken Silverstein has written, "With little public knowledge or debate, the government has been dispatching private companies—most of them with tight links to the Pentagon and staffed by retired armed forces personnel—to provide military and police training to America's foreign allies."[26] The companies involved are generally associated with the Department of Defense's Special Operations Command, which has replaced the CIA's Directorate of Operations as the main American sponsor of covert action in other countries. Nonetheless, these are privately contracted mercenaries who, by their nature, are not directly responsible to the military chain of command. In many cases, these private companies have been formed by retired special forces personnel seeking to market their military training to foreign governments, regardless of the policies of the Defense Department.

One reason privatization appeals to the Pentagon is that whatever these companies do becomes "proprietary information." The Pentagon does not even have to classify it; and as private property, information on the activities of such companies is exempt from the Freedom of Information Act. Given the extreme legalism of American political culture, this is sufficient to shield such companies from public scrutiny, although it would probably not protect them from the new international criminal court. Private companies are at present training the armies of Croatia and Saudi Arabia and are active in Honduras, Peru, and many other Latin American countries. Such firms also purchase weaponry from former Soviet states for distribution to groups that the U.S. government may want to arm without being accused of doing so, such as guerrillas fighting for Bosnia and in Kosovo.

In addition to the Department of Defense's JCET operations, both public and private, its arms sales are a vital component of stealth imperialism. By several orders of magnitude the United States maintains the world's largest military establishment and is the world's biggest arms exporter. According to 1995 figures released by the U.S. Arms Control and Disarmament Agency (whose very name is an Orwellian misnomer and which, in 1998, was absorbed by the State Department), the world spent $864 billion on military forces. Of this amount, the United States accounted for $278 billion, or 32 percent, some 3.7 times more than the then second-ranked country, Russia.[27] The most dramatic cuts in military spending since 1987, the all-time peak year, when $1.36 trillion worth of arms passed from manufacturers to buyers, have come from Russia and other states of the former Soviet Union. The Stockholm International Peace Research Institute (SIPRI) reports that in 1997 the U.S. share of global deliveries of major conventional weapons, worth about $740 billion, had grown to 43 percent whereas Russia's share was 14 percent.[28]

In 1997, total worldwide military and arms spending was approximately one-third lower than ten years ago, at the end of the Cold War. Nonetheless, in addition to being the world leader in arms transfers, the United States continues to dominate the development of military technology. According to SIPRI, the U.S. military research and development budget was more than seven times that of second-place France. In 1997, SIPRI found that the world spent $58 billion on military R&D, of which the United States spent $37 billion. In terms of overall national military spending, the Pentagon's most recent Quadrennial Defense Review, concluded in May 1997, envisaged defense budgets in the range of $250–260 billion until the end of time—an amount vastly greater than anything that might be spent by any conceivable combination of adversaries. The defense budget for the year 2000 was $267.2 billion, plus augmentations in order to pay for the Kosovo war.

Together with NATO, Japan, South Korea, and Israel, the United States accounts for 80 percent of the world's total military spending. In 1995, the United States alone outspent Russia, China, Iraq, Syria, Iran, North Korea, Libya, and Cuba combined, by a ratio of two to one; with its allies, it outstripped all potential adversaries by a ratio of four to one. If the comparison is restricted to only those countries considered regional threats by the Pentagon—the "rogue states" of Iraq, Syria, Iran, North Korea, Libya, and Cuba—the United States outspent them twenty-two to one.

Interestingly enough, maintaining access to Persian Gulf oil requires about $50 billion of the annual U.S. defense budget, including maintenance of one or more carrier task forces there, protecting sea lanes, and keeping large air forces in readiness in the area. But the oil we import from the Persian Gulf costs only a fifth that amount, about $11 billion per annum. Middle Eastern oil accounts for 10 percent of U.S. consumption, 25 percent of Europe's, and half of that of Japan, which contributes in inverse proportion to maintaining a G-7 military presence there. It is not that Europe and Japan are incapable of securing their own oil supplies through commercial treaties, diplomacy, or military activity, but that America's global hegemony makes it unnecessary for them to do so.

One of the things this huge military establishment also does is sell arms to other countries, making the Pentagon a critical *economic* agency of the United States government. Militarily oriented products account for about a quarter of the total U.S. gross domestic product. The government employs some 6,500 people just to coordinate and administer its arms sales program in conjunction with senior officials at American embassies around the world, who spend most of their "diplomatic" careers working as arms salesmen. The Arms Export Control Act requires that the executive branch notify Congress of foreign military and construction sales directly negotiated by the Pentagon. Commercial sales valued at $14 million or more negotiated by the arms industry must also be reported. Using official Pentagon statistics, between 1990 and 1996 the combination of the three categories amounted to $97,836,821,000. From this nearly $100 billion figure must be subtracted the $3 billion a year the government offers its foreign customers to help subsidize arms purchases from the United States.

According to the Stockholm International Peace Research Institute, the five leading arms suppliers for the period 1993 through 1997 were the United States, Russia, England, France, and Germany, though total American sales were some $14 billion greater than those of the other four combined. SIPRI has found that the five leading arms purchasers for that period were Saudi Arabia, Taiwan, Turkey, Egypt, and South Korea, each of which spent between $5 billion and $10 billion on arms over this five-year period.[29] Japan was the second-biggest purchaser of high-tech weapons. All the leading purchasers were close American allies or clients.

Both the United States government and the world's arms dealers claim that the arms trade has declined since 1987, the benchmark year for the Cold War. However, this "decline" is based almost entirely on declining arms sales by the former Soviet bloc—and it is likely that the 1987 estimates of arms sales by the former Soviet Union were as inflated as the estimates of, for example, the Soviet naval threat during the 1980s. American arms sales in any case have actually increased in the years since the Cold War ended. By 1995, according to its own Arms Control and Disarmament Agency, the United States was the source of 49 percent of global arms exports. It shipped arms of various types to some 140 countries, 90 percent of which were either not democracies or were human rights abusers.

In November 1992, presidential candidate Bill Clinton announced that he would make it his policy "to reduce the proliferation of weapons of destruction in the hands of people who might use them in very destructive ways." In February 1995, President Clinton released his new arms export policies. They renewed old Cold War policies even though the Cold War had clearly ended, but they emphasized the commercial advantages of foreign arms sales. According to the Clinton White House, the United States' arms export policies are intended to deter aggression; "promote peaceful conflict resolution and arms control, human rights, [and] democratization"; increase "interoperability" of the equipment of American and allied armies; prevent the proliferation of weapons of mass destruction and missiles; and "enhance the ability of the U.S. defense industrial base to meet U.S. defense requirements and maintain long-term military technological superiority at lower costs."[30] One of the arms industry's chief lobbyists commented, "It's the most positive statement on defense trade that has been enunciated by any administration."[31] But despite the doublethink language of the White House, there are certain essential contradictions in arms sales policy that cannot be papered over. The Pentagon's global industrial policy, which keeps its corporate support system in place and well funded, regularly overrides more traditional foreign policy concerns, creating many potential long-term problems that may, in the end, prove beyond all solution. Arms sales are, in short, a major cause of a developing blowback world whose price we have yet to begin to pay.

In many cases, for instance, the United States has been busily arming opponents in ongoing conflicts—Iran and Iraq, Greece and Turkey, Saudi Arabia and Israel, and China and Taiwan. Saddam Hussein of Iraq, the number-one "rogue" leader of the 1990s, was during the 1980s simply an outstanding customer with an almost limitless line of credit because of his country's oil reserves. Often the purchasing country makes its purchases conditional on the transfer of technology and patents, so that it can ultimately manufacture the items for itself and others. The result is the proliferation around the world not just of weapons but of new weapons industries. On January 10, 1995, former CIA director James Woolsey told Congress that weapons sales "have the potential to significantly alter military balances, and disrupt U.S. military operations and cause significant U.S. casualties."[32] Yet on August 27, 1998, in a typical example of the Pentagon shaping—or misshaping—foreign policy through arms sales, the Department of Defense announced the sale of several hundred missiles and antisubmarine torpedoes to Taiwan for $350 million. China naturally denounced the sale as a violation of agreements it had with the United States. The Defense Department's response was, "The proposed sale of this military equipment will not affect the basic military balance in the region."[33] If that is true, why sell the equipment in the first place? Was it merely to enhance the balance sheets of several defense corporations to which the Pentagon is closely tied? If it is not true, why even bother to suggest that the balance of power is of any interest to the Pentagon?

In August 1996, then Secretary of Defense Perry called for an end to a decades-old ban on arms sales to Latin America on the grounds that most countries in the region were now democracies, so it is inconceivable that they would use newly purchased arms against one another. A year later, on August 1, 1997, the White House announced, "In the past decade, Latin America has changed dramatically from a region dominated by coups and military governments to one of democracy and civilian control. . . . Some Latin American countries are now addressing the need to modernize their militaries." The Clinton administration thereupon authorized the sale of advanced American weapons to any and all buyers south of the border (except, of course, Cuba).

A staple of American thinking about foreign policy is that democracies pose no threat to other democracies. But if the countries of Latin America are now democracies, logically that should mean that they do not need to "modernize their militaries." They might instead follow the example of Costa Rica, which since 1948 has had no military, only a civilian constabulary, and which is one of the most stable, peaceful countries in the area. Its former president, Oscar Arias, who won the 1987 Nobel Peace Prize for negotiating an end to multiple civil wars in Central America, is a strong opponent of the renewed American arms shipments. In 1999, he observed, "Americans have shown great concern about the reported loss of classified nuclear secrets to the Chinese. But they should be just as outraged that their country gives away many other military secrets voluntarily, in the form of high-tech arms exports. By selling advanced weaponry throughout the world, wealthy military contractors not only weaken national security and squeeze taxpayers at home but also strengthen dictators and worsen human misery abroad."[34]

When such contradictions are exposed, the Pentagon falls back on the argument that if it does not sell the arms to Latin America, some other country will. By analogy, Colombia might say to the United States that if it does not grow and sell cocaine to Americans, some other country will. When considered together, the extensive JCET training programs in the region and the new arms sales policy are undoubtedly undermining democracy in Latin America and moving several long-standing conflicts toward war. For example, for some time JCET missions have been training the army of Ecuador while the Pentagon has sold Ecuador military Black Hawk helicopters and A-37 combat jets. Only after the training and the sales were completed did the United States discover that Ecuador was planning to use these forces not against drug dealers and "terrorists" but for a war with Peru.[35]

The United States has justified its contacts with the Ecuadorian military as a means to get to know its leaders personally and to develop long-term relationships of trust. But as *Washington Post* columnist Mary McGrory has observed, many in the Reagan administration and the Pentagon knew practically every crucial figure in the Salvadoran death squads, most of whom were graduates of the School of the Americas at Fort Benning, Georgia. This did not stop the Salvadorans from killing seventy thousand of their fellow countrymen, not to mention raping and killing four American churchwomen in 1980, acts the American ambassador to El Salvador and the secretary of state then covered up. One Salvadoran colonel whom the U.S. ambassador suspected of ordering the murders of the three nuns and a Catholic lay worker was, in 1998, living comfortably with his wife and children in Florida.

The economic benefits of arms sales have been vastly overstated. The world's second-largest capitalist economy, Japan, does very well without them. In the late 1990s, the economy of Southern California started to thrive once it finally got beyond its Cold War dependence on aerospace sales. Many of the most outspoken congressional champions of reducing the federal budget are profligate when it comes to funding arms industries in their localities, often with the expectation of what future export sales will do for their constituents. In January 1998, then House Speaker Newt Gingrich added $2.5 billion to the defense budget for more F-22s and C-130s, which even the air force did not want (or need), only because they were partly manufactured in Georgia. In June 1998, Senate Majority Leader Trent Lott added the construction of another helicopter aircraft carrier (that the navy insisted it did not need) to that year's $270 billion defense appropriations bill because the ship was to be built at Pascagoula, Mississippi.

The American empire has become skilled at developing self-fulfilling—and self-serving—prophecies in order to justify its policies. It expands the NATO alliance eastward in part in order to sell arms to the former Soviet bloc countries, whose armies are being integrated into the NATO command structure, with the certain knowledge that doing so will threaten Russia and elicit a hostile Russian reaction. This Russian reaction then becomes the excuse for the expansion. Similarly, the United States sells advanced weaponry to a country without enemies, like Thailand, which in January 1997 bought $600 million worth of F-18 fighters plus the previously not-for-sale Amraam air-to-air missile. (Purchase of the aircraft was put on hold after the economic crisis erupted.) It then contends that more must be invested in arms development at home for a new generation of American fighter planes and missiles, given the necessity of keeping ahead of the rest of the world.

A classic model of the way this type of circular reasoning can lead to disaster is a U.S. decision to "help" an ally faced with domestic dissidence or even insurrection. First, the "threatened" country is declared part of America's vital interests; next, American military personnel and commercial camp followers are sent in to "assist" the government. The foreignness of this effort as well as its indifference to democracy and local conditions only accelerate the insurrectionary movement. In the end an American protectorate is replaced by a virulently anti-American regime. This scenario played itself out in Vietnam, Cambodia, and Iran in our time. Now it appears it might do so in Saudi Arabia.

Since the Gulf War the United States has maintained around thirty-five thousand troops in Saudi Arabia. Devoutly Muslim citizens of that kingdom see their presence as a humiliation to the country and an affront to their religion. Dissident Saudis have launched attacks against Americans and against the Saudi regime itself. After the June 1996 bombing of the Khobar Towers apartments near Dhahran killed nineteen American airmen, the international relations commentator William Pfaff offered the reasonable prediction, "Within 15 years at most, if present American and Saudi Arabian policies are pursued, the Saudi monarchy will be overturned and a radical and anti-American government will take power in Riyadh."[36] Yet American foreign policy remains on auto-pilot, instead of withdrawing from a place where a U.S. presence is only making a dangerous situation worse.

Ten years after the end of the Cold War, the Pentagon monopolizes the formulation and conduct of American foreign policy. Increasingly, the United States has only one, commonly inappropriate means of achieving its external objectives—military force. It no longer has a full repertoire of skills, including a seasoned, culturally and linguistically expert diplomatic corps; truly viable international institutions that the American public supports both politically and financially and that can give legitimacy to American efforts abroad; economic policies that ef-fectively leverage the tremendous power of the American market into desired foreign responses; or even an ability to express American values without being charged, accurately, with hopeless hypocrisy. The use of cruise missiles and B-2 bombers to achieve humanitarian objectives is a sign of how unbalanced our foreign policy apparatus has become. The American-inspired and -led NATO intervention in Yugoslavia in the spring of 1999 to protect the Albanian majority in Kosovo was a tragic example of what is wrong.

It may or may not be prudent policy to put humanitarian objec-tives above respect for the sovereignty of nations; it is, in any case, a precedent-setting position that could come back to haunt the United States, which is, like Yugoslavia, a multiethnic country. But betraying no doubts whatsoever, the U.S. government disdained to seek U.N. Security Council sanction for its objectives and then chose to commit a defensive military alliance, NATO, to a totally unprecedented offensive role, in violation of the treaty that created it. Its rationale was that its end—humanitarian relief of defenseless civilians under attack by a political leader with an odious record of similar attacks in the past—justified its means: targeting high-flying bombers and cruise missiles on undefended civilian buildings (including the embassy of China) and public infra-structure, such as roads and bridges. It is not surprising that not a single American serviceman was killed. It is also not surprising that the policy produced precisely the humanitarian disaster for the Albanians in Kosovo that its ostensible purpose was to prevent. As former president Jimmy Carter put it, "Even for the world's only superpower, the ends don't always justify the means."[37] The United States's objectives in Kosovo, which were arguably justifiable on their own terms, were compromised by reliance on a technologically phenomenal but utterly inappropriate military machine because it was the only means still available.

Military might does not equate with "leadership of the free world." It is also no substitute for an informed public that understands and has approved the policies being carried out in its name. An excessive reliance on a militarized foreign policy and an indifference to the distinction between national interests and national values in deciding where the United States should intervene abroad have actually made the country less secure in ways that will become only more apparent in the years to come.

What would make the United States more secure is not more money spent on JCET teams or espionage satellites to find and retaliate against terrorists. Instead, the United States should bring most of its overseas land-based forces home and reorient its foreign policy to stress leadership through example and diplomacy. Nowhere is this more true than on the Korean peninsula. American military intervention in Korea dates back to 1945. Most of our commitments in Korea were made before current government leaders were even born. The passage of time, economic development, and the collapse of communism have rendered most of them utterly anachronistic. Yet they remain unchanged, constituting one of our greatest breeding grounds for blowback.

4

SOUTH KOREA:
LEGACY OF THE COLD WAR

There were many differences between the Soviet Union's satellites in Eastern Europe and the United States' satellites in East Asia, most importantly in the area of economic organization. In Europe, Stalin imposed on all seven of his "people's democracies" (Albania, Bulgaria, Czechoslovakia, the German Democratic Republic, Hungary, Poland, and Romania but not Yugoslavia, which was not created by the Red Army) a uniform pattern involving the collectivization of agriculture and an extreme centralization of economic decision making. The USSR demanded that all of these countries industrialize at the fastest possible pace, with absolute priority given to heavy industry. In the period from 1947 to 1952, the Soviet Union imposed its own economic methods uncritically and without taking any cultural or other differences into account. It was a process in some ways similar to the one the International Monetary Fund imposed on the smaller, more open economies of East Asia during and after the financial crisis of 1997—and with similar results.

In contrast with the Soviet Union, the United States was much less doctrinaire about economic arrangements in its satellites during the Cold War. In Japan and South Korea, its two main dependencies in East Asia, it insisted on the institution of private property and opposed any steps toward the nationalization of industry, but it tolerated land reform, state guidance of the economy, protectionism, mercantilism, and the cartelization of industry as long as these methods produced economic growth and blunted the appeal of communism. The United States used aid and preferred access to its vast market to bring these countries into its political orbit and keep them there. It disguised what it was doing— ultimately fooling only its own people—with euphemisms like "export-led growth" and "the separation of politics and economics." The result was that over the years places like South Korea were able to export their way to personal incomes averaging over $10,000 per capita, a process that the Western business press invariably characterized as "miraculous." It was not a process made available to the Latin American dependencies of the United States, because they were not of equal strategic importance in the Cold War.

When it came to the political and military dimensions of satellite creation and maintenance, the Soviet Union and the United States pursued similar policies and for similar reasons. They controlled their dependencies through single-party dictatorships (in Japan's case a one-party "democracy") that either the Red Army or the U.S. Army installed in power and then supported throughout the Cold War against any and all popular efforts to introduce truly democratic regimes. Although rebellions against our military presence in Japan were endemic from 1952 until after the end of the Vietnam War, we helped maintain (often through CIA funds channeled to the ruling Liberal Democratic Party) a single-party regime from 1949 to 1993, a record for stable satellite government (although identical in length to that of the government of East Germany from 1945 to 1989). During this period Japan was led by the same types of "shameless mediocrities" that the French international relations theorist Raymond Aron once said the Soviet Union relied on to govern Eastern Europe.[1]

Democracy finally began to appear in South Korea only in 1987, over four decades after the country came into being, largely because the military dictator, Chun Doo-hwan, had attracted the Olympic Games for the following year and so had trapped himself into behaving in a civilized manner before a global audience when Koreans began to protest his rule. Much as in 1989, when the Russians did not intervene militarily to stop the East Germans from tearing down the Berlin Wall, the United States in 1987 did not encourage its Korean military allies to use force, as it had done in the past. One reason was that American officials still had in mind the traumatic outcome of the Iranian revolution—when their down-the-line support of the Shah's repressive rule had only accelerated the coming to power of Ayatollah Ruhollah Khomeini and an implacably anti-American regime. Just the previous year, in February 1986, they thought they saw similar events unfolding in the Philippines as a popular movement swept away another U.S.-supported but corrupt and incompetent dictator, Ferdinand Marcos. In that case, the United States did not support the repression of the rebels, and the results proved relatively satisfying when Corazon Aquino, the widow of an assassinated Marcos opponent, and a group of middle-class reformers came to power, backed by military men with strong ties to the United States. Thus, the American government again showed restraint in the Korean situation, and the student demonstrators with their middle-class backers, seizing the chance, brought into being what is today the only democracy in East Asia, other than the Philippines, that rests on popular political action from below.

The end of World War II had proved no more a "liberation day" for Korea than for Czechoslovakia or other nations of Eastern Europe. The Japanese had occupied, colonized, and exploited Korea since 1905, just as the Nazis, following the 1938 Munich Agreement, had divided, occupied, and ravished Czechoslovakia. Both countries now underwent transformations into colonies of the victors of World War II. At about the same time in February 1948 when the Communist Party of Czechoslovakia was carrying out a coup d'état in Prague, right-wing forces in the southern half of divided Korea, then under the control of the United States, were slaughtering at least thirty thousand dissident peasants on the island of Cheju. Although the Czech events are much better known (and led to the creation of NATO the following year), the killings in Korea were of essentially the same character as those in

Czechoslovakia. The Cheju massacre was part of a process by which our puppet regime in South Korea, a government every bit as unpopular as Klement Gottwald's Stalinist government in Czechoslovakia, consolidated power. Gottwald, president of Czechoslovakia from 1948 until his death in 1953, and Syngman Rhee, president of South Korea from 1948 to 1960, were, in fact, similar figures: neither could have come to power without the aid of his superpower patron and both were prototypes of the faceless bureaucrats the Soviets and the Americans would use for the next forty years to govern their "captive nations" (a term the Eisenhower administration came to apply to the Soviet Union's satellites).

Between Japan's surrender on August 15, 1945, and the installation of Syngman Rhee (who claimed to be a former Princeton student of Woodrow Wilson's) as president of the Republic of Korea in the southern half of that peninsula on August 15, 1948, the Koreans themselves tried desperately to create a postcolonial government of their own, just as the Czechs struggled to create a democratic government under President Edvard Benes up to February 25, 1948. They were ultimately undone by superpower rivalries. Fearing that the United States was setting up Japan as its chief client in postwar Asia, the Soviets held on to Korea above the 38th parallel as a bulwark against Japanese influence. There, they promoted and endorsed a Communist government made up of former guerrilla fighters against the Japanese.

The Americans were more ambiguous about what they were doing. General John Hodge and his U.S. Army veterans of the Battle of Okinawa were the legal successors to the Japanese in South Korea. Only in 1948 did they hand over power to Rhee, and even then they retained operational authority over the South Korean armed forces and national police for another year. Preoccupied with the security of Japan and indifferent to Korea's status, Hodge ended up thwarting the efforts of patriots such as Kim Ku to reconcile with the North Koreans. Instead, he moved to support Syngman Rhee, who himself was supported by and who staffed his new government with numerous former collaborators with the Japanese whose main credential was their firm and reliable anticommunism. The forces under Hodge's command then trained and supervised Rhee's armed forces in the suppression of any and all dissenters—invariably labeled "Communists"—and waited to see whether Rhee could consolidate his power.

Following the departure of the Japanese, the people of Cheju, a remote island off the extreme southern coast of Korea, governed themselves through patriotic "people's committees" that were socialist but not Communist in orientation, as even General Hodge acknowledged. On April 3, 1948, Rhee's police fired on a demonstration commemorating the Korean struggle against Japanese rule. This incident led to a general insurrection on the island against the police and their attempt to integrate Cheju into the new South Korean regime. Rhee responded with a campaign similar to that of the Indonesian Army in East Timor or of the Serbs in Bosnia and Kosovo. His police carried out a merciless assault on the people of Cheju, killing from thirty thousand to sixty thousand of them in the course of a few months and forcing another forty thousand to flee to Japan. On May 13, 1949, the American ambassador to the Republic of Korea, John Muccio, wired Washington that most rebels and sympathizers on Cheju had been "killed, captured, or converted."[2]

By far the most ruthless of Rhee's agents was a paramilitary vigilante organization called the Northwest Youth League, composed of refugees from North Korea, whom the U.S. Army tolerated with full knowledge of their reputation for brutality. The American occupation authorities, in fact, directly funded and trained a similar organization, the Korean National Youth League, under its leader Yi Pom-sok (known to the Americans as "Bum Suk Lee"), as a right-wing paramilitary organization. The "youths" were aged eighteen to fifty. Northwest Youth League members, who were not funded by the U.S. Army, were, of course, rabidly anti-Communist but they also were interested in securing their own livelihoods by acquiring wealth and wives in South Korea. They were responsible for the widely documented sadistic treatment of Cheju's women, including forcing female survivors of families they killed to marry them and cede their land to them. Some of these men still reside in Cheju today, having profited from the island's contemporary status as a beach and golf resort. In April 1996, when President Kim Young-sam

used the beachfront Cheju Shilla Hotel as the site of his summit meeting with President Clinton, no American journalist mentioned Cheju's
past, much less the similarity between Clinton's mindless visit to Cheju
and former President Reagan's mindless visit to a cemetery for former SS
soldiers in Bitburg, Germany, in 1985.[3] At an August 1998 international
conference on the fiftieth anniversary of the Cheju uprising held in
Cheju City, many speakers noted that Clinton had played golf on the
unmarked graves of Syngman Rhee's victims.

For at least forty-five years after the Cheju massacre, any Korean who
so much as mentioned it was liable to arrest by the Korean Central
Intelligence Agency (KCIA) or its successors, followed by beatings, torture, and a long prison sentence administered under the terms of the
National Security Law, enacted in December 1948 and still on the books
in 1998. Only in that year did the director of the Agency for National
Security Planning, the KCIA's successor, promise that abuse of the law
for political purposes would stop and Koreans would no longer be
arrested for minor violations like praising Communist North Korea.[4]
Only in 1995, after the arrests of former presidents Chun Doo-hwan
and Roh Tae-woo for mutiny, corruption, and murder did the Cheju
Provincial Assembly finally feel secure enough to create a committee to
investigate the massacre, whose research produced the names of 14,504
victims. The committee's best estimate of the total killed was thirty
thousand, about 10 percent of the island's population. Some 70 percent
of the island's 230 villages were burned to the ground and a staggering
39,000-plus homes destroyed.

The consolidation of a pro-Soviet regime in North Korea and a
pro-American one in South Korea led to a war that began in June 1950.
The North Koreans have consistently claimed that this was a war of
national liberation against American imperialism, while Americans
have generally characterized it as an international conflict in which
North Korea invaded South Korea. It was without question a civil war
among Koreans, some of whom in the South had collaborated with the
Japanese colonialists and some of whom in the North had fought against

them. From my personal perspective as a veteran of the period immediately following the armistice of 1953, it was also clearly a war between the United States and China fought on Korean soil.

Shortly after North Korea invaded South Korea on June 25, 1950, the United States intervened in force. In the autumn of that year, after American troops had invaded North Korea, China intervened in force. From June 1950 to early 1951 the war was primarily between U.S. troops and the North Korean army. Starting in March, it became a Sino-U.S. war, and its nature was transformed. The first phase of the war saw massive North Korean, American, and Chinese military movements combined with guerrilla struggles behind the lines. The later Sino-U.S. war bogged down in World War I–style trench warfare along what would later become the Demilitarized Zone (DMZ). Regardless of one's view of the Korean War, the position of South Korea from the war down to the present has been that of a client of the United States.

In June 1950, the United States took its intervention against the North Korean attack to the U.N. Security Council. The USSR was then boycotting the Security Council to protest an American refusal to allow the new People's Republic of China to occupy the seat reserved for China. On July 7, 1950, under conditions never again repeated, the Security Council, free of the threat of a Soviet veto, authorized a "unified command under the United States" to defend South Korea. Fifteen nations other than the United States contributed forces to this "unified command." The United States on its own initiative then created the "United Nations Command" as the operational unit through which it would fight the war. The Republic of Korea also placed its troops under this American-controlled command. Thus, from 1950 to the present, the U.N. commander in Korea was and remains a United States Army general.

The United Nations itself was not, however, a party to the Korean War. There was no U.N. operational control over any aspect of the hostilities, and the United States, the designated occupant of the "unified command," reported to the United Nations only after the fact. Cynics say that the first U.N. commander, General Douglas MacArthur, never sent the United Nations anything other than his press releases. Under international law the U.N. Command is an alliance of national armies commanded by the United States, even though there are today no other members left except for the United States and South Korea. The armistice agreement of July 27, 1953, was signed by General Mark W. Clark, the U.N. commander; Marshal Kim Il-sung of the Korean People's Army; and General Peng Dehuai, commander of the Chinese People's Volunteers—but not by any representative of South Korea. This is one reason why today North Korea insists upon negotiating with the United States, not with South Korea.

Another important result of these arrangements is that the South Korean armed forces—today, some 670,000 men, 461 combat aircraft, and a navy that includes 44 destroyers, frigates, and corvettes as well as 4 attack submarines, with a budget of around US$16 billion—is operationally part of a military command structure headed by an American general. No matter how hard the U.S. government tries to finesse the matter, the South Korean army, except for some elite paratroop and special forces units, is as much under American military control now as it was at the time of the Cheju massacre.

When in 1961 and again in 1979 this South Korean army carried out military coups d'état and in 1980 massacred civilians protesting military rule in the city of Kwangju, ordinary Koreans inevitably saw the Americans as co-conspirators. On November 30, 1994, forty-one years after the armistice and seven years after the birth of Korean democracy, the United States finally transferred *peacetime* control over South Korean forces to the South Korean Joint Chiefs of Staff. In times of war, however, command reverts to a U.S.-dominated Combined Forces Command. China and Russia today have friendly diplomatic and economic relations with South as well as North Korea, whereas the United States still has 37,000 combat troops occupying 65,500 acres of South Korean territory at 96 bases and has no formal relations with North Korea.

In the years since the Korean War, the United States has had to deal with many difficult situations in its South Korean satellite brought about by popular demands for democracy and independence from the United States, which in many ways resembled the 1956 Hungarian and 1968 Czechoslovak uprisings for democracy and independence from the Soviet Union. The major difference was that whereas the Soviet Union relied primarily on its own armed forces to suppress these popular movements, the United States entrusted repression to the Republic of Korea army, whose leaders ruled South Korea from 1961 to 1993. The most important of these situations was the suppression of the Kwangju uprising of 1980, which bore many similarities to the Hungarian uprising of 1956.

The comparison is instructive. At the end of fascist rule in 1945, the Hungarians tried to establish a popularly supported government. In elections held late in that year, six political parties put up candidates. The Independent Smallholders Party emerged with 245 seats, the Communists with 70, the Social Democrats with 69, and the National Peasants with 23. These four major parties formed a coalition government, but power increasingly flowed to the Communists because of the presence in the country of the Red Army—exactly as happened in South Korea because of the presence of the U.S. Army. By 1948, most non-Communist leaders in Hungary had been silenced, sent into exile abroad, or arrested. In 1949, Hungary officially became a people's democracy under Matyas Rakosi, a Communist trained in Moscow, who was secretary-general of the Hungarian Workers Party.

Hungary was, of course, not divided into Soviet and American zones. The Allied powers had concluded a peace treaty with Hungary that came into force in September 1947. It called for the withdrawal of all Allied armies except for the USSR's. Soviet troops were to be stationed in Hungary to maintain lines of communication to Red Army units in the Soviet zone of occupation in Austria. In April 1948, Hungary entered into a treaty of "friendship, cooperation, and mutual assistance" with the USSR in which both parties pledged military assistance to the other if they once again became victims of aggression from Germany or "any state associated with Germany." The Hungarian army was expanded well beyond the limits authorized in the peace treaty.

In July 1955, the occupation of Austria came to an end; the last Soviet units left Vienna on September 19, 1955. Immediately preceding the signing of the Austrian peace treaty, the USSR and its seven people's democracies united in the Warsaw Pact, aimed at NATO and a "remilitarized Western Germany." Under the terms of this alliance, the Soviet Union stationed its 2nd and 17th Mechanized Divisions, with a strength of about twenty thousand men and six hundred tanks, in Hungary.

Rakosi and the Communists ruled Hungary with an iron hand, utilizing mainly the hated State Security Police (the AVH) to crush all dissent. In June 1949, in an interparty struggle, Rakosi arrested the foreign minister, Laszlo Rajk, charged him with an attempt to overthrow the "democratic" order, and had him hanged. Six years later, in March 1956, following the 20th Congress of the Communist Party of the Soviet Union, at which Soviet Premier Nikita Khrushchev revealed the extent of Stalin's tyranny, Rakosi made a similar move to de-Stalinize his own country. He revealed that Rajk had been condemned on "fabricated charges." No doubt Rakosi's mistake was that he was still in political control and revealing his own, rather than someone else's, criminality. Widespread protests followed, and the Russians ousted Rakosi in July 1956, replacing him with Erno Gero, a party hack who did not last out the year. In October 1956, Laszlo Rajk and other victims of the 1949 purge trials were ceremonially reburied, with large Hungarian crowds in attendance.

The autumn of 1956, following the Soviet 20th Congress, saw the first "thaw" in the Communist world. China launched its campaign to "let a hundred flowers bloom" (that is, to invite criticism of the regime); Poland took its first tentative steps toward greater independence from the USSR; and in Hungary, starting with Rakosi's fall, people looked forward to a softening of the regime. This mood lasted no more than a year anywhere in the Communist world, but at the time optimism was prevalent. Gero's regime ordered an end to the compulsory teaching of Russian in Hungarian schools and some other cosmetic reforms. Students and intellectuals felt bold enough to meet and discuss such subjects as ending single-party rule and asking Soviet troops to go home. They called for the return to power of Imre Nagy, who had been premier from 1953 to 1955, following the death of Stalin, and was reputedly a moderate. An old Communist, a member of the party since 1918, Nagy had lived in Moscow for some fifteen years and returned to Hungary with the Red Army in 1944. His moderation consisted primarily of opposition to the secret police and their activities. Rakosi had attacked Nagy as a deviationist and had him expelled from the party.

On October 23, 1956, in the new atmosphere of mild intellectual ferment and optimism, an incident occurred in downtown Budapest that led to a general insurrection and the mobilization of Russian forces in Hungary. The State Security Police, intensely unpopular and universally feared, opened fire on a crowd of demonstrators and killed a number of students. In the melee that ensued, ambulances with red crosses sped to the scene; when their doors opened, AVH reinforcements dressed in the white coats of doctors but armed with machine guns emerged from them.[5] Outrage over the killings and deception led to the Budapest uprising.

Over the succeeding five days fighting broke out between students and workers wielding Molotov cocktails and Soviet tanks trying to negotiate the narrow streets of Budapest. Not a single instance was recorded of Hungarian troops fighting on the Soviet side against their fellow countrymen. Even the Soviet troops themselves seemed reluctant to push forward with the attack. As the U.N. report noted, "Soviet forces normally stationed in Hungary or Romania had been affected by their surroundings. . . . The civilians whom they fought included women, children, and elderly people. [Soviet troops] could see that the people were unanimous in their fight against the AVH and foreign intervention; that the men whom the Soviet Army was fighting and the prisoners who were captured were not fascists, but workers and students, who demonstrably regarded Soviet soldiers not as liberators, but as oppressors."[6]

On the morning of October 24, Imre Nagy, having been readmitted to the party a week earlier, was elected to the Politburo and hastily appointed prime minister. It was a gesture designed to calm the crowds, which by then had broken the power of the AVH, while the Soviets were taking losses in the street fighting. The events of October 24 and 25 were extremely confused, and people did not know whether Nagy was actually in power or even whether he was fully on their side until later in the month. On October 25, Janos Kadar replaced Gero as first secretary of the party, and Gero fled to the USSR. Only on October 27 was Nagy finally able to form a government, into which he invited both Communists and non-Communists as ministers. The people of Hungary then accepted Nagy as their leader, having concluded that although he was a Communist he was also a good Hungarian. In the few days remaining to him, Imre Nagy ordered a cease-fire (which the insurgents honored), asked the Soviet Union to withdraw its forces from Hungary, ordered the AVH abolished, released all political prisoners, withdrew his country from the Warsaw Pact, and asked the international community to defend Hungary's neutrality. This was obviously far more than Khrushchev and the other Soviet leaders had bargained for or were prepared to countenance.

On November 4, 1956, at 5:20 in the morning, Nagy announced over Radio Budapest that Soviet forces in battle formation had invaded the city with the intent to overthrow the legal government of Hungary. This second Soviet attack, using troops from central Asia who had been led to believe that they were being sent to Egypt to fight against British and French "imperialists," was swift and thorough.[7] By eight A.M. that same morning, Soviet tanks were in control of the Danube bridges. Imre Nagy, Laszlo Rajk's widow, and several other democrats and women and children sought refuge in the Yugoslav embassy. The Soviet Union promised them safe passage out of Hungary, but the bus taking them from Yugoslavia's embassy delivered them not to the border but to the headquarters of the Soviet military command. They were never heard from again. In 1958, the Hungarian government announced that Nagy had been secretly tried and executed.

Janos Kadar entered the Hungarian capital in the baggage train of the Soviet invaders and re-created single-party rule under the Hungarian

Workers Party. Kadar and the USSR announced to the world that they had successfully prevented an attempt "to overthrow socialism in Hungary and to restore the capitalists and landowners to power." Kadar thanked the Soviet Union for its assistance in defeating the "reactionary forces." All fighting in Hungary was over by November 6, although in the interim some 190,000 students, liberals, and intellectuals managed to flee the country via Austria. The Soviet Union also deported a large but unknown number of Hungarians to the gulags of Russia.

In Korea, the roots of the Kwangju rebellion went back to General Park Chung-hee's coup d'état of 1961. The previous year, students protesting Syngman Rhee's flagrant corruption and rigged elections had brought down his regime. However, the democratic government they created was ineffective. Park, a graduate of a Japanese military academy in Manchuria, staged a military coup. Once in power he announced as his goals the end of South Korea's extreme dependence on American economic aid and restoring relations with Japan. His economic reforms succeeded beyond anyone's wildest dreams, surprising the Americans in charge of Korean affairs, who despite the evidence from Japan refused to believe that authoritarian guidance of the market could produce high-speed economic growth.

General Park's associate in the 1961 coup was General Kim Jong-pil, who proceeded with the help of the U.S. Central Intelligence Agency to create the Korean Central Intelligence Agency in order to consolidate Park's military rule. The KCIA was and is a secret-police apparatus accountable only to the president of South Korea and has been used over the years to silence any and all calls for a genuine democracy. As the historian Perry Anderson observes, "In the mid-sixties the KCIA had 350,000 agents out of a population of 30 million, dwarfing the NKVD at its height. The dungeons were filled with opponents of every kind; torture was routine. Yet the regime, which as a front line of the Free World could not dispense with the formality of elections, was never able to crush opposition completely."[8]

Despite Park's unquestioned success in overseeing the rapid industrialization of South Korea, his draconian methods and the great inequities of wealth they produced led to opposition to his rule. In the 1971 elections, the dissident leader Kim Dae-jung, who would finally become president in December 1997 and who is from Mokpo, in the same South Cholla region as Kwangju, almost defeated Park. As a result, Park changed the constitution. He ended direct election of the president, allowed the president to be indefinitely reelected, and gave the president the authority to nominate one-third of the National Assembly (the organ that would reelect him). Throughout the 1970s, the KCIA enforced this new "Yushin" constitution (the Korean pronunciation of the Japanese word meaning "restoration") while Park continued to move the country toward an industrialization that favored steel, shipbuilding, petrochemicals, and manufacturing rather than labor-intensive light industries.

Although many economists criticized his new economic initiatives, Park's intention, not unlike that of the Stalinists in Eastern Europe, was to create the industrial foundations for South Korea's own national defense. He deemed this necessary in view of the probable defeat of the United States in Vietnam and its possible withdrawal from Asia. He was, after all, a nationalist and an anti-Communist who did not want the United States to call all the shots when it came to protecting his country. Nixon's opening to China worried him as much as anything the North Koreans did.

By 1979, Park's economic "miracle" in South Korea was considered irreversible. His harsh policies nonetheless continued to elicit student protests, riots, and labor disturbances. On October 16, 1979, over dinner, his KCIA chief, Kim Jae-kyu, pulled out a pistol and shot first Park's bodyguard and then Park himself, allegedly to end his repression of the people. Park's assassination seriously destabilized South Korea and afforded North Korea the most propitious circumstances it had encountered since 1953 to renew the civil war. Yet North Korea did nothing. In South Korea, the United States was suspected of having ordered Park's death, because the assassin was the chief channel of communication between the U.S. government and Park and because it was widely believed that the United States had grown tired of Park's nascent independence.

In a secret cable to Washington, the American ambassador to Seoul, William J. Gleysteen, denied that he had ever so much as hinted to Kim Jae-kyu that his government was exasperated with Park. But the Americans did have one clear motive for wanting to be rid of him: as part of his efforts to ensure a South Korean victory in any new war with the North, Park had launched a program to build his own nuclear weapons, which the United States opposed. According to the prominent Seoul daily *Jungang Ilbo*, his target date for having deployable bombs was 1985.[9] Park's death stopped the program in its tracks. The United States and South Korea had feuded over nuclear research since the mid-1970s, and the United States has never cooperated with South Korea on atomic-power development, as it has with Japan.[10] In response to Park's initiative, North Korea also began to build its own nuclear strike force, a program that did not stop with Park's death. By the 1990s, the possibility that the North might develop nuclear weapons had become a major source of instability in the area.

Our understanding of what happened next in the South Korea of late 1979 owes a great deal to the efforts of an American journalist, Tim Shorrock, who was raised in Seoul as the child of American missionaries. Shorrock has used the Freedom of Information Act to sue the U.S. government, forcing it to divulge some two thousand diplomatic and military cables concerning Korea to and from the State Department and the Defense Intelligence Agency in 1979 and 1980. The documents still contain huge blacked-out areas, and a complete opening of U.S. secret files certainly has not occurred. Most of the cables are from a secret policy-making group that the Carter administration set up ten days after the assassination of Park Chung-hee. Its members were President Jimmy Carter, Secretary of State Cyrus Vance, Deputy Secretary of State Warren Christopher, Assistant Secretary of State for East Asia and the Pacific Richard Holbrooke, Ambassador Gleysteen, and the top intelligence official at the National Security Council, Donald Gregg. Vance gave this group the code name Cherokee.[11]

As revealed in these documents, the primary goal of the United States was to keep South Korea from turning into "another Iran." Toward this goal, the Americans were quite prepared to see General Park replaced by a new, perhaps more malleable general who would effectively suppress the rising calls for democracy that might prove "destabilizing."

Martial law and an interim government under former diplomat Choi Kyu-hah followed Park's death. Choi came up with a plan to spend twenty months writing a new constitution that would guide South Korea from authoritarian to democratic rule. This would put off political reform for a suitably long time. Washington backed the plan despite warnings that ordinary Koreans could not possibly remain politically patient for longer than a year. The extended hiatus in political leadership gave an unknown major general in the army, Chun Doo-hwan, time to prepare his own seizure of power. On December 12, 1979, General Chun, then in charge of defense intelligence at Republic of Korea (ROK) military headquarters, withdrew the 9th Army Division, whose commandant, General Roh Tae-woo, was his co-conspirator, from the demilitarized zone with North Korea and used it to assume control over the rest of the armed forces. These military movements were undertaken without formal approval from General John Wickham, the U.N. commander, but there is every reason to believe that he had been informed and assented to them. The following May, General Wickham readily gave Chun permission to use the 20th Division in the final assault against Kwangju, and at General Chun's trial fifteen years later his main defense was that all his actions in 1979 and 1980 had been explicitly approved by Washington.

Ambassador Gleysteen's characterization in the Cherokee cables of what happened is accurate enough: "We have been through a coup in all but name. The flabby façade of civilian constitutional government remains but almost all signs point to a carefully planned takeover of the military power positions by a group of 'young Turk' officers. Major General Chun Doo-hwan, advantaged by his powers of security and investigation, seems the most important figure of a group of men who were very close to President Park. . . . The organizing group planned its actions for at least ten days and drew support throughout the armed forces among younger officers." Gleysteen was concerned that General Chun had "totally ignored the Combined Forces Command's responsibilities, either ignoring the impact on the United States or coolly calculating that it would not make any difference." "At the same time," he added, "I do not think we should treat the new military hierarchy as so bad that we decide to risk seriously alienating them." A few days after the coup, Gleysteen wrote, "Whatever the precise pattern of events, they did not amount to a classical coup because the existing government structure was technically left in place." And at the end of December, he added hopefully, "If the new leaders handle themselves with moderation, there may be no violent repercussions." (These quotations are all from Shorrock's documents.)

As the administrator of the martial law then in effect, Chun became the de facto ruler of the country. He had to move carefully, however, because he lacked legitimacy within the South Korean legal system and because he could not be certain that all of the armed forces were behind him. Not unlike the "thaw" in Eastern Europe in 1956, there was widespread anticipation that the next election, whose date had not yet been set, would usher in the democracy that had failed to develop after the overthrow of Syngman Rhee in 1960.

On April 14, 1980, acting president Choi, now totally subordinate to Chun, promoted him to the rank of lieutenant general and appointed him acting director of the KCIA. These actions prompted student demonstrations throughout the country. Molotov cocktails were hurled at police formations, and the police retaliated with hypervirulent CS tear gas (the same type used by the FBI at Waco in 1993). Everyone knew that Chun had to consolidate his position before the National Assembly convened for the first time since Park's death on May 20, when the Democratic Republican Party, the façade behind which Park had ruled, was likely to join with the opposition in ending martial law. That would have destroyed any legal basis for Chun's political ambitions.

In a secret cable dated May 7, 1980, preceding a scheduled meeting with General Chun, Ambassador Gleysteen wrote to his superiors in

Washington: "In none of our discussions will we in any way suggest that the USG [U.S. government] opposes ROKG [Republic of Korea government] contingency plans to maintain law and order, if absolutely necessary, *by reinforcing the police with the army* [italics added]." The next day Warren Christopher cabled back, "We agree that we should not oppose ROK contingency plans to maintain law and order." Pat Derien, who was President Carter's assistant secretary of state for human rights, later said to Shorrock that this was "a green light as far as I could see then and as far as I can see now." She went on to accuse Holbrooke of "pandering to dictators" and of "national security hysterics."[12]

General Chun did not wait long after talking with Gleysteen to complete the coup d'état he had begun the previous December. Late on the night of May 17, 1980, General Chun expanded martial law, closed the universities, dissolved the National Assembly, banned all political activity, and arrested thousands of political leaders.[13] Unlike Park, Chun had no following whatsoever outside the army. All Korean cities were tense with fury at his usurpation of power, but only in Kwangju did the situation explode, much in the same way it had in Budapest twenty-four years earlier. What resulted was, in the words of historian Donald Clark, "the most notorious act of political violence in South Korea's history." Professor Clark adds that the explicit American endorsement of Chun's recapture of the city "forever associated the United States with the Kwangju Massacre."[14]

On May 18, 1980, a few hundred demonstrators in Kwangju took to the streets to protest the imposition of martial law. They were met by paratroopers of the 7th Brigade of the Korean special forces, known as the "black berets," who had a well-known reputation for brutality going back to their service on the American side in the Vietnam War. The 7th Brigade also included a battalion of infiltrators and provocateurs, who wore their hair long and dressed to look like students. According to eyewitnesses, the special forces troops set about bayoneting all the young men and women they could find and attacked others with flamethrowers. In a May 19 cable to Washington, Gleysteen wrote, "Rumors reaching Seoul of Kwangju rioting say special forces used fixed bayonets and inflicted many casualties on students. . . . Some in Kwangju are reported to have said that troops are being more ruthless than North Koreans ever were."

In reaction to these acts of state terrorism, the whole population of Kwangju and sixteen of the twenty-six other municipalities of the South Cholla region rose in rebellion. They drove the paratroopers from the city, which citizens' councils controlled for the next five days. They appealed to the U.S. embassy to intervene, but General Wickham had already released from his United Nations Command the forces Chun would use to retake the city. Gleysteen later claimed that he was unable to verify the authenticity of the mediation request and therefore decided not to act. "I grant it was the controversial decision, but it was the correct one. Do I regret it? I don't think so."

On Wednesday, May 21, martial law command headquarters in Seoul broke its near total censorship of what was going on in Kwangju and reported that 150,000 civilians, about one-fifth of the city's population, had gone "on a rampage" and that they had seized 3,505 weapons and 46,400 rounds of ammunition from arsenals and had commandeered 4 armored personnel carriers, 89 jeeps, 50 trucks, 40 wreckers, 40 buses, 10 dump trucks, and 8 tear-gas-firing jeeps.[15] On the same day, Ambassador Gleysteen wrote to Washington that a "massive insurrection in Kwangju is still out of control and poses an alarming situation for the ROK military." He said that the Korean military was "concentrating defense on two military installations and a prison containing 2,000 leftists. . . . The December 12 generals obviously feel threatened by the whole affair."

In the cables released to Tim Shorrock, there is ample evidence that the American embassy knew about the transfer of the special forces to Kwangju and what was likely to happen when they applied their well-known skills to civilians. In cables dated May 7 and May 8, Ambassador Gleysteen had gone into detail on the numbers of special forces brigades brought into Seoul and around Kimpo Airport "to cope with possible student demonstrations." On May 8, the U.S. Defense Intelligence Agency had sent a cable to the Joint Chiefs of Staff at the Pentagon saying that all Korean special forces brigades "are on alert." "Only the 7th Brigade remained away from the Seoul area," and "was probably targeted against unrest at Chonju and Kwangju universities."

Under the Combined Forces Command (CFC) structure, Korean special forces (as distinct from all regular army units) were outside joint U.S.-Korean control and did not need U.S. approval to be moved. However, it was routine for the Koreans to inform the CFC of any troop movements. In Gleysteen's May 7 cable, he speculates that the Koreans might ask for approval to move the ROK 1st Marine Division. "There has been no request for such approval yet, but CINCUNC [Commander in Chief of the United Nations Command] would agree if asked." In a May 22 cable, Gleysteen describes "the extent to which we were facilitating ROK army efforts to restore order in Kwangju and deter trouble elsewhere." However, he told the South Korean foreign minister, "We had not and did not intend to publicize our actions because we feared we would be charged with colluding with the martial law authorities and risk fanning anti-American sentiment in the Kwangju area."

In Washington, D.C., on May 22, the newly created Policy Review Committee on Korea met at the White House to consider what the United States should do. Its members included newly appointed secretary of state Edmund Muskie, President Carter's national security adviser Zbigniew Brzezinski, the director of central intelligence Admiral Stansfield Turner, and the secretary of defense Harold Brown, plus Christopher, Holbrooke, and Gregg. Brzezinski, himself a Polish-American and an authority on the Soviet Union's satellites in Eastern Europe, summarized the consensus of the meeting: "In the short-term support, in the longer term pressure for political evolution." According to the minutes transmitted to Gleysteen, "There was general agreement that the first priority is the restoration of order in Kwangju by the Korean authorities with the minimum use of force necessary without laying the seeds for wide disorders later."

On May 23 Gleysteen met with the acting prime minister and told him that "firm anti-riot measures were necessary." He agreed to release "CFC [Combined Forces Command] forces to Korean command for use in Kwangju." General Wickham withdrew the Korean 20th Division from its duties on the DMZ and turned it over to the martial law authorities. General Chun broadcast news of the American decision to release the troops throughout South Korea, thus cleverly bolstering the view that the United States backed Chun. At 3:00 A.M. on the morning of May 27 the 20th Division entered Kwangju, killing anyone who did not lay down his or her weapons. This was a highly disciplined unit, and the city was quickly secured, much as Budapest had been in 1956.

The endgame of the Kwangju uprising dragged on for another two years. In the summer of 1982, two special forces brigades were moved from the border with North Korea to the cities of Kwangju and Chongju in order to hunt down rebels who had fled into the hills when the 20th Division entered the city. The U.S. Defense Intelligence Agency has acknowledged that these remnants were not Communist-inspired but were reacting against the brutality of their own country's army.

Back in Seoul, General Chun arrested dissident leader Kim Dae-jung on trumped-up charges of favoring North Korea—Kim had spoken of a federal system for the future of a unified Korea—and on May 22 charged him with instigating the protests in Kwangju even though he was in jail when they occurred. The martial law authority sentenced him to death. Richard Allen, Ronald Reagan's first national security adviser, takes credit for saving Kim's life. He claims that he traded a presidential invitation to Chun Doo-hwan to visit the White House—in February 1981 Chun was the first head of state to be received by the new president—in return for a life sentence. (Allen actually ended the article in which he described this achievement with the sentence "Chalk up one for the Gipper!")[16] In 1982 Chun allowed Kim Dae-jung to go into exile in the United States.

On May 24, 1980, Chun took care of some old business and had Kim Jae-kyu, Park's assassin, hanged, since dead men tell no tales. He then put together an "electoral college" under the authority of the Yushin constitution and had himself elected president of the republic. By August 1980, the Carter administration was more than satisfied that Chun Doo-hwan would serve nicely as the leader of one of America's oldest satellites.

It is hard to calculate how many people were actually killed at Kwangju. There was no United Nations investigation as there was into the Hungarian uprising. The United States has remained even more close-mouthed about what happened there than the Chinese Communists are about the 1989 massacre in and around Tiananmen Square. There were only a few Western eyewitnesses. Jurgen Hinzpeter, a German television reporter, reached the city on May 20 and photographed bodies being loaded onto trucks, terrified citizens being led away by troops at gun-point, and burning buildings. His films circulated underground in South Korea for years among student and Christian groups.

Norman Thorpe of the *Asian Wall Street Journal* was so appalled by what he saw at Kwangju that he retired from being a journalist in East Asia. In 1996, he protested Richard Holbrooke's nomination for a Nobel Peace Prize stemming from his work in Bosnia. "Mr. Holbrooke argues that stability was important," writes Thorpe about Holbrooke's role in Korea, "because of the North Korean threat. Nonetheless, under the U.S. policies he helped develop, the military prolonged its rule in South Korea, delaying the transition to democracy and taking the lives of many demonstrators."[17]

Following the attack on the city on May 27, Sam Jameson of the *Los Angeles Times* rented a car and driver to get to Kwangju. He reported that although there was no way to confirm a death toll, at least 200 armed insurgents were said to have made a final stand in the provincial head-quarters building. He counted 61 caskets on the floor of a gymnasium across the street from provincial headquarters, victims from the early days of the protest who had been identified by relatives. Photographs placed on the coffins showed the faces of mostly young men, but there was also a middle-aged woman and a child identified as seven years old. The South Korean government later settled on a figure of at least 240 killed; Kwangju sources claim more than 3,000 killed or injured.

General Chun ruled South Korea as president from 1980 to 1988 and then was succeeded by his co-conspirator General Roh, who held office until 1993. Finally, under the subsequent civilian presidency of Kim Young-sam, prosecutors developed bribery and corruption cases against both generals. They produced evidence that while in office the two had shaken down the *chaebol* (the large conglomerates that dominate the Korean economy) to the tune of $1.2 billion for Chun and $630 million for Roh. In December 1995, in one of the clearest signs of South Korea's maturing democracy, the government arrested both generals and charged them with accepting bribes. President Kim then made the decision to indict them as well for the military mutiny of December 1979 and for the massacre of hundreds of pro-democracy demonstrators at Kwangju in May 1980. The South Korean state charged that their purpose at Kwangju had simply been to consolidate their own power, which they had acquired illegally.

In August 1996, a South Korean court found both Chun and Roh guilty of sedition. Chun was sentenced to death and Roh to twenty-two and a half years in prison. In December, an appellate court reduced the sentences to life for Chun and seventeen years for Roh, and in April 1997, the South Korean Supreme Court unexpectedly upheld both sentences. Only in December 1997, after Kim Dae-jung (himself sentenced to death by Chun) had been elected president did outgoing president Kim Young-sam pardon both Chun and Roh, with the new president's consent.

When asked about the 1996 convictions of Chun and Roh, a spokesman for the U.S. State Department, Nicholas Burns, replied, "This [the Kwangju massacre] is an obvious tragedy for the individuals involved and an internal matter for the people of the Republic of Korea."[18] No one in the U.S. government seemed to remember that the events in Kwangju deeply implicated them and that Messrs. Gleysteen, Wickham, Holbrooke, Christopher, and others might well have belonged in the dock alongside their Korean colleagues.

In 1989, when the Korean National Assembly sought to investigate Kwangju on its own, the Bush administration refused to allow Ambassador Gleysteen or General Wickham to testify; and the interagency task force assembled to review Shorrock's requests for documents under the Freedom of Information Act specifically refused to release any of General Wickham's communications with his Korean counterparts or with the U.S. government, even though he was the official closest to the Korean military. The *New York Times* never once mentioned the results of Shorrock's FOIA suit, and most Americans remain in the dark about what happened at Kwangju or the American role in it. They know much more about the Chinese government's violent clearing of protesters from Beijing's Tiananmen Square in 1989 than they do about their own government's cover-up of the costs of military rule in South Korea. Blowback from these American policies is one of the most volatile ingredients in South Korean politics today.

5

NORTH KOREA:
ENDGAME OF THE COLD WAR

North Korea long claimed a greater legitimacy in the struggle against Japanese colonialism than South Korea, a claim that many students in South Korean universities and historians of the Korean War accept. Moreover, until at least 1975, North Korea was considerably richer than South Korea in terms of per capita gross domestic product, a situation that slowly changed with South Korea's extraordinary economic achievements.

The Seoul Olympics of 1988, which the North boycotted, brought worldwide attention to the prosperity of South Korea. Russia and China, both of them caught up in domestic-reform movements, took notice. The only Communist country that respected the North Korean boycott was Cuba. In 1990, Russia opened diplomatic relations with the Republic of Korea; in 1992, China followed suit. On December 18, 1992, Kim Young-sam was popularly elected president of the Republic of Korea, the first civilian head of state since 1961.

The North did not like any of this, but did not totally foreclose adjusting to the new southern realities. Ever since the end of the Cold War, North Korea had very tentatively signaled an increased openness to discussions with unofficial South Koreans about the future of the peninsula, while also trying to shield itself from the infinitely greater economic power of the South. In 1990, a North Korean commented to a Chinese official, "What we have hung out is not an iron curtain, but a mosquito net. It can let in breezes, and it can also defend against mosquitoes."[1] The North's dictator for life Kim Il-sung died on July 8, 1994, just before he was scheduled to attend a first-ever Korean summit meeting with Kim Young-sam.

The U.S. news media have dismissed North Korea as a "rogue state" and its leader Kim Jong-il, Kim Il-sung's son and successor, as a "mad prince . . . whose troops (and nukes) make him the Saddam Hussein of North Asia."[2] What we know about that land, however, suggests that it is less a rogue state than a proud and desperate nation at the end of its tether. Having been driven into a corner, it has offered the world a text-book example of how to parlay a weak hand into a considerable diplomatic and economic victory over a muscle-bound but poorly informed competitor.

The tearing down of the Berlin Wall in 1989 and the collapse of the USSR in 1991 precipitated an acute crisis in North Korea. Even if it was not prepared to abandon its ideology and reform its economic system of *juche* (self-reliance), the northern leadership still could not help noting that the endgame of the Cold War was particularly dangerous for players on the Communist side. The former leaders of Romania were put up against a wall and shot; the former leaders of East Germany were tried and given heavy sentences by the courts of a newly unified Germany. Meanwhile, in another sign of the North's potential fate, the United States persisted in its boycott and embargo of Communist Cuba even though that island's regime no longer posed any kind of threat to it. Asked why the United States was willing to engage North Korea while still maintaining a strict embargo against Cuba, a "senior administration official," speaking on condition of anonymity, said with a smile, "To my knowledge [the Cubans] do not have a nuclear weapons program."[3] This difference, in a nutshell, is the secret of how North Korea caught the Americans' attention.

As the 1990s began, it became clear to North Korea that it had to try something short of war to break out of the trap in which the end of the Cold War—which had stripped it of its main allies and their economic support—had left it. It began by trying to open relations with Japan, inviting a delegation led by a senior Japanese politician to visit Pyongyang. In September 1990, only a few weeks after President Roh Tae-woo of South Korea had met with President Mikhail Gorbachev of the USSR in San Francisco and obtained Soviet diplomatic recognition, the then vice president of the Liberal Democratic Party in Japan, Shin Kanemaru, led a joint Liberal Democratic Party–Socialist Party delegation to the North Korean capital. The idea of going to North Korea was entirely Kanemaru's and was vigorously opposed by the Japanese Ministry of Foreign Affairs. At the time, however, it was widely assumed in South Korea that Japan was deliberately trying to undermine its increasingly friendly relations with the USSR, just as the North Koreans naturally assumed that Kanemaru, as a representative of Japan's long-standing, one-party government, was coming as an official spokesman.

As it turned out, Kanemaru's visit was just the last hurrah of one of Japan's most corrupt politicians trying to further line his pockets. As Tokyo political commentator Takao Toshikawa has put it, "It was very much a personal initiative: a last chance for diplomatic glory in old Shin's declining years, and also a brazen attempt to generate huge kickbacks out of the flow of grants, yen credits, etc., that would flow to Pyongyang once the principle of paying reparations [for Japanese colonial and wartime acts of brutality] was established." While in Pyongyang, Kanemaru, "drunk and slightly senile, is suspected of having promised the North Korean strongman [Kim Il-sung] grants and low-interest loans totalling ¥100 billion."[4]

Ever since this meeting the Japanese Ministry of Foreign Affairs has denied that what took place in any way represented official policy. More important, from a North Korean point of view, Kanemaru was arrested in March 1993 on bribery and corruption charges and died shortly thereafter. His downfall seemed to convince Pyongyang that its Japanese initiative was not viable. Kim Il-sung then evidently decided to see if he could deal directly with the United States.

As a result of the end of the Cold War, North Korea had lost the patronage of the USSR. For the previous forty years, the Soviet Union had competed with the People's Republic of China to curry favor in Pyongyang, and this was the chief international structural condition that allowed the North to prosper and become somewhat independent of both. In 1974, following the first OPEC oil crisis, North Korea's Soviet ally sponsored its entry into the International Atomic Energy Agency so that the Soviets could help North Korea develop a nuclear-power-generating capability. In 1985, North Korea adhered to the Nuclear Non-Proliferation Treaty, also at the Soviet Union's behest. With the collapse of the Soviet Union, North Korea lost not only Soviet nuclear aid and any continuing reason to participate in Western-dominated atomic control regimes, but also its second most important source of fuel oil. China, previously its leading source, now compounded these difficulties by asking North Korea to pay largely in hard currency for Chinese oil imports (though they also accepted some barter payments).

Under these circumstances, in March 1993, North Korea gave notice of its intention to withdraw from the Nuclear Non-Proliferation Treaty. Whatever its reasons—including fear of Japan, energy demands, post–Cold War isolation, and thoughts of possible "posthumous retaliation" (Raymond Aron's phrase) against Japan and a triumphant South Korea—North Korea developed the foundations for a small future nuclear-weapons capacity, or at least convinced the International Atomic Energy Agency (IAEA) that it had. It has never actually tested a nuclear device. (It is highly unlikely, in fact, that it yet has one to test.) The initial American reaction was belligerent. The Pentagon talked about "surgical strikes," à la the 1981 Israeli attack on an Iraqi reactor being built at Osisraq. Patriot missile brigades were transferred to Seoul, and the United States seemed poised once again to use force on the Korean peninsula.

American policy on nuclear nonproliferation has long been filled with obvious contradictions, and the officials in charge of the Korean branch, through overreaction and an almost total ignorance of their adversary, played right into the North's hands. Until the five Indian nuclear tests of May 1998, the United States had more or less refused to acknowledge that in addition to Britain, France, China, and the Soviet Union, proliferation had already occurred in Israel, India, Pakistan, and South Africa; that South Korea, Japan, Sweden, Brazil, Argentina, Algeria, and Taiwan had technologically proliferated without testing; and that Iraq—perhaps Iran, too—was almost surely pursuing a clandestine nuclear-weapons program. The U.S. doctrine of nonproliferation also ignores the fact that there is something odd about a principle that permits some nations to have nuclear weapons but not others and that the United States has been only minimally willing to reduce its own monstrously large nuclear strike forces.

North Korea has ample reason to build a nuclear-power-generating capacity, given its vulnerability to a cutoff of crude oil. From a national security standpoint, Japan's nuclear power capacity, its fast-breeder reactor program, its plutonium stockpile, and its solid-fuel rockets with ICBM capabilities could all plausibly appear threatening to a country that it once colonized and exploited. Japan has some forty-one nuclear plants generating 30 percent of its electricity, with another ten under construction. It has set a goal of meeting 43 percent of its demand for electricity through nuclear power by the year 2010.

The North Koreans must also have come to the conclusion that, whatever the American threats, a military strike against it was wholly unlikely. For one thing, South Korea is deeply opposed, not least because of memories of the way its capital, Seoul, only thirty-five miles from North Korean troops at the DMZ, was totally destroyed during the Korean War. In March 1999, when the United States was once again stridently issuing warnings about possible North Korean weapons of mass destruction and insisting that Pyongyang was developing ballistic missiles to deliver them, the South Korean defense minister ruled out participation by his country in a U.S. plan to create a regional missile shield, the theater missile defense (TMD). He further stated in the clearest possible terms that Seoul was opposed to any preemptive attack on North Korea even if war tensions were to rise to unbearable heights on the peninsula.[5]

Equally important, a new Korean war would almost certainly end the

Japanese-American alliance. Since the Americans would inevitably take some casualties and the Japanese would refuse to participate at all militarily, the American public would want to know why. The Japanese-American Security Treaty was badly strained by a similar pattern during the Gulf War; a repetition in Japan's "backyard" might well snap it. The American military therefore tacitly gave up on a military option and turned to the idea of imposing sanctions against North Korea if it did not rejoin the control regime created by the Nuclear Non-Proliferation Treaty and allow the IAEA to resume inspections of its nuclear facilities.

The threat of sanctions also proved meaningless, although it did reveal to the American government how little its strategic thinking fits the actual complexities of the region. The legal basis for imposing sanctions would have to be Articles 41 and 42 of the United Nations Charter, which authorize the Security Council to impose interruptions of economic and diplomatic relations and militarily enforced blockades to give effect to its decisions. China would have vetoed the use of either article. Nor was it clear that there had ever been any legal basis for sanctions, because North Korea had formally and in a legalistic sense quite properly declared its intent to withdraw from the Nuclear Non-Proliferation Treaty. Such sanctions would have involved some combination of acts that would include interrupting North Korean telecommunications, cutting off desperately needed remittances of money from Koreans in Japan, prohibiting people and vessels from going there via a blockade, and stopping all trade. North Korea promptly announced that it would regard any blockade as an act of war and would retaliate directly against Seoul. This caused the South Koreans to lose their enthusiasm for sanctions. The suggestion that Japan join in the use of sanctions against North Korea proved acutely embarrassing, revealing as it did both the extent to which Japan was already involved in propping up North Korea economically and the extent of the Japanese guilty conscience over its mistreatment of its own sizable resident Korean population, many of whom support North Korea.[6]

Once the Americans had started to talk about sanctions, the Japanese government ordered a full-scale analysis of what might be involved. The secret report that resulted was subsequently leaked to the press and published in the monthly magazine *Bungei Shunju*.[7] It revealed Japan as North Korea's second most important trading partner after China, and the organization of Koreans in Japan allied with North Korea, Chosen Soren, as a remitter of huge amounts of foreign currency to the North, as well as large shipments of prohibited cargo such as computers and integrated circuits. All the large Japanese banks, including Daiichi Kangyo, Fuji, Mitsubishi, Sumitomo, Sakura, Asahi, Sanwa, and the Bank of Tokyo, have correspondence agreements with North Korean banks. Individual Japanese contributions to North Korea amount to at least ¥60 billion to ¥70 billion per annum—an amount equal to the value of North Korea's total trade with China—and Korean operators of *pachinko* (pinball) parlors, many of whom are allied with Japan's Socialist Party, have in the past contributed as much as ¥100 million on Kim Il-sung's birthday. Any Ministry of Finance attempt to freeze these assets in Japan, the government report stated, would be ineffective since most private remittances and shipments go through third countries and then through China before reaching North Korea. Thus, even if the Americans had gotten U.N. approval of sanctions and avoided a Chinese veto, Japan concluded, they could not have successfully been implemented.

As is often the case, American policy toward North Korea in 1994 was belligerent but ineffective. The threat of a military intervention to destroy possible North Korean nuclear facilities lacked credibility, was not supported by either the South Korean or Japanese people, and might have destroyed relations with China. In this context former president Jimmy Carter undertook a mission of personal diplomacy to resolve the situation. Carter had long been interested in Korea. As president he had advocated withdrawing American military forces from the peninsula as part of a post-Vietnam reassessment of the failures of American policy in East Asia. He had been forestalled by implacable opposition from cold warriors in Washington, the assassination of Park Chung-hee, the anti-U.S. revolution in Iran, and the USSR's invasion of Afghanistan.

In 1994, the American ambassador to South Korea, James T. Laney, a former missionary in Korea and president of Emory University in

Atlanta, was a close friend of Carter's and was aware of the former president's willingness to undertake personal diplomacy whenever it seemed he might be helpful. Laney also knew that Kim Il-sung regarded Carter as less hostile than most American officials because of his aborted attempts in the late 1970s to bring peace to Korea. Although without evident enthusiasm, the Clinton White House did finally approve a Carter visit to Pyongyang.

As it turned out, Carter almost surely kept the United States from making a tragic mistake in a region long dominated by the military. His mission was quite comparable to the Nixon-Kissinger opening to China twenty years earlier. Whether Kim Il-sung was personally satisfied with a former president rather than a sitting president, we do not know, but clearly it was a better opportunity than negotiating with the International Atomic Energy Agency, which had nothing to offer him in return for his compliance with its inspection requirements. The Americans, on the other hand, could deliver goods North Korea badly needed, and also wring concessions and economic assistance from the Japanese and the South Koreans. Carter's visit, like Nixon's to China, was also testimony to the legitimacy of an isolated regime, something the United States had long denied. Kim Il-sung therefore agreed to freeze his nuclear program and opened negotiations on what he would require in order to permanently stop his weapons project and shift to a Western-approved form of nuclear power generation.

So ended the first phase of one of the potentially most serious confrontations of the post–Cold War era. Had the United States government followed the advice of its military, it might have produced its own version of the Russian catastrophe in Chechnya (as it may yet at some point in the future). Had the North Koreans pursued their nuclear program (as they may still decide to do), they would have achieved their own Iraq-like status as the true pariah of East Asia. The United States could have avoided this confrontation had it opened some constructive channel of communication with Pyongyang years ago; instead, our soldiers continue to glare at theirs across the table at Panmunjom, within the Demilitarized Zone between the two parts of Korea. The West's master theorist of war, Karl von Clausewitz, once argued that even after hostilities have commenced it is desirable to keep some channels of communications open among belligerents; failure to establish diplomatic ties in peacetime was, he thought, inexcusable. American–North Korean relations have been an apt example of his point.

Talks to implement the Carter-Kim agreement opened on July 8, 1994, the day Kim Il-sung unexpectedly died, and as a result were immediately suspended. His death and the lack of credible information about his son and successor, Kim Jong-il, which might have set back the negotiations, actually seemed to have little effect on the discussions. But they did create serious problems in South Korea, where the government prohibited any public expressions of grief over Kim's death and banned a church-sponsored human chain that was to extend to the Demilitarized Zone on the anniversary of Korea's liberation from Japan. The South Korean government also released letters that Russian president Boris Yeltsin had given to President Kim Yong-sam on a visit to Moscow in June 1994 allegedly proving that Kim Il-sung had started the Korean War. The police even entered elite Seoul National University's campus to arrest some 1,400 students who were calling for U.S. troops to get out of Korea and quit blocking unification.

On August 5, 1994, talks between North Korea and the United States resumed in Geneva, leading to an "Agreed Framework," which the two sides signed that October 21. According to this agreement the United States was to arrange for the construction by the year 2003 of two 1,000-megawatt light-water reactors in North Korea to replace its current graphite-moderated reactors (a Soviet design from which plutonium can rather easily be extracted for possible use in nuclear weapons). The United States was also to provide fuel oil to replace energy lost by the closing of North Korea's current reactors, and it was to guarantee that it would not use or threaten to use nuclear weapons on the Korean peninsula. Finally, the United States pledged to open trade and some form of diplomatic relations. For its part North Korea agreed to stop using and then dismantle its Russian reactors, ship its used nuclear fuel rods out of the country, remain a party to the Nuclear Non-Proliferation Treaty, and allow IAEA inspections of its nuclear sites.

The new reactors the United States was to provide were estimated to cost in the range of $4 billion to $4.5 billion. By March 1995, South Korea had agreed to pay about 70 percent of their cost and Japan 20 percent (with the remainder covered by various, mainly European countries). Although the United States negotiated the agreement, it agreed to pay nothing. All three nations—the United States, the Republic of Korea, and Japan—set up a new organization called the Korean Energy Development Organization (KEDO) to do the construction work.

The Japanese government supplied an initial $5.8 million so that KEDO could go into operation, but it has since regularly suspended funds whenever something has happened in North Korea that has not met its approval. In addition, elements in the U.S. government keep undercutting the agreement. U.S. Secretary of Defense William Cohen, for instance, said in Seoul in April 1997 that the United States intends to keep its forces stationed in Korea even if the two Koreas reunite. He gave no reason for this astonishing one-sided commitment, which implies an unending American imperial role in East Asia. He also predicted that North Korea was on the verge of collapse, which may explain why the United States has been so slow to implement the agreement. Instead of delivering fuel oil, as promised, or opening diplomatic and economic relations, as the North Koreans expected, the U.S. government has vacillated, often blaming Congress for its failure to fund the new relationship. Its impulse seemed to be to provide North Korea with just enough food to keep it from starving while hoping that its collapse would be "soft," relatively nonviolent, and controllable. Unexpectedly, with the onset of the global economic crisis in 1997, South Korea itself came close to collapse and proved incapable of paying its share of the new North Korean reactors. The American government made no effort to find or raise replacement funds.

It is important to understand that the war scare of 1994, temporarily relieved by Jimmy Carter's mediation and the subsequent Agreed Framework, sprang from two sets of related causes. The first was, of course, North Korea's flirtation with nuclear brinkmanship in the context of the collapse of the Communist world that had sustained it since its creation. The second was a kind of military machismo on the part of the Pentagon and its assorted cronies and clients around the world. Without any regard at all for Korean and East Asian realities, the American military leadership and its political backers seemed intent on having another "splendid little war" in Korea, a rerun of the 1991 Gulf War, with all of its medals, promotions, and new post–Cold War assignments for the armed forces. Needless to say, the Pentagon strategists who abstractly think of Korea as a potential East Asian Iraq give no heed at all to Korea as a real place in time and space—it is not, for example, an uninhabited desert, and any use of force there will produce catastrophic casualties on all sides. Despite its being one of the most heavily armed places on earth, there is no plausible military "option" in Korea. The temporarily favorable resolution of the 1994 threat of nuclear proliferation in North Korea, once direct negotiations and diplomacy were given a chance to work, did not eliminate either of the contending forces that had caused it, and at the end of the 1990s they reerupted to produce a festering political-military sore.

Frustrated by the failure of the United States to deliver on what Pyongyang expected to get from the Agreed Framework, North Korea continued development of a medium-range and potentially an intercontinental-range missile force. The North had long worked on copying, improving, and manufacturing the Soviet-designed Scud short-range liquid-fueled battlefield missile, which it then exported to earn hard currency or barter wherever it could. Throughout the 1980s, it traded weaponry to Iran for oil, accounting for as much as 40 percent of all Iranian arms imports during the Iran-Iraq War.[8]

After the Scud, the North's next big project was to build an intermediate-range missile that conceivably might deter the massive forces the United States arrayed against it at bases in Japan and on the ships of the Seventh Fleet. It is not clear whether this effort was technologically serious or whether it merely aimed at deterrence by raising anxieties. The first North

Korean IRBM (intermediate-range ballistic missile), the Nodong 1, was a Scud with additional engines bolted to its waist, giving it enough thrust to reach parts of Japan. The North only tested the Nodong once, in June 1993, when it went three hundred miles into the Sea of Japan. The accuracy of the Nodong and how many it has are unknown. Equally unknown is whether North Korea has even one nuclear warhead that it might attach to one of its missiles. The presumption is that the Agreed Framework interrupted its movement toward a nuclear device and that its missiles, even if they conceivably might arrive over their targets, are not armed with nuclear weapons.

However, in August 1998, a truly explosive development transformed this relatively benign environment into a paroxysm of Japanese and American overreaction and worst-case scenarios. On August 31, 1998, the United States government announced that North Korea had test-fired a two-stage (later revised to a three-stage) liquid-fueled missile over Japan. The United States knew about the North Korean missile launch as it occurred; indeed one of the Air Force's two RC-135S Cobra Ball surveillance aircraft, both assigned to the 55th Wing at Offutt AFB, Nebraska, was on station above the Korean peninsula to observe it.[9] The Japanese, at least metaphorically, went ballistic. They condemned North Korea for a dangerous military provocation and an implied threat to Japan's security. They cut off all contacts with the North and announced that they would launch their own spy satellites specifically to keep track of what was going on in North Korea and to end their dependence on military intelligence from the United States. They even professed to be thinking about withdrawing from the Agreed Framework.

It turned out that the North Koreans had used a three-stage rocket to launch a rather modestly designed satellite in connection with the celebration of the country's fiftieth anniversary. Like the famous 1970 Chinese satellite that broadcast the Maoist anthem "The East Is Red" into outer space, Pyongyang Radio announced that its satellite was transmitting the "Song of General Kim Il-sung" and "Song of General Kim Jong-il," which it labeled "immortal revolutionary hymns." The satellite seems to have malfunctioned, and no one ever recorded these melodies.

The North Korean foreign ministry also pointedly added, "We have never criticized the United States and Japan for having launched artificial satellites. We are well aware that these satellites have been used for espionage on our country."[10] Japan has in fact launched at least twenty-four satellites since its National Space Development Agency was founded in 1969. The Japanese (and Americans) also failed to mention that this was only the fourth North Korean missile firing on record and only the second in the 1990s, five years after the test of the Nodong 1 in May 1993. It also did not mention Japan's own highly developed rocket program, including a behemoth called the H-2, which has a payload of 5 tons, considerably greater than the 3.8 tons the United States' MX Peacekeeper ICBM can lift. This is not to imply that the North's missile was not threatening, only that it was most plausibly an attempt to deter much more formidable strategic forces deployed against it by the United States and Japan.

The United States has continued to harp on the threat posed by North Korea's missile capability. It ostentatiously flew B-52 and B-2 strategic bombers to its Pacific bases in Guam. Among the reasons for this belligerence was a desire on the part of the Defense Department and the arms industry to continue working on an antimissile defense system, an idea now considerably scaled down from the Reagan administration's lasers in outer space but still devoted to intercepting an incoming missile by firing a defensive missile at it. The technological requirements of hitting a bullet with another bullet are fierce, and there is always a possibility that nuclear fallout and debris from a successful interception will kill more people than if the warhead had been allowed to proceed to its target.

The American government has so far spent billions trying to make the theater missile defense (TMD) work but has repeatedly met with failure. One of the things it had most wanted was to get the Japanese to help fund the project (which even if it does not work will be very lucrative for the companies trying to build it) and provide technical input into it. The Japanese had consistently balked. The TMD seemed to them a probable violation of the Anti–Ballistic Missile Treaty and, in terms of deterrence theory, utterly destabilizing. If one country should ever achieve a successful missile defense (or believe that it had), it would have a strong incentive to launch a preemptive strike against its opponents before they too achieved such a defense. This is the main reason why China has consistently denounced America's infatuation with the TMD, as well as because it does not want to be drawn into a ruinously expensive arms race to develop it.

North Korea's launch of a missile with a range of several thousand miles transformed this debate. The Japanese finally agreed to buy into the TMD. On September 20, 1998, to the jubilation of Secretary of State Madeleine Albright and Secretary of Defense William Cohen, Japan reversed itself and joined the missile defense research program. Whether Japan and the United States together will ever overcome the stupendous technological problems, not to mention the strategic issues of decoys, reliability, lack of defense against cruise missiles (because they fly too low), the ability to deliver weapons of mass destruction through much less sophisticated ways than missiles (for example, via boats, helicopters, airliners), and the likelihood that civilian populations will never actually trust defensive missiles are all open questions, to say the least. The history of the Cold War demonstrated that stable, credible deterrence is the only rational answer to weapons against which there is no defense. Nonetheless, the North Korean missile launch, together with evidence that North Korea is working on even longer-range missiles, gave great renewed impetus to the TMD idea.

The unraveling of the Agreed Framework was not entirely caused by Pyongyang. The drumbeat demonizing North Korea has continued unabated in Washington. In February 1999, Republican congressman Benjamin Gilman, chairman of the House International Relations Committee, was convinced that "North Korea could nuke Seattle," and the director of central intelligence, George Tenet, testifying before the Senate Armed Services Committee, told the senators, "I can hardly overstate my concern about North Korea."[11] It seemed evident in the spring of 1999 that North Korea was being groomed as Public Enemy Number One until events in Yugoslavia overtook this campaign.

Even though it remains a small, failed Communist regime whose people are starving and have no petroleum, North Korea is a useful whipping boy for any number of interests in Washington. If the military needs a post–Cold War opponent to justify its existence, North Korea is less risky than China. Politicians seek partisan advantage by claiming that others are "soft" on defending the country from "rogue regimes." And the arms lobby had a direct interest in selling its products to each and every nation in East Asia, regardless of its political orientation.

There is considerable evidence that since the signing of the Agreed Framework in 1994, a series of mysterious incidents has been created deliberately to undermine diplomatic efforts to reduce tensions. In September 1997, for instance, the United States, South Korea, China, and North Korea were scheduled to hold negotiations on replacing the forty-five-year-old Korean armistice with a peace treaty. In the same month the United States also said it hoped to obtain North Korea's adherence to an international agreement first negotiated in 1987 called the Missile Technology Control Regime. This agreement sought to bring under control the transfer of technologies that could be used to make intercontinental ballistic missiles. The United States had indicated in advance that it would lift some of its economic sanctions against North Korea if it would halt deployment and sales of its missiles.

On August 22, 1997, the eve of the talks, the North Korean ambassador to Egypt, a key player in North Korea's missile sales to the Middle East, "defected" to the United States. R. Jeffrey Smith, a reporter for the *Washington Post*, quoted a CIA source as saying, "There will be people in the intelligence community who will be salivating to see this guy."[12] In the *New York Times* Steven Lee Myers noted that the defection threatened the peace talks but quoted another U.S. official as saying, "The alternative of turning down a bona fide plea for asylum from a state like North Korea is pretty unthinkable."[13] Jamie Rubin, a State Department spokesman, insisted that the defection "will not affect the four-party peace talks."[14] Then *Newsweek* revealed that the former ambassador had in fact long been on the CIA's payroll.[15] Informed observers concluded that he had not so much defected as been called in from the cold at a time of the CIA's choosing and with an eye toward scuttling the upcoming talks. North Korea in retaliation declined to attend either set of scheduled meetings.

A year later, amid reports that North Korea had grown frustrated with the failure of the United States to normalize relations, the *New York Times* published a front-page article by David E. Sanger—"North Korea Site an A-Bomb Plant, U.S. Agencies Say"—which revealed that "United States intelligence agencies have detected a huge secret underground complex in North Korea that they believe is the centerpiece of an effort to revive the country's frozen nuclear weapons program, according to officials who have been briefed on the intelligence information."[16] Congressional sources later revealed that Sanger's source was unanalyzed intelligence photographs probably leaked by Lt. Gen. Patrick Hughes, chief of the Defense Intelligence Agency. According to congressional aides, General Hughes regularly passed on information about the site, later identified as Kumchang-ri, to Republican congressmen.[17] None of the *Times*'s reporting on this incident ever cited a single government official by name, relying instead on the "blind quote": "high government officials say," "sources close to the White House reveal," "members of the intelligence community disclose," and so forth.

Two days after the article appeared, the Pentagon announced that the underground A-bomb plant actually seemed to be a large hole in the ground—one of thousands of such holes, some of them containing whole factories that were sited underground after the devastating American bombing during the Korean War—and that the United States had no evidence the North Koreans had ceased to comply with the Agreed Framework. Analysts in Asia speculated that if North Korea did decide to pull out of the agreement, it need only restart its reactors at its nuclear research center at Yongbyon instead of building a brand-new, inherently risky and expensive underground reprocessing plant. In Europe, the IAEA's spokesman said that the international monitoring agency first heard of the alleged new nuclear site from the *New York Times*.

Dr. C. Kenneth Quinones, who from 1992 to 1994 was the State Department's desk officer for North Korea and subsequently the Asia

Foundation's representative in South Korea—as well as the American who probably has visited the North more often than any other—wrote, "This . . . story is centered in Washington, not in Pyongyang. It involves America's intelligence community and not North Korea's nuclear program. . . . The recent leak of unsubstantiated 'intelligence' certainly appears to have been an irresponsible effort by a 'pessimist' within the American intelligence community. . . . The U.S. government has officially denied the accuracy of the reports."[18] Nonetheless, Secretary of State Madeleine Albright called the "suspected nuclear facility" a "huge threat" and demanded the right of the United States to conduct inspections in North Korea when and where it chooses.[19] North Korea agreed to let Americans look into Kumchang-ri in return for food aid. When the inspection was completed, American officials disclosed that it was a huge, empty tunnel and that there was no evidence of any preparations to construct a nuclear reactor or install machinery of any kind in it.[20]

In addition to these and other North Korean alarums, 1999 saw a number of strident but ultimately overstated U.S. claims about Chinese missile deployments and nuclear espionage, and unfortunate "accidents" (the U.S. bombing of the Chinese embassy in Belgrade during the Kosovo war). These raised serious questions about whether the armed and intelligence services were either out of control or being manipulated for political ends.

This is not to say that North Korea's nuclear and missile programs are not serious problems. Since there is as yet no worldwide treaty banning them, nor an effective defense against them, *all* programs to develop nuclear weapons and long-range missiles, including those of the United States and Japan, are "destabilizing." They constitute the most dangerous offensive weapons in existence at the present time. The issue is what to do about them. North Korea remains isolated in part because of policies the United States has pursued over the past forty-five years. To be sure, these policies were first formulated during the Cold War, but with the end of the old postwar order in East Asia, we finally have a chance to help promote a peaceful reunification of the Korean peninsula. Instead, the Pentagon is promoting a ballistic missile defense system.

Surely no better illustration exists of our continued imperial ambitions and delusions.

It is also worth remembering that what we call the Korean War ended as a war between the United States and China fought on Korean soil. Had it been strictly a "Korean" war in which only the United States intervened, the side we supported would have been militarily victorious and Korea today would not be divided. If the Korean peninsula ever erupts again into open warfare, China, an active participant in the Korean War, would undoubtedly once again consider intervention. China today actually seems most interested in a perpetuation of the status quo on the Korean peninsula. Its policy is one of "no unification, no war." Not unlike the eighth- and ninth-century Tang dynasty's relations with the three Korean kingdoms of Koguryo, Silla, and Paekche, China presently enjoys diplomatic relations with both Koreas and may prefer a structurally divided peninsula. A Korea unable to play its obvious role as a buffer between China, Russia, and Japan would give China a determining influence there. China's greatest worry has been that the Communist state in the North may collapse due to economic isolation and ideological irrelevance, thereby bringing about a unified, independent, and powerful new actor in northeast Asian politics, potentially the size of and as rich as the former West Germany and defended by a good army, possibly armed with nuclear weapons—not a development the Chinese would necessarily welcome.

For all of these reasons, the United States should cultivate North Korea and become an active supporter of Korean unification. In return for unification, the United States should withdraw its forward-deployed land forces from East Asia but retain its role as a balancer and provider of a "nuclear umbrella." A unified, economically successful Korea would help ensure a genuine *balance* of power in East Asia rather than the hegemony of either China, Japan, or the United States. Such a policy would also be a more effective way of instilling prudence in the foreign policy of an emerging China than our current pretense that we have the will, money, or patience to "contain" China.

6

CHINA: THE STATE OF THE REVOLUTION

On June 29, 1998, on a state visit to China, President Bill Clinton addressed the students of Beijing University in a speech carried live by television to all parts of China and then responded to their questions. One young man asked, "With a friendly smile, you have set foot on the soil of China. . . . So we are very excited and honored by your presence. What the Chinese people really aspire for is the friendship between China and the United States on the basis of equality. And I know that before your departure from the States, you said that the reason for you to visit China is because China is too important and engagement is better than containment. I'd like to ask you whether this is a kind of commitment you made for your visit, or do you have any other hidden things behind this smile? Do you have any other design to contain China?"[1]

This was a good question. Two years earlier the president had mobilized two carrier task forces when China launched a dramatic rocket barrage as part of its "military exercises" in the vicinity of Taiwan. These symbolic gestures were clearly aimed by the People's Republic at the upcoming Taiwanese presidential elections, and were a response as well to an unprecedented visit by the Taiwanese president to the United States the previous year. The exercises were meant as reminders to both governments that the mainland would never look on Taiwan as anything other than a province of China, and the American response, equally symbolic and crude, was a sobering reminder to the Chinese of the massive military forces the United States maintains and is capable of deploying just off their coast. Ironically though, from the point of view of American policy goals, Clinton's show of force had the unintended effect of helping the government in Beijing overcome its loss of legitimacy following the collapse of communism in Europe and its repression of its own students and workers in Tiananmen Square in 1989. Much as did Japanese aggression in the 1930s, American saber rattling rallied ordinary Chinese behind their government.

Since those aircraft carriers appeared in the waters off Taiwan in the spring of 1996, the United States has signed agreements with Japan enlarging the latter's military commitments, undercutting its pacifist constitution, and securing its acquiescence in remaining a privileged sanctuary for American military operations. The issue of the territories and waters in East Asia covered by these agreements has been deliberately obscured: the U.S. government insists the area to be "protected" includes the Taiwan Strait, while the Japanese government insists it does not (and neither government has been candid with its citizens about the major ambiguities in the new agreements).

China has protested vigorously any intrusion by the United States and its Japanese client into Taiwanese affairs, but to no avail. The United States continues to sell arms to Taiwan in violation of agreements the Reagan administration signed with China during the 1980s (in the communiqué of August 17, 1982, the U.S. government promised gradually to reduce the quantity and not improve the quality of arms sold to Taiwan). These sales include 150 F-16 advanced fighter aircraft, which President Bush agreed to sell during the 1992 presidential election campaign in order to appeal to voters of Texas, where the airplanes are manufactured. Combined with 60 Mirage fighters from France and sophisticated fighter aircraft that it manufactures itself, Taiwan has an aviation capability superior to anything possessed by the mainland. Taiwan's ability to threaten Chinese coastal cities, including Shanghai, is an effective deterrent against any mainland attempt to invade the island. This is one reason why mainland China's leadership seeks to intimidate Taiwan through the threat of a missile attack rather than an invasion and why the U.S. proposal to develop and station antimissile missiles on Taiwan is so alarming to them.

Slightly more than a week after Clinton had reassured his Chinese audience that the United States had no designs on their country, Secretary of Defense Cohen, at a joint news conference with his South Korean counterpart, outlined a military role in East Asia as dangerous as the one the USSR planned in Cuba in 1962—which almost led to nuclear war. Cohen indicated the United States intended to maintain combat troops on the Korean peninsula indefinitely, offering no reason why American troops should remain in a potentially unified Korea or who exactly they were meant to defend against. He also spoke of how any pullout of forces from Japan would create a dangerous power "vacuum" that "might be filled in a way that would not enhance stability but detract from it." This was interpreted at the time in the Japanese and Korean media as a barely veiled reference to China as a future enemy and as a warning against the possibility that Japan might undertake a foreign policy independent of the United States.

The friendly relations the United States enjoyed with China during the last eighteen years of the Cold War era, following the historic Nixon-Kissinger realignment, were based on a common opposition to the USSR. The collapse of the Soviet Union therefore ended China's main usefulness to the United States as an ally, while enhancing its new status as a possible long-term rival to American hegemony. In the wake of the Cold War, with the Pentagon intent on maintaining near Cold War levels of military spending, enemies on the global horizon were much needed. With the Soviet army increasingly seen as a disintegrating "paper tiger," China's economic emergence as a major power in the Pacific offered one possible fit with the Pentagon's need for a major enemy. Moreover, China's continuing disputes with Taiwan, its claims to islands in the South China Sea, its friendly relations with North Korea, its occasional armed disputes with Vietnam, and its modest ICBM forces armed with nuclear weapons all seemed to give evidence—in American eyes at least—of its aggressive intentions; all seemed to indicate that it might someday menace American imperial interests in the region.

In the years from the end of the Cold War to the present there has clearly been disagreement, even bitter acrimony, within the highest levels of the American government, from the White House to Congress to the Pentagon, over policy toward China. The question largely has been whether, like President Clinton, to espouse a policy of "engagement" with the People's Republic—that is, to emphasize trade as a tool of bringing the country into a regional system still dominated by the United States—or, like Republican congressman Christopher Cox, to espouse a policy of "containment"—that is, to make China the enemy around which an American regional system is to be organized—or even some at present inconceivable combination of the two. In pursuing various aspects of these policies and fighting out internecine, intragovernmental, intrabureaucratic struggles over them, various factions in American officialdom have highlighted issues ranging from human rights abuses to trade policy to potential atomic spying, leaking material to the media, holding inflammatory hearings, and making subtle military gestures.

What no American official seems to have considered is what a policy of "adjustment" to the reemergence of China might look like. To make space for or alter American policies in order to accommodate China's legitimate concerns as a potential future superpower seems beyond the policy horizons of American officialdom. Adjustment would hardly mean "appeasement"; it is possible that China might miscalculate and undertake some initiative so damaging to the rights of others that retaliation would indeed be appropriate. But the United States seems to assume that such an outcome is preordained, rather than undertaking diplomacy and statecraft to head it off.

The American president says one thing, but the American military presence in East Asia implies another. During the first half of the twentieth century, China often found itself in a similar situation in relation to the Japanese, whose central government expressed a desire for peace while its military simultaneously launched armed attacks on Chinese territory. A distrust of public protestations of peace and the need to draw conclusions from concrete military acts are part of China's heritage of international relations. They played a role in Chinese thinking during the Korean War, when differences between General MacArthur's strategic decisions in Tokyo and President Truman's statements in Washington contributed to China's decision to intervene. In the same way, the discrepancies between the American military's bombing of the Chinese embassy in the Yugoslav capital, Belgrade, on May 7, 1999, and the White House's subsequent protestations that the attack by a B-2 bomber using precision-guided munitions was an accident based on an "outdated map" are particularly hard for the Chinese to overlook. Contemporary American actions in East Asia, as distinct from statements by Washington, help trigger these old memories in Beijing.

The Chinese were sufficiently alarmed by our self-appointed post–Cold War mission of maintaining stability wherever we declared it to be threatened that, according to Helmut Sonnenfeldt (an executive of the Atlantic Council in Washington, D.C., and a close associate of Henry Kissinger's), they began studying George Kennan's early reports from the Soviet Union. At the dawn of the Cold War, Kennan was the State Department's foremost specialist on Russia. In a famous 1947 article in the magazine *Foreign Affairs* written under the pseudonym "X" and entitled "The Sources of Soviet Conduct," he first suggested a postwar policy of attempting to "contain" the expansion and influence of the USSR. According to Sonnenfeldt, the Chinese were interested because "now that the United States was turning containment against China, they wanted to learn how [the policy] had started and evolved."[2]

U.S. policy toward China, whatever the disagreements about it within the government, is driven by a familiar global agenda aimed at preserving and enhancing a Washington-centered world based on our being the "lone superpower." Whether it is called "globalization," the "Washington consensus," "soft power," or the "indispensable nation," it still comes down to an urge to hold on to an American-inspired, -financed, and -led world order. Whereas such hegemonism vis-à-vis Germany, Japan, Latin America, Russia, or the United Nations is only likely to result in imperial overstretch and the probable long-term decline of the United States, attempts to establish American hegemony over China hold out more explosive futures and are in any case doomed to failure.

As the histories of previous empires demonstrate, imperial overstretch can be a long-drawn-out process if all sides are careful to avoid confrontation (the Russian and Ottoman empires come to mind). But such hegemonic policies applied to China are likely to precipitate a crisis. China is the world's most populous country and has recently achieved an economy that promises to provide it with commensurate wealth and power. It is also an old civilization, whose humbling by foreign imperialists over the past two centuries led to the most sweeping and complex of all the modern revolutions. Its leaders are still working out whether they should seek parity on a global stage as defined by Western conceptions of international relations or try to re-create an older Sinocentric world of tributary states that existed before the arrival of the European imperialists, or perhaps some amalgam of the two.

In any case, China owes no obeisance to the United States. From 1950 to 1953, at great cost to itself, it fought the American military to a stalemate in Korea. A new policy of containment toward China once again implies the possibility of war, just as it did during the Cold War vis-à-vis the former USSR. The balance of nuclear weapons prevented that war, but this may not work in the case of China, where great asymmetries in manpower between China and any single external power or alliance will always exist. China has the capacity to deter an American use of nuclear weapons by threatening retaliation against U.S. cities, and the United States could never mobilize a large enough army to defeat China in a land invasion. There is also a much firmer foundation for a Chinese government's resistance to external threats in Chinese nationalism than there was at the time of the British, French, Russian, or Japanese depredations over the past 150 years. Many Americans do not evaluate Chinese nationalism correctly, thinking it is whipped up by Communist Party propaganda to suit its purposes. But like American nationalism after Pearl Harbor, it is actually rooted in concrete historical experiences of victimization, including Japan's attempt to establish a protectorate over China in 1915, its creation of a puppet regime in Manchuria in 1931, and its invasion of the whole country in 1937. The Chinese pose no threat to the territory of the United States, but the Americans (and the Japanese) have done so in the past and conceivably still could directly threaten China. A war with China would almost certainly bankrupt the United States, radicalize China, and tear Japan apart.

Military containment of China is a particularly dangerous policy for Japan (as an American ally) to espouse, since its own emergence onto the world stage began a century ago with its invasion and defeat of China in 1895 and its seizure of the island of Taiwan, which it held as a Japanese colony until 1945. Moreover, because Japan's devastation of China in the 1930s and 1940s was the crucial factor leading China into the civil war from which the Communist Party emerged victorious, politically aware Chinese remain acutely sensitive to any hint of revived Japanese militarism, just as Russians do to any hint of revived German militarism.

According to a Hong Kong wisecrack, China has just had a couple of bad centuries and is back. The question is whether the United States can adjust to the emergence of a new great power in Asia. Will it deal more effectively and less bloodily with China than, say, the former hegemon Great Britain did in the early twentieth century, when it failed to adjust to the emergence of new centers of power in Germany, Japan, and Russia? The current trend of events is not promising.

In 1949, in proclaiming the birth of the Chinese People's Republic from atop the Gate of Heavenly Peace overlooking the square of the same name, Tiananmen, in Beijing, Mao Zedong announced that finally "China has stood up." He was wrong. China had only risen to its knees. Of the two great objectives of the Chinese revolution—ending imperialistic interference in China's domestic affairs and overcoming China's economic weakness in relation to the developed world—the Chinese Communists proved able to deliver only on the first. The latter had to wait another forty years, until China finally discovered the secret of the enrichment of East Asia—Japanese-style, state-guided capitalism—and began to act on it. Its economy then started to grow at double-digit rates, threatening to alter the global distribution of power. Without question, the most important element in the current phase of Asia's empowerment has been China's belated discovery of the market and its consequent candidacy as the second great power in East Asia, perhaps as *the* super-power of the twenty-first century.

Ever since the industrial revolution, the cardinal source of friction in world politics has been the economic inequality it produced. This inequality allowed the first industrializers to use their new power to colonize or in other ways subjugate and exploit the nonindustrialized areas of the world. Nationalistically awakened elites among these subjugated peoples then sought in various ways to overcome their relative backwardness, to equalize relations with or achieve supremacy over their victimizers.

But how can peripheral societies, even when they achieve national independence, break out of their economic and political dependency? In the view of the prominent political scientist Andrew Janos, history offers examples of two grand strategies for dealing with this issue.[3] The first was for dependent or "late-developing" countries to attempt through war and revolution to reconstruct their environments. This strategy required a militarization of society and the use of a mobilized people to attack and transform the environment. The execution of this strategy has taken the forms of aggression and conquest (Nazi Germany, Japan from 1931 to 1945), support for world revolution (Lenin's and Stalin's Russia), fomenting "people's wars" (China and Cuba), aggressive neutralism (India), and other projects aimed at altering an environment in which "advanced" countries exploit "developing" ones.

The second strategy has been, in Janos's words, a "drive to imitate the technological innovations of the advanced countries." This strategy has generally been internally oriented. It is best illustrated by Japan's state-guided industrialization from 1868 to approximately the Great Depression and again from 1949 to the present. It may involve only the state's use of tariffs to shelter its own economy from the penetrative power of stronger national economies. This was the strategy of the United States during the nineteenth and early twentieth centuries, in accordance with the ideas of Alexander Hamilton and Friedrich List. A version of this strategy also became policy in West Germany after its defeat in World War II. But such a strategy involving state guidance of the economy, cartelization, and the strategic allocation of industrial finance may so come to dominate a social system that development itself becomes the main legitimating and organizing principle of society, replacing or displacing democratic representation, tradition, or any other set of political or cultural principles. When that happens, the ensuing regime can be termed a "developmental state."[4]

Needless to say, in comparing the ways each strategy has been used during the twentieth century, it seems clear that the developmental state has proven far more successful than any attempt to forcibly reconstruct the external world, although it is a tricky strategy to execute and has many hidden consequences. It is critically dependent on a permissive international environment, such as the one the United States enjoyed in the nineteenth century or Japan vis-à-vis the United States after 1952.

These two strategies also define the history of the People's Republic of China since its birth in 1949. From the time Mao discovered that it would not be easy to duplicate a Stalinist program of development in China—that is, when he discovered that his Great Leap Forward campaign to move the country toward heavy industrialization through extreme levels of collectivization had by 1962 resulted in the deaths by starvation of some thirty million people—he experimented with altering the external environment on the cheap. He tried to militarize (he called it "revolutionize") his own society and to reconstruct the external world by sponsoring or endorsing "people's wars." Even though in Vietnam this approach succeeded in tarnishing the image of the United States as a superpower, it did not really alter the balance of power, and the Vietnamese soon resented Mao's claims of paternity to a strategy they had embarked on without Chinese help. Mao's massive domestic upheaval, the "Great Proletarian Cultural Revolution," which started in 1966 and lasted in one form or another almost a decade, was his revenge against the Communist Party after he lost control of it in the wake of the Great Leap Forward. It further discredited him, and communism, in the eyes of his main supporters; after his death in 1976 and the return to power of the purged Deng Xiaoping in 1978, the country devoted itself to reform and recovery from the Cultural Revolution. China began, in short, to experiment with the second strategy for breaking out of its backwardness.

By the end of the 1980s, China had begun seriously to incorporate the lessons of high-speed economic growth pioneered in American-dominated East Asia. Its still ruling Communist Party also began tacitly to stress nationalism rather than communism, which was then collapsing in Russia, to garner political support. On the basis of this new nationalism, China began to reach out and accept investment and other forms of assistance from the fifty-five million overseas Chinese, particularly those living in Hong Kong and Southeast Asia. It also slowly opened the country to foreign trade and investment with capitalist countries, so long as the terms were mutually beneficial. This strategy held the possibility of ultimately delivering on the second goal of the Chinese revolution—namely, the creation of a per capita income approaching that of the other major powers. Since China is by far the world's largest society in terms of population, if it succeeds it may also become the world's most powerful nation.

China's attempt to emulate the economies of Japan, South Korea, Taiwan, and Singapore is, however, fraught with difficulties, above all how to control the increasing gap between rich and poor in a previously Communist country. In terms of relations with the rest of the world, China's products will never enjoy the virtually unrestricted access to the American market and its sources of technology that Japan and others enjoyed in exchange for their support during the Cold War. This was made clear during 1999 when the United States was caught up in a politically driven panic over allegations of Chinese industrial espionage and imports of technologically advanced equipment for purposes of reverse engineering. On the other hand, China has one major asset not available to most developing nations: the overseas Chinese. This reservoir of talent, capital, and experience is open to a China that stresses nationalism rather than communism. China has so far been very cautious in lifting currency controls and import barriers that protect it from the full pressures and volatility of the international market, a precaution that served it well during the East Asian financial crisis of 1997 and after. China has no choice but to continue to open up to international trade; its development strategy will not work if, as in the Maoist days, it once again isolates itself from the rest of the world. At least for now, however, the news from China is reasonably positive. The peaceful reversion of Hong Kong to mainland rule in 1997 and its maintenance as a global financial center were a clear sign of China's determination and its capacity to succeed economically.

Throughout much of recorded history China was the world's largest economy. Today, as it reemerges on the world scene, the World Bank estimates that it has already passed Germany to become the world's third-largest economy, after the United States and Japan, as well as the fastest-growing economy. The Chinese State Statistical Bureau has calculated that during 1995 it grew by some 10.2 percent, down from the 11.8 percent increase of 1994 but still above the government's target growth rate of between 9 percent and 10 percent. The global economic crisis that began in 1997 has slowed but certainly not stopped growth. Even if in the future China grows at only 7 percent a year, it will surpass a U.S. economy growing at a 3 percent rate sometime between 2020 and 2030. Needless to say, extending present trends statistically into the future is a deeply perilous activity. It is perfectly possible that environmental degradation, or natural disasters, or a downward spiral into depression and poverty due to fast and messy industrial modernization will cause pressures of a sort we cannot even imagine today and sooner than we think. But thus far, China has a better development strategy than any it has experimented with since 1949.

Since economic reform began in 1978, China's annual average per capita income has risen 6.7 times but still remains unimaginably small: $464 in China's cities and $186.75 in rural areas, according to 1995 official estimates (but perhaps as much as $2,000 per capita in terms of purchasing power, given the low prices of basic human necessities). By contrast, Japan's per capita income in 1993 was $31,450 and that of the United States $24,750. China's labor costs are still just 10 to 15 percent of those in Hong Kong, Taiwan, and South Korea but on a par with those in India.

The Chinese Communist Party, the world's largest political organization, no longer has much legitimacy in the eyes of the Chinese people. Although it came to power in 1949 as the leader of the largest and most complex revolution of all, it squandered its great popularity: in rural China because of the famine that followed the Great Leap Forward; among hard-core Communist revolutionaries because of the Cultural Revolution; and, finally, among urban intellectuals and a burgeoning middle class because of the repression at Tiananmen Square in 1989 and the nearly simultaneous collapse of communism in Europe.

The Chinese Communist Party continues to rule through a combination of inertia, improving economic conditions, favorable comparisons with the past, nationalism, and a complex set of inducements and penalties. There is every reason to believe that it will be able to do so for the foreseeable future, despite occasional periods of instability. Taiwan, whose government comes from a similar background (single-party rule by Sun Yat-sen's political party, the Kuomintang, which Chiang Kai-shek inherited), offers strong evidence that the mainland could also slowly evolve into a prosperous, relatively open society. Pressure for democratization will probably become a serious internal issue, if it ever does, only around the year 2010, when some 30 percent of the mainland population might have reached a per capita income of about $4,000. Until then, the bulk of the Chinese population will probably remain content with economic progress, better health care, and other practical concerns.

From the Politburo down, most Chinese now believe in pursuing economic reforms, even if different groups support the reform process for different reasons. There is also something of a consensus on the necessity of maintaining a powerful, independent political authority to implement such reforms. The Chinese leaders are firmly convinced that authoritarian rule is indispensable to the success of their market-driven policies, and there is evidence that the Chinese population accepts this view because of the economic achievements of recent years. In this view, without authoritarian political control, economic reform will rapidly breed new economic interests and corruption, already a serious problem. Long-term success requires some authority capable of occasionally cracking down on corruption, complete with public executions as warnings to others. The more corrupt interests become entrenched, the more resentment against them is likely to generate a cycle of political protest, followed by economic instability. Always before the Chinese leadership is the example of the virtual collapse of the former Soviet Union and the resulting impoverishment of large sectors of the Russian population when authoritarianism was allowed to lapse and the economy was "reformed" in accordance with the theories of American economists.

In general terms, the greatest weakness of the development-state strategy is that it both causes and can be crippled by domestic political turmoil. In the other East Asian economic success stories, turmoil has been kept in check by authoritarian political systems of various sorts, the reasonably equitable distribution of incomes, and the promotion of distinctive "Asian values" focused on condemning the alleged selfishness of Western individualism and sometimes of Western democratic institutions as well. Asian leaders have often argued that democracy undercuts development. Lee Kuan Yew, the legendary first prime minister of the rich city-state of Singapore and a persistent critic of U.S. foreign policy in Southeast Asia, is the most articulate exponent of this view. As Lee has put it, "With few exceptions, democracy has not brought good government to new developing countries. Democracy has not led to development because the governments did not establish [the] stability and discipline necessary for development."[5] It should be noted that in the 1990s, Singapore, which may not be as pleasant a place for an individualist to live, nonetheless has had a higher per capita income ($23,565) than Australia ($19,960), something that lends a certain credibility in Asian eyes to what its leader has had to say.

All of the Asian capitalist developmental states have been characterized by what I call "soft authoritarian" governments.[6] Democracy—understood as a political system in which the force of public opinion makes a difference, a balance of powers exists within the government (what Americans call the "separation of powers"), and free elections can actually remove unsatisfactory officials—exists only partially in Japan, South Korea, and Taiwan, thanks to the pervasive, potent influence of unelected bureaucrats. In none of the three has an independent judiciary or the rule of law ever fully developed. In South Korea and Taiwan, movements for democratic reform have in recent years finally succeeded in bringing formerly "hard" authoritarian governments under more popular controls. In Japan, public opinion exerts a powerful influence over the government, but mainly through informal and traditional channels rather than the formal institutions of parliament and the courts.

If the government of Japan and its emulator states—South Korea, Taiwan, and even Singapore—can be characterized as soft authoritarian, at least during their decades of high-speed economic growth, then China may be an example of "soft totalitarianism," on a par with governments like Suharto's in Indonesia or Chiang Kai-shek's in Taiwan, and considerably softer than the truly totalitarian worlds of Hitler, Stalin, and Mao.

A soft totalitarian regime directly restricts freedoms of speech and the press, thereby curbing the effect of public opinion on the government. Under soft authoritarianism (as in Japan, for example), such freedoms exist on paper but are attenuated in part by cartelization of the news media—press clubs in Japan can impose collective or individual penalties on journalists who report news that irritates the state—and also by narrow channels of access to advertising, state-owned broadcasting, and state licensing of school textbooks. The public is better informed in soft authoritarian countries because there are always ways around press clubs and cartels, but public opinion remains only a mild constraint on the government. Whereas a soft totalitarian state will employ direct suppression of offending books, imprisonment of authors, state control of Internet servers, and dismissal or imprisonment of dissidents, soft authoritarianism achieves its ends through peer pressure, bullying, fear of ostracism, giving priority to group norms, and eliciting conformity through social sanctions of various kinds. Under both types of regimes, elections are usually to one degree or another only formalities, behind which permanent state officialdoms actually govern.

An ideological shift from an all-embracing communism to an all-embracing nationalism has also helped to hold Chinese society together, giving it a certain intellectual and emotional energy and stability under the intense pressures of economic transformation. One of the weaknesses of communism was its quasi-religious claim to scientific truth, which, once exposed as fraudulent, undermined the values and ideological cement of the regimes that had embraced it. Since the collapse of communism in Eastern Europe and Soviet Russia, the Chinese Communist Party has tried to foster a consensus among mainland and overseas Chinese based not on scientific but on historical claims to power, prestige, and wealth—as well as on a belief that China is once again destined to reclaim its position as the preeminent civilization in Asia and become a global superpower. The People's Republic of China used to proudly call itself Communist China. Today, the term commonly used is just China, and this new "China" borrows endlessly from its past glories but also plays powerfully on its century-long experience of humiliation at the hands of European, American, and Japanese imperialists. Present-day China is clearly in transit toward some new self-concept, not to speak of a new system of relationships with other countries; it is not yet clear, however, what form or forms these will take.

To be sure, there are factors that could derail China's emergence as a major power, the most obvious of which are inadequate education and uneven development within the country. In the Republic of China on Taiwan during the 1990s, for example, the president, premier, and half the cabinet had doctoral degrees. In fact, its impressive record in producing a college-educated populace is one explanation for Taiwan's increasingly successful transition to democracy in a context of high, reasonably equitable per capita income distribution and huge reserves of foreign currency. Such educational achievements—close to 40 percent of Taiwanese aged eighteen to twenty-one are enrolled in institutions of higher learning—are almost unimaginable on the mainland. China, with a total population of 1.2 billion, has the staggeringly low total of about 7 million college graduates to help run a massive and massively modernizing economy and society. There are a total of 1,065 institutions of higher learning in China today, with about 2.5 million students.[7]

China also sends thousands of students abroad for advanced degrees, but many of them do not come home. This means China has no access to the sort of meritocratic officialdom with which Japan, South Korea, Taiwan, and Singapore have managed their systems of privately owned but publicly guided enterprises. The Communist Party itself currently has a total of about fifty million members, but only some two million of them are college educated. It can compensate for this educational weakness to some extent by tapping into the talents of overseas Chinese and of interested foreign investors, but such a lack of widespread technical competence may in the long run prove a serious and potentially catastrophic constraint.

Uneven development is a potentially explosive problem. Although in times of dynastic decline or internal weakness China has been prey to strong centrifugal forces, warlordism, and regional movements for independence, this is unlikely to be a major concern in the foreseeable future. A wealthy province like Guangdong, adjacent to thriving Hong Kong, for example, has nothing to gain and much to lose in the civil war that would undoubtedly result from any attempt to separate itself from the rest of the country. The issue of the present moment is not so much keeping wealthy provinces in line as keeping poor provinces quiet and functional with not much more in the way of compensation than the promise that sooner or later the wealth of the country is bound to begin to trickle down to them.

An estimated one hundred million people, more than the entire population of Mexico, are now adrift in China, largely migrants from the interior looking for work in rich coastal areas. They represent what "trickle down" there may be for the poorest rural areas, remitting part of their meager earnings to the interior. The vast and controversial Three Rivers Dam under construction on the Yangtze River will aid interior areas more than any other part of the country by providing cheap electric power to them; for the time being, however, the migrants tend to evade taxes and ignore the country's draconian one-family, one-child policy. There is also the danger, from the ruling party's point of view, that they might organize. This would not only reduce their value as an ultra-cheap labor force contributing to the present export-driven boom but also raise the possibility that migrant groups could grow into a Chinese version of Solidarity, the union movement that largely dismantled communism in Poland. This would be the regime's worst nightmare and is the primary reason for the sometimes harsh application of its otherwise soft totalitarian policies to political dissidents of all sorts, but to union organizers and religious movements in particular. Part of the unholy alliance between China's domestic autocrats and its foreign investors is that both hate unions and any movement toward workers' rights, even if for different reasons.

The global economic crisis that began in 1997 in East Asia and subsequently spread elsewhere threatens China almost as much as other Asian nations. But there are several factors in the Chinese situation that leave it in a more advantageous position than many other developing nations. As a start, the country is insulated from currency speculators because its currency is not freely traded on world markets. A year after the crisis began Malaysia, one of East Asia's earliest-stricken economies, in order to regain control over its own economic affairs, took a page out of China's book and imposed controls over capital flows so that foreign speculators could no longer freely bring in or take out huge amounts of Malaysian currency. China has one of the highest levels of external debt in the world, of around $120 billion; but more than 85 percent of that debt is in medium- and long-term loans, not the short-term ones that bankrupted South Korea, Thailand, and Indonesia when international lenders began demanding immediate repayment. Most foreign investment in China is also in major manufacturing projects, not in stocks, so there is less danger of sudden capital flight. In addition, China holds the world's second-largest foreign currency reserves (after Japan), around $130 billion, which exceed its external debt.

China's main structural weakness is its banking system. The People's Bank of China estimated that during 1997 at least 22 percent of the nation's loans, worth more than $200 billion, were nonperforming—that is, they were not being repaid. The borrowers of these funds are the one hundred thousand sometimes woefully inefficient and unprofitable state-owned enterprises left over from the Maoist era, which together employ some fifty-six million people. These companies are the main legacy of the old Soviet-type economic system that the Communists adopted in the 1950s. In 1996, the state-owned sector turned in an overall loss for the first time. By contrast, collective enterprises, owned by local political units but subject to market forces, have doubled their productivity since 1978, while the privately owned sector now accounts for more than 11 percent of all Chinese industrial output.

At the 15th Congress of the Chinese Communist Party, held in September 1997, the party launched a new drive to transform the majority of state-owned enterprises into share-holding or limited-liability companies. If they remain unprofitable, they can then be closed one by one. Zhu Rongji was appointed prime minister primarily to manage this delicate operation, endangering as it does the previously guaranteed lifetime jobs of so many workers. His main problem has been that if he restricts bank credit to state-owned enterprises in order to rehabilitate the banking system, he risks soaring unemployment when many such enterprises go under. Despite the "no pain, no gain" ideology being urged on China by the Western business press, officials are proceeding very slowly with these changes, for overzealous liquidation of state-owned enterprises, with its ensuing massive unemployment and dislocation, could destabilize the entire society. In July 1998, as part of the effort to reform the old economic structure, President Jiang Zemin ordered the People's Liberation Army to liquidate the fifteen thousand commercial enterprises it runs, often of much greater interest to officers and troops than military preparedness. A distinctive characteristic of the Chinese economy has long been the extensive business activities of the armed forces (and the widespread corruption that has followed in their wake). Intended to increase the competitiveness of state-owned enterprises by stamping out corruption and smuggling, getting the army out of business will not be easy.

China's long-range economic strategy is to transform its state-owned enterprises into versions of Japan's industrial groups, the *zaibatsu* (renamed *keiretsu* after the war), or South Korea's *chaebol* (which, unlike Japan's groups, are more likely to be family-owned). By grouping profitable and risky enterprises together into developmental conglomerates and supplying bank credit to them on a preferential basis, China hopes to forge its own versions of Mitsubishi, Sumitomo, Daewoo, and Samsung. Needless to say, this will divide the labor force into labor aristocrats working for strategic corporations and ordinary workers in medium and small enterprises who sell intermediate goods to the big companies. This structural feature has long inhibited labor solidarity in Japan and South Korea, and it will have the same effect in China. While American economic theorists generally disapprove of the *zaibatsu*-type of corporate organization, something Japan invented in the late nineteenth century, the postwar descendants of the original *zaibatsu* were crucial to the economic development of Japan, South Korea, and Taiwan. China has every reason to try to emulate them.

The real economic model for mainland China, although never mentioned for all the obvious reasons, is undoubtedly neither Japan nor South Korea but Taiwan, where the state and the ruling Nationalist Party own outright or directly control about 50 percent of all corporate assets and account for close to 30 percent of Taiwan's gross national product. Numerous and successful state-owned enterprises are the single most striking feature of Taiwan's economic landscape. Even though one of the richest places on earth, largely untouched by the economic meltdown of the late 1990s, it is structurally less orthodox in terms of the American model of capitalism than any other East Asian country.[8]

But Taiwan is not just a covert economic model for China; it is also one of China's greatest political conundrums. Although an unquestioned part of China according to international law, the island has become so rich that many of its inhabitants would far rather see their country secede and become independent than find themselves integrated into the poorer, more politically repressive mainland. If Taiwan did declare its independence, any number of dreadful developments could follow, ranging from a nationalistic backlash in China that could lead to the overthrow of the regime to an attempted invasion of Taiwan to keep China's territory intact and a possible larger war involving the United States. The Taiwan problem at the end of the twentieth century is, as it was at the midpoint of the century, still the single most complicated issue of Chinese foreign policy and the most dangerous place where Chinese and American interests intersect. If it is mishandled by either side, the various kinds of blowback that might result could dominate global politics in the next century.

7

CHINA: FOREIGN POLICY, HUMAN RIGHTS, AND TRADE

In addition to its desire to maintain national security, advance its economic interests, and repress dissidents, China's ruling Communist Party emphatically plays upon the country's experience as a victim of imperialism and on its newfound nationalism. In its foreign policy, its primary focus has not been on expanding its territory or influence at the expense of other nations but on settling old, irredentist claims. The term "irredentism" derives from the name of an Italian political party of 1878 that sought to recover adjacent regions inhabited largely by Italians but under foreign control; by extension it now refers to any policy aimed at recovering territories lost to foreigners.

In the Chinese context irredentism applies to places formerly claimed by Imperial China, whose last dynasty ended in 1912, and allegedly lost due to foreign activity. Without regard to their relative importance, the primary ones in question have long been 1) Hong Kong, 2) Taiwan, 3) various island groups in the South China Sea, and 4) Tibet. The issues surrounding these contested areas have varied depending on whether each was occupied by China or others, on the nature of the historical record that lay behind each claim, and on the relative power of the claim holders. In addition, there is the question, seldom directly raised by the Chinese but to one degree or another taken into consideration, of the costs today of pursuing old claims, no matter how well founded. Each of the remaining claims—the Hong Kong one having been peaceably settled in 1997—is much exacerbated by the regime's increasing reliance on nationalism to solidify a base of support for its rule. The need to invoke the inviolable nature of "the Chinese motherland" as a basis for power has spurred the government to right old wrongs even when doing so violates another nation's sovereignty or tramples on the human rights of peoples who were never in any sense part of the Chinese empire. This is only complicated by China's stated willingness to use military means to achieve its irredentist aims.

Hong Kong is indeed no longer at issue. It began its colonial existence in the nineteenth century as the booty of the English opium cartel after a successful war fought to prevent China from cutting off trade in the substance. On June 30, 1997, it was returned to China by the British government in an elaborate, ceremonial, and nondisruptive manner. Consistent with their penchant for publishing only bad news about China, the *New York Times*, the *Wall Street Journal*, the *Washington Post*, *Time*, and *Newsweek* all predicted that the reversion of Hong Kong would go badly and questioned whether Beijing could administer the territory successfully as the capitalist financial hub it had long been. And yet nothing out of the ordinary has happened. The government of Hong Kong is today similar to the colonial one under British rule from 1841 to 1989. Only after the Tiananmen repression, with reversion in sight, did Hong Kong's British rulers introduce elements of democracy to the colony. China has retained some of these late democratic reforms but rescinded others. Much was at stake for the Chinese government in a peaceful and successful reversion. Hong Kong was certainly seen as a model for the future incorporation of Taiwan into the Chinese nation and evidence to the Taiwanese that the process, despite disparities between the two societies, need not be painful or punitive.

Taiwan is, in fact, similar to Hong Kong in one respect: the cultural gap between citizens of the mainland and of either Hong Kong or Taiwan is now far greater than it was fifty years ago, when the Communists came to power in Beijing. Taiwan was settled by immigrants from Fujian province in the seventeenth century and then became a Japanese colony from 1895 to 1945. For China, the "liberation" of Taiwan remains a fundamental goal, a final task left over from the revolution that Mao led in the 1930s and 1940s against Nationalist Party leader Chiang Kai-shek, who retreated to Taiwan with what was left of his defeated forces at the end of a bitter war.

The Nationalist exiles who evacuated to Taiwan in 1949 have slowly died off or been assimilated into the island's preexisting Chinese population. Today, the Nationalist Party (the Kuomintang) is led by a native Taiwanese, who must compete for power against other Taiwanese not hobbled by old Nationalist affiliations. The hostility that existed after World War II between mainland exiles and long-resident Taiwanese has been slowly ameliorating, not only due to the deaths of first-generation exiles but also to intermarriage, the growing wealth of both groups, and a gradual political democratization that has in its own way been a form of decolonization. The emergence of Taiwanese-led political parties has signaled the end of a mainlander monopoly over politics. One result of this is that today few Taiwanese of any stripe particularly want to "rejoin" the mainland. Yet they do not dare declare their independence, fearing that this would force the hand of the mainland government. Serious political instability on the mainland, however, might prompt a unilateral declaration of independence, which would probably draw China and the United States into a war that neither wants and neither could win.

In the spring of 1995, the U.S. government permitted a visit by the president of the Republic of China on Taiwan, Lee Teng-hui, a native Taiwanese, even though the United States had broken diplomatic relations with Taiwan in 1978, when it recognized the People's Republic. He was ostensibly to attend an alumni gathering at Cornell, his alma mater. Although this was billed as a private visit, the House of Representatives had voted 396–0 and the Senate 97–1 in resolutions calling on President Bill Clinton to admit Lee. To add insult to injury, Chinese officials first heard the news on CNN rather than through diplomatic channels. They were outraged and said so, pointing out that China has a legal claim to

Taiwan older than the United States itself and accusing Congress and the president of meddling in their "internal affairs."

Lurking here, as elsewhere, is a classic American error: the superpower's mistaken belief that its role is pivotal in any context. Taiwan has been actively complicating the mainland's decision making in ways far more effective than bluster from Washington. Taiwan is, for example, by far the largest investor in Vietnam and has risked more than $15 billion on Southeast Asian projects. Vietnam, a member of the Association of Southeast Asian Nations (ASEAN), has the longest and best record when it comes to countering Chinese pressures on its southern neighbors. The Taiwanese, in other words, have done their best to ensure that any Chinese attack on the island would involve the region as a whole, including ASEAN, which is slowly emerging as one of three major poles, along with Japan and China, in East Asia's new balance of power.

Meanwhile, America's cold warriors continue to exacerbate tensions between the mainland and Taiwan through incessant saber rattling of various sorts. Some of this is done largely for partisan political advantage in the United States, some in hopes of selling extremely expensive if sometimes untested advanced weapons systems in the area. Some of it is instigated by paid lobbyists for Taiwan, which seeks to ensure that the United States would be drawn into any conflict in the area, even if Taiwan's own policies provoked it. It must be stressed here that the United States has no basis in international law for intervening on Taiwan's behalf in what is essentially a not-yet-fully-resolved civil war. Thus the tactics of American provocateurs in leaking false intelligence reports, prodding Japan into closer military cooperation with the United States, and promoting a theater missile defense (TMD) for the region are not only dangerous but potentially illegal.

On February 11, 1999, for example, American newspapers quoted unnamed sources at the Pentagon claiming that the "Chinese government has deployed more than 120 ballistic missiles, and possibly as many as 200, on its side of the Taiwan Strait.... Analysts said the deployment—at least a doubling of the previous number of missiles massed on China's southern coast—is sure to fuel calls in the U.S. for including Taiwan in . . . the TMD."[1] The following day, navy Captain Michael Doubleday, a Pentagon spokesman, publicly contradicted this by declaring that "China has not increased the number of missiles aimed at the island . . . since an early 1990s buildup."[2] On February 26, Taiwan's Ministry of Foreign Affairs, fearing perhaps being pressured into a major investment in an unproven, essentially nonexistent antimissile system, proclaimed its appreciation of U.S. concerns about peace and stability in the Taiwan Strait but added, "The policy of the ROC government is that cross-strait issues should be resolved with peaceful means." On the other hand, in a statement typical of Taiwanese pressures in the area, Shaw Yu-ming, a high-ranking ROC official now affiliated with the Institute of International Relations at National Chengchi University, suggested that Taiwan might want to use the (false) Pentagon assessment as a basis to seek more arms sales from the United States.[3]

A missile defense system, if at all effective, would be particularly threatening from a mainland point of view. China lacks the capability to successfully invade and conquer Taiwan, but in the present highly nationalistic domestic climate, no mainland government could acquiesce in Taiwanese independence and survive. As a way to deter the island from declaring independence, China therefore threatens to respond with missiles. It does not want to do so, and it understands that Taiwan, in the face of an unprovoked attack from the mainland, would retaliate with massive force. The way to avoid conflict in the area is thus to perpetuate the status quo: continued self-government for Taiwan without a formal declaration of independence.

The American government's attempt to promote the TMD in this context is an unwelcome provocation. Its untested technology will not, in the end, reassure the Taiwanese, while the Chinese fear it as the basis for a strengthened military alliance between Taiwan and the United States. Wang Daohan, a senior adviser to President Jiang Zemin, said to the press of a possible future deployment of the TMD in Taiwan, "It is like playing with fire. That will completely disrupt the current world situation, and instead a new Cold War will appear."[4]

None of this is even slightly necessary. The United States needs to bring its own security apparatus under control and stop exaggerating the Chinese military threat. With regard to nuclear warheads, for example, between 1964, when China first tested a nuclear device, and 1996, when China signed the Comprehensive Test-Ban Treaty, it conducted 45 nuclear tests. The United States, in contrast, has conducted 1,030 nuclear tests, not including the actual atomic bombings of Hiroshima and Nagasaki. Robert Walpole, the CIA's national intelligence officer for strategic and nuclear programs, testified in September 1998 that China had at most twenty ICBMs, which were being maintained in an unfueled state and with their warheads unattached.[5] Admiral Dennis C. Blair, commander in chief in the Pacific, testified before Congress in March 1999 that "China is not a military threat to U.S. interests. It will be many years before the People's Liberation Army presents a major challenge to U.S. forces."[6] And yet, in that same month, the Senate voted 97–3 to build a "national missile defense" essentially against China and North Korea, and President Clinton endorsed spending some $10.6 billion on it over the coming five years. This is American overstretch, not a responsible national defense policy.

Some members of Congress and Pentagon officials are also promoting worst-case scenarios about Chinese moves in the South China Sea. Through this waterway passes virtually all of the oil from the Middle East intended for China, Japan, South Korea, and Taiwan. There are two sets of about a thousand islands, reefs, and rocks in the South China Sea, the Spratlys (Nansha in Chinese) and the Paracels (Xisha), which are claimed in part or in whole by seven different governments—those of China, Vietnam, Taiwan, the Philippines, Malaysia, Brunei, and Indonesia. It was only in late 1987 that sovereignty over the Spratlys first became an issue in Chinese foreign policy, reflecting a shift to nationalism as the main legitimating principle of the regime. Most of these barren bits of land are unoccupied, but during the late 1980s and early 1990s, in pursuit of their various claims, China occupied six of them, Vietnam twenty-one, the Philippines six, Malaysia three, and Taiwan one.[7]

In March 1988, China first occupied its six locations; later that same year it separated its large southern island, Hainan, from Guangdong Province, making it a special economic zone and a major military base. In February 1992, it passed the "Law of the People's Republic of China on the Territorial Sea and the Contiguous Zone," which laid down an exclusive claim to the entire Spratly archipelago, about 340,000 square miles of ocean, and authorized the Chinese navy to evict "trespassers" by force. In February 1995, China built a structure on a rocky formation claimed by the Philippines about 135 miles west of that country and hundreds of miles from the Chinese mainland. At that time the aptly named Mischief Reef was unoccupied. Although China has been verbally belligerent on the issue of the Spratlys, it has also been careful not to seize a rock or reef already occupied by some other nation.

China and Vietnam have already clashed twice in the South China Sea, once in 1974 over the Paracels and again in a short but bloody naval battle over the Spratlys in 1988. China has staked its claim to the islands on a series of fifteenth-century voyages by Ming dynasty admiral Cheng Ho. According to Vietnam, China was even then infringing on its territory. Meanwhile, Malaysia is building a tourist resort on its island, known as Terumbu Layang-Layang. All the nations of the area have increased their defense postures significantly.

China's island policies certainly reflect the force of its new nationalism and its commitment to defend all claims to Chinese territory as a way of dramatizing its previous humiliations at the hands of imperialist powers. It is a policy that may also reflect incipient Chinese hegemonism, a response to the breakup of the USSR and to the American claims of being the "indispensable nation" in East Asia. And there may be oil under the Spratlys. China is now a net oil importer, reflecting its advancing industrialization and motorization, so it is interested in any potential new source of oil. Many experts doubt, however, that any significant reserves in the South China Sea will ever materialize, as the waters separating the Spratlys are about 2,000 meters deep. The deepest oceanic drilling for oil at present is only to a depth of 872 meters in the Gulf of Mexico.

It is more than likely that the issues surrounding the South China Sea will be contained by ongoing negotiations between China and ASEAN, focusing not on sovereignty but on "confidence-building measures." China has actually moderated its claims to the area over time. To date, this dispute is a classic example of the dangers of worst-case analysis— that is, of treating possibilities as probabilities or inevitabilities, particularly when doing so, in the American case, may someday contribute to a larger military budget.

Tibet is another matter. As an independent state or even culture, it is probably doomed. China is currently implementing what the Dalai Lama calls its "final solution" for Tibet—an openly racist policy of state-sponsored Chinese emigration to the area and forced "assimilation" (the word used in the Chinese press is *hanhua*, literally "to make Chinese") of what is left of the Tibetan people. Tibet's only hope lies in the extraordinary efforts of the Dalai Lama, Tibet's priest-king, and his followers in exile in Dharamsala, India, to internationalize their struggle. Combined with continuing Chinese blunders, it is possible (though not likely) that global concern will raise the costs to China of its obstinate and destructive behavior. Meanwhile, Sinophiles at many foreign academic institutions and ministries of foreign affairs continue to advise their political leaders that Tibet has always been a part of China, which is simply not so.

The concept of irredentism does not apply to Tibet. It was never a province of China, nor was it even involved in the normal tributary relationships that vassal states of Imperial China traditionally maintained with Beijing. The Tibetans are of Mongol origin; their country emerged as a distinct place in the seventh century, when an early version of Mahayana Buddhism took root there. China first established relations with Tibet during the Tang dynasty (618–906). In the twelfth and thirteenth centuries, Tibet was heavily influenced by Indian Buddhists fleeing ahead of the Muslim invasion of the subcontinent. During the thirteenth century Mongol power came to predominate in Lhasa, just as the Mongols also ruled at that time in Beijing, but Mongol influence persisted in Tibet until the eighteenth century, much longer than in China itself. In 1270, Kublai Khan was converted to Lamaism by the abbot of the Sakya lamasery.

In 1720 the Manchu dynasty in China replaced Mongol rule in Tibet, and from that time on China claimed a limited suzerainty over Tibet— actually a loose arrangement in which Beijing was responsible for foreign relations and defense while Lhasa was left entirely in charge of domestic affairs. After imperial rule collapsed in 1912, Tibet became something like an independent state with its own governing institutions and even a small army, although its nationhood was not recognized by any other country. During this period the Tibetans expelled most Chinese. All this changed with the Chinese Communist invasion in 1950.

The legal status of Tibet today is clear and is similar in nature to the kind of colonial rule Japan imposed on Korea in 1910. A seventeen-point agreement, signed by Beijing and Tibetan representatives in 1950 at a moment when the Chinese People's Liberation Army had occupied much of the country, incorporated Tibet into the Chinese state as a "national autonomous region." This was an unprecedented status. Even then, the Tibetans never expected the Chinese to interfere in the actual running of their country. But a brutal occupation—including mass executions, forced labor, confiscations of property, and destruction of religious sites—led to a low-level revolt in the mid-1950s that exploded in March 1959 into open rebellion. The CIA covertly aided this rebellion, which may be part of the reason why the Chinese have shown so little flexibility in dealing with Tibet.[8] Blowback from CIA support, which was cut off at about the time that President Nixon decided to pursue an opening to China, has been very costly to the Tibetans. In 1959, the Dalai Lama was forced into exile in India, where he has ever since devoted himself to a campaign to publicize the Tibetans' plight. He turned sixty-three years old in 1999—and there is every sign that the Chinese will simply try to wait him out, believing that on his death they will be able to appoint a youthful successor, as they have done with the Panchen Lama, the second-holiest lama in the Tibetan hierarchy.

China will probably succeed in maintaining its imperium over Tibet and ultimately assimilate both the Tibetan people and their culture. There are no powerful interests to save them. The Tibetans are in this sense similar to the pre-Columbian inhabitants of North and South America. A continuing propaganda barrage from both Beijing and Taipei argues that the Tibetans are "feudal" and do not deserve to be saved. But the Chinese are very nervous about what they are doing and regularly make stupid mistakes.

A typical example was the spectacle of officially atheist China attempting to name a pro-Chinese Panchen Lama. On May 15, 1995, from Dharamsala, the Dalai Lama designated a six-year-old shepherd boy as a "living Buddha" and the successor to the Panchen Lama, who had died in China in January 1989. The Chinese government responded that the Dalai Lama was interfering in China's domestic affairs and in elaborately staged ceremonies in Beijing and Lhasa anointed a different six-year-old (evidently placing the Dalai Lama's choice and his family under house arrest). They formally installed him on December 9, 1995, as the Eleventh Panchen Lama; he was quoted in the newspapers as having said, "Thank you, Jiang Zemin. Thank you, government of China. I will study hard and love the motherland."[9]

It is possible that, as they regain their national self-confidence, the Chinese will invite the Dalai Lama to return and allow him to re-create something like the relationship that existed in the past between Lhasa and Beijing. This would be clever of them. As matters stand now, people in Buddhist countries like Japan and Korea (or in Hollywood) could well become as emotionally involved with the fate of Tibet as others have been with the pandas, whose fate seems destined to be similar. The most likely scenario, unfortunately, is that Tibet will become Sinified and its lamaseries will be left as nothing more than crumbling museums, as most already are.

A particular focus of foreign concern over Tibet as well as other areas of Communist Party rule is China's record on human rights. This is a subtle and complex issue. As the prominent sociologist Irving Louis Horowitz wrote at the height of the Cold War,

Politics is a game of vulnerabilities, and the human rights issue is clearly where the "socialist" world has proven most vulnerable, just as the economic rights issue is where the "capitalist" world is most open to criticism. . . . The debate on human rights can be conceptualized in part as a struggle between eighteenth century libertarian persuasions [the West] and nineteenth century egalitarian beliefs [China]—that is, from a vision of human rights having to do with the right of individual justice before the law to a recognition of the rights of individuals to social security and equitable conditions of work and standards of living.[10]

During the Cold War, the West consistently used the issue of human rights as a weapon against the Communists—but always only in its first, eighteenth-century sense. The Communists consistently returned the favor, using the issue of human rights—but always in the second, nineteenth-century sense—as a weapon against the West. We in the United States may sometimes abuse our citizens' political rights through police wiretaps or sting operations, but we are much more sensitive to these abuses than to economic abuses. The Chinese have generally taken an opposite stance.

Americans hold that human rights are a universal matter, and in a philosophical sense of course they are, but we ignore how that universalism can sometimes disguise very specific agendas and the ways in which it can be wielded as a political weapon to advance our own interests. We conveniently fail to classify civilian safety from land mines, for example, among human rights; and we are regularly indifferent to or conveniently look the other way when human rights as we define them are suppressed by regimes like those in Turkey, Chile, or Guatemala that are important to us for political, strategic, or economic reasons. The selective linking of Most Favored Nation (MFN) trade status (that is, giving or withholding access to our market on the most preferential terms) to a regime's human rights record is a prime example of this process. In December 1974, Congress first attached the Jackson-Vanik amendment to Nixon's 1972 trade agreement with the USSR (which granted the Soviet Union MFN status, as well as access to U.S. Export-Import Bank financing) in order to help Jews emigrate from Russia. The amendment specified that the president had to certify annually that trade with Communist countries was consistent with freedom of emigration. In 1979, China was also granted MFN status, and Jackson-Vanik automatically applied because China is a Communist country. When Deng Xiaoping, on his first visit to the United States after we recognized the Beijing government, was asked about the freedom of Chinese to emigrate, he smiled broadly and replied, "How many do you want?"

In the autumn of 1989, however, following China's use of army troops to disperse demonstrators in Tiananmen Square and kill workers and students in the surrounding streets, Congresswoman Nancy Pelosi of California sponsored legislation giving thousands of Chinese students in the United States permission to extend their stays. Congress later amended these provisions to require annual presidential certification that China was making "overall significant progress" in its human rights policies, in trade practices, and in weapons nonproliferation, backing all this with the threat of MFN withdrawal. But that threat was never credible, since its implementation would have meant putting at risk extensive American investments in China. Thus the withdrawal of MFN remains primarily a rhetorical device used by members of Congress for partisan political advantage at home without the serious intent of altering policy at all.[11]

The selective way the U.S. government has wielded the human rights issue has had an unintended consequence. It has stimulated Asians of many different persuasions to develop an "Asian concept of human rights" and to attack the United Nations' Universal Declaration of Human Rights as not "universal" at all but only another manifestation of Western cultural imperialism. As so often is true whenever invidious comparisons between Asia and the West are involved, former prime minister Lee Kuan Yew of Singapore gained a certain prominence as a spokesman for the Asian point of view. "Americans believe their ideas are universal—the supremacy of the individual and free, unfettered expression. But they are not. Never were . . . ," he insisted. "The ideas of individual supremacy and the right to free expression, when carried to excess, have not worked. They have made it difficult to keep American society cohesive. Asia can see it is not working."[12]

Lee's emphasis on American society's internal cohesion was telling in an Asian context. China's leaders remain preoccupied by the disintegration of societies pressured to adopt Western-style economic and political practices like the former Soviet Union and Suharto's Indonesia. In their eyes a decision to permit free association when there are so many inequalities of many different kinds left over from the old order or created by the new one is more likely to lead to a political revolution than to produce political harmony. On March 15, 1999, in a news conference that included foreign reporters, Prime Minister Zhu Rongji said, "Don't support these so-called pro-democracy activists. They will bring neither democracy nor the rule of law to China."[13]

Chinese leaders—and foreign investors—also ignore human rights in their mutual exploitation of a cheap labor market. One prime way of doing so and of justifying what they are doing is to spread the idea that human rights (as conceived by Westerners) have no basis within Chinese culture. This kind of rhetoric is very common throughout Asian ruling circles today. The Burmese military (and their Japanese financiers) use it to keep Nobel Prize winner and National League for Democracy leader Aung San Suu Kyi under house arrest even though her party won 82 percent of the seats in the 1990 Burmese election; the Singaporean government and courts used it in 1995 to execute a Filipina housemaid, Flor Contemplación, for murders probably committed by her Chinese employer;[14] and the Chinese government used it in sentencing Democracy-wall activist Wei Jingsheng to prison for a second fifteen-year term merely for suggesting that there might be a fifth modernization (democracy) in addition to the four favored by then party leader Deng Xiaoping. The Chinese government finally released Wei, deporting him to the United States after President Jiang Zemin's visit in 1997, but the governments of Burma and Singapore have proved to be deaf to foreign criticism on human rights grounds. The Chinese government's record of releasing political detainees when the issue is raised with it discreetly has not been bad. In his press conference of March 1999, Premier Zhu said, "We welcome foreign friends criticizing us in our work, but don't be impatient," noting that he has grown accustomed to "friends from abroad pulling out lists" of pro-democracy activists whom they want released from jail.[15]

In the final analysis, two aspects of human rights policy transcend mere political rhetoric and deserve our attention over the long haul. First, the United States must strive to retain the respect of the relatively small group of Chinese elites who will eventually come to have influence or hold power in the next century. Tibet's exiled leader, the Dalai Lama, divides the Chinese people into three broad categories in terms of their attitudes toward politics.[16] The first category is made up of the leaders of the Communist Party. "Their main concern is keeping power in their hands," says the Dalai Lama, and they are in that sense no different from other Asian ruling elites, like the Liberal Democratic Party in Japan or the military in Burma, whose main concerns are preserving their own positions of power.

The second category is made up of intellectuals and students. "This is the group which ultimately will bring democracy in China. . . . No outsider, not the United States, nobody, can bring democracy to China, except those people." A sound human rights policy would attempt to maintain the respect of these people through appropriate, supportive activities in our own country and in international organizations without continually pretending that something is being accomplished by "constructive engagement," the current euphemism for the ineffective sermonizing and browbeating tactics used by the State Department and others to attack China verbally on the issue. Personal diplomacy by officials who are well informed and sensitive to Chinese society is always more effective when we are trying to win freedom for people who have risked their lives for ideals we support.

The Dalai Lama's third category is made up of the masses, concerned with "daily livelihood," for whom "democracy is not much relevant in their day-to-day life." The Dalai Lama argues that those engaged in a positive human rights policy toward China should seek advice from the second group on what ought to be done about preserving the rights of this third group.

Human rights must be an important dimension of any American policy toward China that truly addresses Chinese problems and is sensitive to the Chinese record in particular cases. Such a policy is best implemented by trained and experienced diplomats, not by politicians speaking in generalities to domestic audiences for political advantage. Inevitably, demands for political reform will grow in China over time, just as they have in Taiwan and South Korea, so long as the regime's basic policies remain what they are today. In the meantime, the U.S. government should exercise patience and firmness, while discreetly intervening in particular cases where we might make a difference.

The second aspect of human rights in China we must recognize is to ensure that poor working conditions and prison labor in China (and elsewhere) do not end up destroying the livelihoods of American workers. Without question the most powerful human rights tool the United States could wield would be to deny access to the American market to products from multinational companies that have abandoned American workers to seek out low-wage foreign workers lacking in economic or political rights of any sort, not to speak of human rights. The economics profession may attack such policies as "protectionism," but the time is long past when the United States should allow corporations to use the bottom line, "globalization," or the pressures of competition—"Adam Smith made me do it"—as excuses for their indifference to basic human rights at home or abroad. Failure to consider this dimension of the rights question leaves the United States open to a charge of hypocrisy.

The United States is formally as well as emotionally and intellectually committed to an academic textbook definition of "free trade," which it believes (or pretends to believe) was the foundation of the General Agreement on Tariffs and Trade (GATT). Created in 1948 as a specialized agency of the United Nations, GATT governed trade among the so-called free-market economies during the era of the Cold War. Its greatest accomplishments were a series of multilateral negotiations among its members to reduce or eliminate tariffs on many different products, which greatly stimulated international trade over the years. It was replaced on January 1, 1995, by the World Trade Organization (WTO). Actually, for most of the Cold War, GATT was part of an American grand strategy vis-à-vis the USSR in which the United States traded access to its market and its technologies in return for support against communism by nations like Japan, South Korea, and Taiwan. The WTO has no similar strategic purpose; it must either deliver the allegedly *mutual* benefits of free trade or else it is a menace to the livelihoods of all working Americans. Far too often free trade has meant in practice free access to the American market for foreign products but American toleration of closed foreign markets regardless of the damage this has done to U.S. industries and good jobs in manufacturing.

China's primary trade goal is to gain admission to the WTO with the status of a developing country. As a developing country, China would not have to open its markets to foreign competitors on an equal basis and would be exempt from the provisions of the WTO treaty concerning national subsidies for industries and intellectual property rights covering items like foreign films and books. If it achieves that—as the ideological myopia of American trade negotiators of both parties and the economists who advise them makes likely—its mercantilism will ultimately do serious damage to the American economy, not to speak of the WTO system. Like Japan before it, China will run up huge trade surpluses with the United States rather than generating a balanced and mutually beneficial trade. Managed trade is the antidote to this, and it need not hamper China's economic development, but it is anathema to the economic ideologists of the United States. Management of trade with China would require the kind of political leadership and a governmental capability that the country may simply not be able to muster in the post–Cold War world. After all, the United States has never given the same priority to trade as to human rights, arms sales, or territorial disputes.

Before the economic crisis that began in 1997, which greatly expanded global dependency on the American market, the United States was already absorbing about 25 percent of all exports from East Asia and running annual trade deficits with the area well in excess of $100 billion. China's trade surplus with the United States, more than $60 billion in 1998, is second only to Japan's and growing much faster. When China launched its economic reforms in 1978, its overall foreign trade totaled $20.6 billion; by 1993 the figure was $195.8 billion, an increase of 950 percent. Some 80 percent of China's exports are manufactured goods, and China is the world's largest textile exporter as well as the largest source of American textile and apparel imports. The Europeans and Japanese also run trade deficits with China, but the U.S. deficit is approximately two to three times theirs.

In a sense, this "trade problem" is really a matter of "systems friction," the clash of different forms of capitalism, exactly as one might expect given the developmental-state strategy that China is pursuing. The point of this strategy is to bend the rules and norms of laissez-faire capitalism in order to achieve national wealth and power, since economics in this view is inevitably a zero-sum game in which some nations win and others lose. China has never tried to become a "free-market economy" but rather to engage and exploit other market economies to become a great power. Economic reform, after all, was undertaken in the first place in order to preserve the Communist Party's political control and to achieve through other means what it had failed to achieve through Stalinism and then Maoism.

The U.S. response to this challenge has primarily been to try to induce or cajole China into "reforming" its economy to give it the look of American-style capitalism. Thus, in 1994, reflecting the attitudes of Washington's economic theorists and trade bureaucrats, the *Washington Post* editorialized that in order to be allowed into the WTO, China must 1) publish its trade regulations in a transparent form accessible to importers, 2) ensure that all foreign and domestic companies receive the same treatment from the legal system, and 3) stop using artificially low exchange rates to boost exports and impede imports.[17] These proposals, of course, were not only culture-bound but thoroughly at odds with

China's chosen strategy of economic development as well. Even if China were to abandon its strategy of economic development, it would never do business the way the United States does.

The answer to these problems, in the sense of helping to promote China's economic development while preventing its predatory trade policies from provoking international conflict, is managed trade. All this means is the use of public policy to manage outcomes rather than procedures. It assumes that when either public or private companies in different economic systems trade with and invest in each other's economies, a mutually beneficial outcome cannot be assured merely through agreement on rules. Managed trade is not nearly as uncommon as professional economists imply. In 1960, at the height of the Cold War, when the United States began to trade with Poland, Romania, and Hungary, it set goals that these Leninist countries had to meet. It required, for instance, that Polish imports from GATT countries rise 7 percent per year or trade would be cut off.[18]

The economic challenge of China is likely to be the most difficult test not just for American economic policy but for its foreign policy in general in the first quarter of the twenty-first century. Unfortunately, Americans still remain confused by the idea that the foundations of power no longer lie in military but in economic and industrial strength. They tolerate, even applaud, irrationally bloated defense budgets while doing little to rebuild and defend the industrial foundations of their own nation. When the world economic crisis began in Asia in 1997, the United States responded with the stale formulas of the International Monetary Fund, only worsening the situation. Inadequate political leadership, inappropriate staffing of the government, and an inability to redirect the foreign affairs, defense, technological, and intelligence agencies to pay more reasonable attention to Asia in general and China in particular seem endemic problems for the foreseeable future.

8

JAPAN AND THE ECONOMICS
OF THE AMERICAN EMPIRE

During the Cold War the Soviet Union lost any number of friends and potential allies by forever hectoring them about Marxism and the stages of economic growth they would have to go through in order ever to hope to live like Russians. Such Marxist rigidity clearly benefited the American side in the superpower face-off of that era. Ideological arrogance turned many countries, like Tanzania and Egypt, against their Soviet economic advisers, and overbearing Soviet behavior contributed heavily to the Sino-Soviet dispute. Unfortunately, in the post–Cold War era it is the United States that is exhibiting a capitalist version of such heavy-handedness and arrogance.

Ideology—that is, the doctrines, opinions, or way of thinking of an individual, a class, a nation, or an empire—is as tricky a substance to use in international conflicts as poison gas. It, too, has a tendency to blow back onto the party releasing it. During the late 1950s, in the depths of the Cold War, many Americans began to suspect that the Soviet Union was actually a third-rate economy; but it still had the world's most alluring ideology, a body of thought capable of attracting more people in the Third World than the "possessive individualism" (to use the philosopher C. B. Macpherson's term) espoused by the United States. Soviet intellectual appeals were built around the ideas of Karl Marx—indubitably a man of the West and properly buried in Highgate Cemetery, London—which attracted even the most chauvinistic people on earth, the Chinese. Marxism-Leninism, as espoused by the Soviet Union, provided explanations for the inequities of colonialism, a model of economic development based on the achievements of Russia under Stalin, and the promise of world peace when all nations had passed beyond imperialism, which was the "final stage of capitalism."

Part of what gave Soviet ideology such power to convince whole peoples in the Third World was the way it assimilated and invoked the single most uncontested ideology of our century, that of science. It claimed to rest not on the hopes of idealistic reformers but on the logic of "scientific socialism." The Soviets insisted that they were acting in accordance with laws of human development discovered by their patron saints, Marx and Lenin. By contrast, the ideology of the "free world" looked at best like a rationalization of the privileges enjoyed by Americans because of their exceptional geography and history.

Not surprisingly, American leaders came to feel that somehow they had to match the ideological claims of communism in what they saw as a great global battle for the souls of earth's contested majority. Nowhere did this need seem more acutely necessary than in East Asia, where Communist regimes had come to power in China, North Korea, and Vietnam despite the fact that Marx's analysis of class conflict in industrializing societies bore only the faintest relation to the actual conditions in any of these countries. At the time, communism was also an active competitor in every other country of the region. Asians were attracted to it precisely because it claimed to be based on science—the ingredient that seemed to undergird the industrial and military might of their European, American, and Japanese colonizers—and because the example of the Soviet Union held out the hope of a solution that might someday be within their own revolutionary grasp.

The American response, never expressly articulated but based on the total mobilization of the American people for the Cold War by President John F. Kennedy and other leaders, was twofold. First, we would do everything in our considerable power to turn Japan into a capitalist alternative to mainland China, a model and a showcase of what Asians might expect if they threw in their lot with the Americans instead of the Communists. Second, academic economics as taught in most American universities was subtly transformed into a fighting ideology of the "West." From each of these transformations would come fateful consequences for the American empire after its competition with the Soviet Union ended. Because most Americans never understood either policy to be a strategy for pursuing the Cold War, they took both Japan's achievements and the wealth of the West to be evidence of an ineluctable destiny that made the United States a singularly appropriate model for the rest of the world. Any doubts raised about these propositions were seen as undermining the pretensions of the American empire. Thus, what began as tactical responses to temporary, often illusory or misleadingly interpreted Soviet "advantages" ended up as ideological articles of faith for the "sole superpower" of the post–Cold War world.

From approximately 1950 to 1975, the United States treated Japan as a beloved ward, indulging its every economic need and proudly patronizing it as a star capitalist pupil. The United States sponsored Japan's entry into many international institutions, like the United Nations and the Organization for Economic Cooperation and Development, well before a post–World War II global consensus in favor of Japan had developed. It also transferred crucial technologies to the Japanese on virtually concessionary terms and opened its markets to Japanese products while tolerating Japan's protection of its own domestic market. It even supported the Japanese side in all claims by individual American firms that they had been damaged by Japanese competitors. In addition, the United States allowed Japan to retain an artificially undervalued currency in order to give its exports a price advantage for well over a decade longer than it did any of the rebuilt European economies.

We proclaimed Japan a democracy and a model of what free markets could achieve while simultaneously helping to rig both its economic and political systems. We used the CIA to finance the ruling party and engaged in all manner of dirty tricks to divide and discredit domestic socialists.[1] In this process there was much self-deception. For far too long

America's leading officials insisted that Japan could never be an economic competitor of the United States'. President Eisenhower's secretary of state John Foster Dulles was, for example, convinced that while
the Japanese might be able to sell shirts, pajamas, "and perhaps cocktail
napkins" to the American market, little else was possible for them.[2]
Americans did not wake up to Japan's competitive challenge until their
steel, consumer electronics, robotics, automotive, camera, and semiconductor industries were virtually extinct or fighting for their lives.

After the "security treaty riots" of 1960, when a Japanese mass movement tried to prevent the signing of a treaty that would perpetuate the
basing of American troops in Japan and Okinawa, the United States
moved its campaign to portray Japan as a model democracy into high
gear. It appointed as ambassador the well-known Harvard historian of
Japan Edwin O. Reischauer, who was married to a Japanese woman from
a distinguished political family. His job was to repair the damage to the
image of Japanese-American amity caused by the 1960 riots, which to
many Asians appeared to be a Japanese equivalent to the Budapest uprising of 1956. Reischauer was to "reopen a dialogue" with the alienated
Japanese left while shoring up the conservative Liberal Democratic
Party, its aging rightists from prewar and wartime governments now
screened from public view while it emphasized economic growth over
democracy.

Perhaps Reischauer's most influential step was to endorse in his own
extensive writings and speeches of the time a movement among American academic specialists to rewrite the history of modern Japan as
a case study of successful "modernization." So-called modernization
theory flourished in the United States during the 1960s just as the
Japanese economy "took off" (to use that famous term of the modernization theorists), achieving double-digit growth rates. This new approach
to Japan traced the country's course of development from the Meiji
Restoration of 1868, which was Japan's debut as a unified nation rather
than a collection of feudal states. It contrasted Japan's achievement of
great-power status with the dependency and susceptibility to colonialism
of the rest of Asia, particularly China. It stressed how the initial author-

itarianism of the Meiji oligarchs evolved into a toleration of political parties during the 1920s, producing at least the possibility of parliamentary democracy. The theory drew attention to how the "liberal" 1920s, although ultimately destroyed by reaction and militarism after 1931, provided precedents for reform that many Japanese leaders seized upon when genuine democratization got under way during the American occupation.

Japan emerged from this stirring tale of political and economic development as an exemplary nation, the only country in Asia that avoided being colonized. The fact that it did so by joining the Western colonialists in victimizing the other countries of Asia was underemphasized in such accounts. Japan's *kuroi tanima*, or "dark valley," from 1931 to 1945, in which it warred with China and the United States, was explained away as due to a unique concatenation of international factors—the Great Depression, the closing of European and American colonies to Japanese exports, Japan's fear of bolshevism, and American isolationism. What actually went on in the "dark valley," from the rape of Nanking to the Bataan Death March, was incidental to the tale of economic growth and political consolidation and best forgotten, since Japan's aggression was now understood to be but a temporary sidestep on a long march toward modernization. The emperor of Japan, who had reigned since 1926 and presided over much military aggression and brutality, emerged as a simple marine biologist and pacifist who had opposed the war from the beginning and had actually brought it to an end in 1945 through his own decisive action. It was said that he was a man of few words in view of the fact that from the end of the war to his death in 1989 he was never again allowed to utter many in public.

The American public, like its policy elites never very well informed about Japan to begin with, bought this rosy picture of that country as the chief bulwark against communism in Asia. John Dower and a few American academic specialists argued that modernization theory was incomplete and that Japan's militarism had domestic roots every bit as deep as its commitment to modernity, but they were easily ignored.[3] Japan was now entrenched in American consciousness as a full-fledged democratic ally with a system rooted in free-market capitalism and certain eventually to "converge" with the United States as a liberal, consumer-based state.

To be sure, there were occasional "misunderstandings" as one nation's capitalists sought competitive advantage over the other. In dealing with such "unfortunate" developments, the task of diplomacy and the mission of the American embassy in Tokyo became not to champion American interests but to ameliorate the conflict itself, usually to Japan's advantage. Nothing seriously wrong could come of such policies, it was argued, because, as modernization theory taught, the two societies were on the same developmental path toward common economic ends.

The second aspect of the ideological challenge to the Soviet Union was the development and propagation of an American economic ideology that might counter the promise of Marxism—what today we call "neoclassical economics," which has gained an intellectual status in American economic activities and governmental affairs similar to that of Marxism-Leninism in the former USSR. Needless to say, Soviet citizens never understood Marxism-Leninism as an ideology until after it had collapsed, just as Americans like to think (or pretend) that their economics is a branch of science, not a fighting doctrine to defend and advance their interests against those of others. They may consider most economists to be untrustworthy witch doctors, but they regard the tenets of a laissez-faire economy—with its cutthroat competition, casino stock exchange, massive inequalities of wealth, and a minor, regulatory role for government—as self-evident truths.

Until the late 1950s, academic economics remained one of the social sciences, like anthropology, sociology, and political science—a non-experimental, often speculative investigation into the ways individuals, families, firms, markets, industries, and national economies behaved under different conditions and influences. It was concerned with full employment, price stability, growth, public finance, labor relations, and similar socioeconomic subjects. After it became the chief ideological counterweight to Marxism-Leninism during the Cold War, its practitioners tried to extract it from the social sciences and re-create it as a hard science.

Its propositions were now expressed less in words than in simultaneous equations, the old ideas of Adam Smith reappearing as fully mathematized axioms, increasingly divorced from empirical research. Its data were said to be "stylized facts," and economists set out to demonstrate through deductive reasoning expressed in mathematical formulas that resources could be allocated efficiently only through an unfettered market. By now all these terms ("resources," "efficiency," "markets") had been transformed into abstractions, not unlike the abstract formulations ("the proletariat," "the bourgeoisie," "class conflict") of its Soviet opponents. English-speaking economics became such a "hard science" that in 1969 the central bank of Sweden started giving Nobel Prizes to its adepts, virtually all of them American academicians. This ensured that virtually all aspiring economists would in the future try to do so-called theoretical economics—that is, the algebraic modeling of markets—rather than old-fashioned empirical and inductive research into real-world economies.

Economics split from the social sciences and took up a new position somewhere close to mathematics. Economists were now endlessly called upon by governmental bodies to testify that the American economy was unmatchable, even if it sometimes behaved badly because of overspending liberals, pork-barrel politics, or greedy monopolists. Alternatives to it were understood to be either converging with it or destined to fail. Economics no longer studied the economy; it spoke ex cathedra about what was orthodox and what was heresy. Meanwhile, empirical research on economic phenomena migrated to business schools, commercial think tanks, and the other social sciences.

Unquestionably, after the first two decades of the Cold War, in a purely dichotomous choice between an economy based on Marxism-Leninism and one based on free-market capitalism—as exemplified by the economies of the Soviet Union and the United States—most people around the world would have chosen the free market. But in East Asia, at the height of the Sino-Soviet dispute and the American war in

Vietnam, neither ideology was working out according to either super-power's script. The Chinese were discrediting forever whatever attractiveness might have remained in the forced-draft economic achievements of the Soviet model. Through bungling, megalomania, and deep ideological confusion about what Marxism and the Soviet experience taught, the Chinese Communist Party managed to kill thirty million of its own citizens and then, in a paroxysm of mutual blame, came close to destroying its unmatchable cultural legacy in the so-called Cultural Revolution. Today this period is recognized—even in China—as a monumental disaster, but at the time many Americans, from idealistic leftist students to presidents and other political leaders, failing to understand what was happening, retained a sentimental attraction to Mao Zedong and Zhou Enlai, the mismanagers of the Chinese revolution.

The truly surprising development in East Asia, however, was that America's "non-Communist" satellites, protectorates, and dependencies were starting to get rich and to compete with their superpower benefactor. All of this was camouflaged by the Cold War itself, so that the enrichment of East Asia occurred almost surreptitiously. The year-in, year-out record-breaking growth rates of such previously poor places as Japan, South Korea, and Taiwan were not precisely what American elites had expected, but they were explained away as nothing more than confirmations—even overconfirmations—of officially espoused free-market ideology and so were greeted with parental pride.

If the capitalist economies of East Asia were starting to perform better than the United States itself, this anomaly was usually attributed to mysterious Japanese or Asian cultural or even spiritual factors or to complacency on the part of American managers and workers. By the time the Western world awoke to what had actually happened, economic growth in East Asia was self-sustaining and unstoppable by external actions (although many Asians thought this was exactly what the United States was attempting when its policies toward the area led to the meltdown of 1997). The enrichment of East Asia under the cover of the Cold War was surely the most important, least analyzed development in world politics during the second half of the twentieth century. It remains to this day intellectually indigestible in the United States.

The fundamental problem is not simply that in the Cold War era Japan attained a $5 trillion economy—although that alone was an unexpected competitive challenge to American economic preeminence—but how it did so. It had found a third way between the socialist displacement of the market advocated by Soviet theorists and an uncritical reliance on the market advocated by American theorists. The Japanese had invented a different kind of capitalism—something no defender of the American empire could accept. It was therefore assumed either that the Japanese were cheating (and all that we needed to compete successfully against them was a "level playing field") or that they must be headed for a collapse similar to the one that had overtaken the USSR.

In turning neo-classical economic theory into a fighting ideology, American ideologues encountered one element of capitalist thought that they could not express in abstract, seemingly "scientific" mathematical terms. This was the set of institutions through which competitive market relationships actually produce their benefits. Institutions are the concrete, more-or-less enduring relationships through which people work, save, invest, and earn a living—such things as stock exchanges, banks, labor unions, corporations, safety nets, families, inheritance rules, and tax systems. This is the realm of the legal, political, and social order, where many considerations that govern the economy other than efficiency contend for primacy. For economic theorists institutions are "black boxes," entities that receive and transmit economic stimuli but are themselves unaffected by economic theory.

In attempting to forge a fully numerical, scientific-looking model of the capitalist economy for purposes of the Cold War, Western ideologues simply assumed that the institutions of modern capitalism must be those that existed in the United States in the late Eisenhower era. This meant that savings were typically moved from the saver to industry through a capital market (such as the New York Stock Exchange) rather than, for example, through the banking system. They assumed that industrial-labor conflicts were settled by interminable strikes, and not by, for example, offering some workers career job security; and they assumed that the whole purpose of an economy was to serve the short-term interests of consumers, instead of some overarching goal such as the wealth and power of the nation as a whole.

These American assumptions were almost identical to the Soviet assumption that the institutions of "socialism" must be those that existed in the USSR during, say, the Khrushchev era. Neither side ever produced an ideological model to sell to others that could be divorced from their own country. Because of this inability to express the institutions of either socialism or capitalism in some culturally neutral—or at least more varied—way, it is understandable that many observers simply reduced the claims of Marxist-Leninist ideology to the USSR and those of free-market capitalism to the United States.

In finding a third way, Japan's postwar economic "miracle" reinvented not economic theory but the institutions of modern capitalism so that they would produce utterly different outcomes from those imagined in the American model. Given Japan's history of catch-up industrialization, its overarching need to avoid the victimization and colonialism to which every other area of East Asia had succumbed, its virtual dearth of raw materials, its dependence on manufacturing and international trade to sustain its large population, and its overwhelming defeat in World War II, it could not ever have become a clone of the United States. Its postwar planners and technocrats instead organized a capitalist economy intended to serve the interests of producers over consumers. They forced Japan's citizens to save by providing little in the way of a safety net; they encouraged labor harmony regardless of what it did to individual rights; and they built industries based on the highest possible human input rather than simply on some naturally given comparative advantage, such as cheap labor or proximity to a large market like China's. Their goal was to enrich Japan, if not necessarily the Japanese themselves. They viewed all economic transactions as strategic: theirs was to be an economy organized for war but now directed toward ostensibly peaceful competition with other countries.

Since the 1950s, the United States had seen the entire world in Cold War terms. This meant that Japan was far more important as an anti-Communist ally than as a potential economic competitor. In order to keep U.S. troops and bases in Japan, the Americans provided open access to their market and the government pressured private American firms to relinquish ownership rights to technologies being transferred to Japan. As Japanese trade and industrial bureaucrats took advantage of this deal, trade disputes became inevitable. From the "dollar blouses" that flooded into the United States during the Eisenhower era to the textile disputes of the Kennedy and Nixon administrations, complaints about the costs of "alliance" with Japan became a permanent feature of Washington politics. They also produced a lucrative new field for former government officials turned lobbyists, whom the Japanese hired in increasing numbers to ameliorate or paper over the disputes. Even though Washington remained more or less ignorant of how the government in Tokyo actually worked, the government in Tokyo took a life-or-death interest in Washington's role in regulating the American economy. Japanese officials also did everything in their power to maintain the artificial separation between trade and defense that the U.S. government had invented and to see that the Pentagon was happy with its facilities.

This artificial separation between trade and defense has been a peculiar characteristic of the half-century-long American hegemony over Japan. Official guardians of the Japanese-American Security Treaty and their academic supporters have maintained an impenetrable firewall between what they call, using the Japanese euphemism, "trade friction" and the basing of one hundred thousand American troops in Japan and South Korea. There was no reason why these two aspects of the Japanese-American relationship should been dealt with as if they were separate matters except that, had they not been, the actual nature of the relationship would have been far easier to grasp.

Until the 1980s, the United States officially ignored all evidence that this compartmentalization of its massive military establishment and its growing trade deficits with Japan was going to be very costly. From about

1968 on, trade deficits began to rise just as the hollowing out of certain industries that the Japanese government had targeted became more visible. U.S. officials then consulted with their Japanese counterparts about these problems and accepted fig-leaf agreements that offered the pretense of remedies to distressed American businesses and communities. With the exception of President Nixon's 1971 decision to force an ending to Japan's artificially undervalued exchange, nothing else of significance was done.

During the 1980s, however, pressures for action of some sort markedly increased. The Japanese economy, now a major competitor, was starting to erode the industrial foundations of the United States. Moreover, the Cold War was settling into its final Reaganesque rituals. Despite inflated CIA estimates of Soviet strength, it became increasingly clear to many, even before the rise to power of Mikhail Gorbachev, that the two sides were starting to accommodate each other and that the threat of a super-power war was declining. In this context, a new way of thinking developed about Japan itself and about the nature of America's relationships with newly rich Asia. *Business Week* dubbed it "revisionism" and wrote:

> No less than a fundamental rethinking of Japan is now under way at the highest levels of the U.S. government, business, and academia. The standard rules of the free market, according to the new school, simply won't work in Japan. . . . Some people call the new thinking "revisionism," departing as it does from the orthodox view that Japan will eventually become a U.S.-style consumer-driven society.[4]

The Japanese, who had been very proud of their "developmental state" and its guided economy and who readily wrote about it for domestic consumption, suddenly became concerned when American revisionists, myself included, began saying that "leveling the playing field" was not the issue, since the two economies were different in such fundamental ways. It was one thing for Japan and its lobbyists to parry complaints about their country's closed markets and the numerous barriers it raised against foreign products ranging from automobiles and semiconductors to grapefruit and rice. It was quite another for Americans to claim that they were playing by entirely different rules. Accusations that the "revisionists" were Japan bashers or racists rose quickly to the surface.

Meanwhile, a number of Japanese politicians and industrialists added insult to injury by claiming that the trade deficit resulted from the laziness of American workers or resorted to racism by pointing to the racially mixed nature of the workforce while characterizing American minorities as indisciplined and ineducable. In 1989, a prominent Japanese politician, Shintaro Ishihara, and the president of Sony, Akio Morita, cowrote a book, *The Japan That Can Say "No,"* in which they suggested that their country should not share Japanese-developed technologies that the Americans regarded as of national security significance unless the Americans reined in their critiques. In 1998, Ishihara, angry about an economy that seemed to be heading into decline, wrote a sequel, *The Japan That Can Say "No" Again*, suggesting a halt in investment in U.S. government securities to teach a lesson to Americans who had pushed Japan to open its economy. These views made him sufficiently popular that in 1999 he was elected mayor of Tokyo.

Nonetheless, the American government continued its typical Cold War style of doing business into the early 1990s. In 1988, for example, State Department and Pentagon leaders proposed transferring to Japan the technology of the F-16 fighter aircraft in order to allow the Japanese to build their own fighter, the FS-X. A huge controversy erupted over why the Japanese did not simply buy the F-16 fighters they needed from the manufacturer, thereby helping to balance the trade deficit and keep manufacturing in the United States. One State Department official, Kevin Kearns, who was in Tokyo at the time the FSX deal was negotiated, agreed with the critics and wrote in the *Foreign Service Journal*, "As long as the Chrysanthemum Club [of pro-Japanese American officials] continues to skew the policy process in our government and paid Japanese lobbyists and academics-for-hire continue to influence disproportionately the treatment of Japan in the public realm, the United States will continue its approach to Japan in the same tired, self-defeating way."[5] Following these remarks, Deputy Secretary of State Lawrence Eagleburger publicly denounced Kearns and in February 1990 forced his resignation from the State Department. The Bush administration then transferred the F-16 technology to Japan.

In an equally telling incident in 1990, the Matsushita Electric Company of Japan bought MCA Inc., the giant Hollywood-based entertainment conglomerate, for $7.5 billion, one of the biggest purchases ever of an American company by a foreign firm. This was less than a year after Sony had acquired Columbia Pictures for $3.4 billion and Newsweek had run a cover showing Columbia's torch-bearing female icon wearing a kimono.[6] In addition to by-then-widespread worries about Japanese capital invading the United States, there was the further complication that MCA owned a lucrative concession that serviced visitors to Yosemite National Park. In order to avoid the public relations embarrassment of having a Japanese company own part of a national park, the Department of the Interior suggested that Matsushita donate the concession to the park service. The Japanese, however, did not want to let it go and instead hired an elite corps of Washington lobbyists, lawyers, and public relations specialists to escort their purchase past congressional and government critics.

Leading the Matsushita team was former U.S. trade representative Robert Strauss. According to the Washington Post, he was paid $8 million for successfully brokering the deal and seeing to its public relations aspects, including getting the Department of the Interior to back off. When asked by reporters why he was being paid such an enormous fee for a minimal amount of work, Strauss nonchalantly replied, "I don't work by the hour anymore. I don't do windows."[7] This remark greatly puzzled the Japanese, although they were pleased enough with what their largesse had bought them. They concluded that Washington was as corrupt as Jakarta or Seoul and that anything could be had if the price was right. Rather than devoting attention to the potential pitfalls of their own brand of capitalism, the Japanese in this instance followed a distinctly American path and convinced themselves that they were invincible, while the United States was in a terminal decline. They therefore marched steadily toward their own decade-long economic downfall.

These alarms and diversions were also effective in turning American attention away from the most distinctive trait of Japan's type of capitalism—namely, the major role given to governmental industrial policy and its role in a capitalist economy. Industrial policy refers to the attempt by the government to nurture particular strategic industries that are thought to be needed by an economy for reasons of national security, export competitiveness, or growth potential.[8] As a result, most Americans failed to grasp how crucially Japan's industrial policy depended on its political and military relationship with the United States and on access to its vast market. Nor did they understand that the Japanese were investing the huge trade profits in American Treasury securities that were, in turn, helping to finance America's huge debts and making the American financial system critically dependent on Japanese savings. This growing dependency made American officials reluctant to criticize the Japanese in any way. Even when they did so, the Japanese rationalized such criticism as meant only for U.S. domestic consumption.

What Americans, including the revisionists, failed to see was that the Japanese economy, still devoted to exporting a vast array of ever more sophisticated and technologically advanced manufactured goods primarily to the American market, was generating an industrial overcapacity that would eventually threaten the health of the world economy. Moreover, as much of Asia began to emulate the Japanese form of capitalism or become offshore manufacturing platforms for Japanese corporations, this overcapacity threatened to reach crisis proportions. The crisis came to a head in 1997 and has been a continuing feature of the international economy ever since.

Political developments helped precipitate the crisis. In 1992, the Americans elected Bill Clinton on a slogan of "It's the economy, stupid," and in 1993, the Liberal Democratic Party in Japan, no longer needed as a bulwark against communism, simply collapsed of its own corruption and redundancy.

The Clinton administration did experiment briefly with policies advocated by the revisionists, including managed trade. The new administration even toyed with convincing the Japanese to join in helping manage Japanese-American trade, but its heart was never in it. The actual work was left to the usual array of Washington lawyers and economists, who had no East Asian knowledge or experience whatsoever, with the easily predictable outcome that the Japanese, much more experienced and better informed than their American adversaries, simply ran circles around them.

Using their huge leverage over American debt financing and Clinton's need for the appearance of domestic economic prosperity in order to be reelected in 1996, the Japanese got the Americans to back down on most trade issues. The administration covered its tracks by claiming that it could not allow economic disputes to interfere with security and military matters. The difficulty was that except for the bellicose statements and deployments of the United States itself, peace was breaking out in East Asia. In 1992, for example, China recognized South Korea; that same year the government of the Philippines asked the U.S. Navy to leave the major base it had long occupied at Subic Bay. Still, the U.S. government claimed to see threats from North Korea and China, and the Japanese went along, doing whatever they could to satisfy the Pentagon.

In 1993, the Liberal Democratic Party lost its majority in the Japanese Diet for the first time in thirty-eight years. Increasingly irrelevant to Japan's need to reinvigorate its economy and assume control over its foreign policy, it was not voted out of office but simply disintegrated. At first, a popular coalition government formed among the many new parties in the Diet. It seemed that a long overdue political realignment might be at hand. As it turned out, the Socialist Party, long feared by the United States because of its advocacy of "neutralism," was so beguiled to be in office that it ultimately abandoned everything it had ever claimed to stand for and forged a cynical coalition with the LDP to control parliament. In the end, all the LDP's loss of power revealed was that the party system itself had largely been postwar window dressing. In

1997, the LDP returned to power and resumed its stewardship over Japan's old Cold War relationship with the United States.

At least, though, the rise to power in the 1993–97 interregnum of nonmainstream LDP and opposition party leaders opened up an important debate over how and why the country had become so rich and yet had such an ineffective elected government. Bureaucratic insiders as well as intellectuals and academics began publicly to acknowledge and elaborate on the very points the American revisionists had made. *New York Times* correspondent James Sterngold reported from Tokyo, "Five years ago, some Western critics were derided by the Japanese establishment as wrong—and probably racist—for declaring that Japanese policy was set by bureaucrats, not politicians, and that Japanese politics was often corrupt. . . . Suddenly, expressions and criticism previously regarded as blasphemous when uttered by 'revisionists' and 'Japan bashers' are spoken with a surprising matter-of-factness."[9] In the process they opened up whole new perspectives for viewing the interlocking Japanese governmental, social, and economic systems. They affirmed that a corps of unelected elite bureaucrats actually governed the country under a façade of democracy. They laid out the ways in which, working within a Cold War framework and guided by their government, the major corporations had invested in productive capacity many times greater than domestic demand could possibly absorb, thereby becoming totally dependent on continued sales to the American and Asian markets. They detailed the methods of the cartels, of restrictive licensing practices, of the underdeveloped system of judicial review, and of myriad other "nontariff barriers" to trade that kept American and European corporate penetration of the domestic market to a minimum.

One impetus for such new, self-critical attitudes could be found in the changed economic atmosphere. Following a binge of big-ticket investments at the end of the 1980s and a bubble of real estate speculation that accompanied newfound wealth, the economy began to falter. After eight years of stagnation, in 1998 it finally plunged into real recession. In an ironic twist, American ideologists used these developments to argue as always that American free-market capitalism was the globe's one and only path to success. However, they now incorporated revisionist analyses without acknowledgment into their critiques of the Japanese economy. For example, the *Wall Street Journal's* Paul Gigot had long maintained that Japan's economy operated just like the U.S. model. "Japan's miracle, like Britain's and America's before it," he wrote in 1986, "was largely the product of creativity and enterprise by individuals and their businesses."[10] A decade later, in a column entitled "The Great Japan Debate Is Over: Guess Who Won?," he could be found deriding Japan's "model of bureaucratic-led economic growth," as distinguished from "American-style capitalism." His new point: the revisionists may have been right about how Japan worked but they were wrong to think it was a success. To the extent that the Japanese economy might ever stage a comeback, Gigot argued in a fashion typical of his colleagues, it would have to do business "in a framework that more resembles the American model."[11] Put another way, these economic ideologues found convincing proof in Japan's economic fate that a hegemonic America would continue to dictate the rules of international commerce into the distant future, even if that hegemony were disguised with catchphrases like "globalization."

As the Cold War receded into history, the United States, rather than dissolving its Cold War arrangements, insisted on strengthening them as part of a renewed commitment to global hegemony. Japan was supposed to remain a satellite of the United States, whether anyone dared use that term or not. Meanwhile, annual American trade deficits with Japan soared. American manufacturing continued to be hollowed out, while a vast manufacturing overcapacity was generated in Japan and its Southeast Asian subsidiaries. Capital transfers from Japan to the United States generated huge gains for financiers and produced an illusion of prosperity in the United States, but in 1997, it all started to unravel. The most severe economic crisis since the Great Depression hit the East Asian economies and began to spread around the world.

9

MELTDOWN

Each year approximately ten thousand American troops descend on Thailand for a joint military exercise called Cobra Gold. The military part of these visits is largely make-work for the American and Thai staffs, but the troops love Cobra Gold because of the sex. According to the newspaper *Pacific Stars and Stripes*, some three thousand prostitutes wait for the sailors and marines at the South Pattaya waterfront, close to Utapao air base. An equal number of young Thai girls from the country-side, many of whom have been raped and then impressed into the "sex industry," are available downtown in Bangkok's Patpang district. They are virtually all infected with AIDS, but the condom-equipped American forces seem not to worry. At the time of the 1997 war games, just before the economic crisis broke, sex with a Thai prostitute cost around fifteen hundred Thai baht, or sixty dollars at its then pegged rate of twenty-five baht to one U.S. dollar. By the time of the next year's Cobra Gold the price had been more than halved.[1] This is just one of many market benefits Americans gained through their rollback operation against the "Asian model" of capitalism.

The global economic crisis that began in Thailand in July 1997 had two causes. First, the built-in contradictions of the American satellite system in East Asia had heightened to such a degree that the system itself unexpectedly began to splinter and threatened to blow apart. Second, the United States, relieved of the prudence imposed on it by the Cold War, when any American misstep was chalked up as a Soviet gain, launched a campaign to force the rest of the world to adopt its form of capitalism. This effort went under the rubric of "globalization." As these two complex undertakings—perpetuating Cold War structures after they had lost their purpose and trying to "globalize" countries that thought they had invented a different kind of capitalism—played themselves out around the world, they threatened a worldwide collapse of demand and a new depression. Whatever happens, the crisis probably signaled the beginning of the end of the American empire and a shift to a tripolar world in which the United States, Europe, and East Asia simultaneously share power and compete for it.

During the Cold War, the Communists routinely charged that the United States used the Marshall Plan for rebuilding wartorn Europe and subsequent economic aid programs to advance the interests of American companies and to keep the Third World dependent on the First. According to the Communist theory of economic colonialism, capitalist states enforce an inherently discriminatory division of labor on less developed countries by selling them manufactured goods and buying from them only raw materials, an extremely profitable arrangement for capitalists in advanced countries and one that certainly keeps underdeveloped countries underdeveloped. This is why revolutionary movements in underdeveloped countries want either to overthrow the capitalist order or to industrialize their economies as fast as possible.

Such economic colonialism has long existed in many aspects of America's relations with Latin America. During the Cold War, the United States wrapped this system of dependency in the rhetoric of anticommunism, labeling elected leaders Communists if they seemed to endanger American corporate interests, as in Guatemala in 1954, and ordering the CIA to overthrow them. Campaigns against the influence of Fidel Castro, for instance, often proved of great usefulness to American companies south of the border. But this pattern of relationships did not cause the global economic crisis of the late 1990s.

The fundamental structural cause was the way the United States for more than forty years won and retained the loyalty of its East Asian satellites. These non-Communist countries accepted the American deal as offered and worked hard at "export-led growth," primarily to the American market. If the Japanese led this movement, behind them were three ranks of followers: first, the "newly industrialized countries" of South Korea, Taiwan, Hong Kong, and Singapore; then, the late developers of Southeast Asia, Malaysia, Indonesia, Thailand, and the Philippines; and finally, China, at present the world's fastest-growing economy. The Japanese found this so-called flying-geese pattern appealing. They were flattered to be the lead goose and the inspiration for those that followed. The leaders of each of these countries assumed that their economic destination—Los Angeles (and from there the rest of the American market)—was a permanent feature of the international environment; and so long as the Cold War existed, it was as permanent as anything ever is in interstate relations.

Over time, however, this pattern produced gross overinvestment and excess capacity in East Asia, the world's largest trade deficits in the United States, and a lack of even an approximation of supply-and-demand equilibrium across the Pacific. Contrary to Communist analyses of how neocolonialism should work, these terms proved surprisingly costly to the imperial power. They cost American jobs, destroyed manufacturing industries, and blunted the hopes of minorities and women trying to escape from poverty.

Judith Stein, a professor of history at the City College of New York, has detailed how the de facto U.S. industrial policy of sacrificing American workers to pay for its empire devastated African-American households in Birmingham, Alabama, and Pittsburgh, Pennsylvania. This is, of course, but another form of blowback. She writes, "At the outset of the Cold War, reconstructing or creating steel industries abroad was a keystone of U.S. strategic policy, and encouraging steel imports became a tool for maintaining vital alliances. The nation's leaders by and large ignored the resulting conflict between Cold War and domestic goals. Reminiscing about elite thinking in that era, former Federal Reserve

Board chairman Paul A. Volcker recalled that 'the strength and prosperity of the American economy was too evident to engender concern about the costs.' "[2] Moreover, American economic ideologues always dominated what debate there was, couching the problem in terms of protectionism versus internationalism, never in terms of prosperity for whites versus poverty for blacks. The true costs to the United States should be measured in terms of crime statistics, ruined inner cities, and drug addiction, as well as trade deficits.

U.S. officials did finally start to negotiate more or less seriously with the Japanese and the other "miracle economies" to open their markets to American goods. But the attempt always collided with the security relationship. In order to level the economic playing field, the United States would have had to level the security playing field as well, and this it remains unwilling to do.

In East Asia, to create industries that could export to the American market, design the right products, and achieve competitive prices and levels of quality, governmental industrial policies became the norm. Japan was the regional pioneer in creating model collaborative relationships between government and industry. In part, it drew on its history as one of the world's most successful late industrializers and on its wartime production system, in which the government and the huge *zaibatsu*, or corporate combines, had worked together to produce the weapons that Japan needed. After the onset of the Cold War, the Americans did very little to prevent the Japanese from re-creating the combines (now called *keiretsu*) and the legal structure that supported them, largely because occupation officials either failed to recognize what was happening or were blind to its implications.

To base a capitalist economy mainly on export sales rather than domestic demand, however, ultimately subverts the function of the unfettered world market to reconcile and bring into balance supply and demand. Instead of producing what the people of a particular economy can actually use, East Asian export regimes thrived on foreign demand artificially engineered by an imperialist power. In East Asia during the Cold War, the strategy worked so long as the American economy remained overwhelmingly larger than the economies of its dependencies and so long as only Japan and perhaps one or two smaller countries pursued this strategy. But by the 1980s the Japanese economy had become twice the size of both Germanies. Anything it did affected not just the American but the global economy. Moreover, virtually everyone else in East Asia (and potentially every underdeveloped country on earth) had some knowledge of how to create such a miracle economy and many were trying to duplicate Japanese-style high-speed growth. An overcapacity for products oriented to the American market (or products needed to further expand export-oriented economies) became overwhelming. There were too many factories turning out athletic shoes, automobiles, television sets, semiconductors, petrochemicals, steel, and ships for too few buyers. The current global demand for automobiles, for example, seems to have peaked at around 50 million vehicles at a moment when capacity has already grown to 70 million. To make matters worse, as a result of the global economic crisis, auto sales in Southeast Asia fell from 1.3 million in 1997 to 450,000 in 1998.

This is not to say that all the barefoot peoples of the world who might like to wear athletic shoes or all the relatively poor people who might someday be able to afford a television set or an automobile are satisfied. But for now they are too poor to be customers. The current overcapacity in East Asia has created intense competition among American and European multinational corporations. Their answer has been to lower costs by moving as much of their manufacturing as possible to places where skilled workers are paid very little. These poorly paid workers in places like Vietnam, Indonesia, and China cannot consume what they produce, while middle- and lower-class consumers back in the United States and Europe cannot buy much more either because their markets are saturated or their incomes are stagnant or falling. The underlying danger is a structural collapse of demand leading to recession and ultimately to something like the Great Depression. As the economic journalist William Greider has put it in his book *One World, Ready or Not*, "Shipping high-wage jobs to low-wage economies has obvious, immediate economic benefits. But, roughly speaking, it also replaces high-wage consumers with low-wage ones. That exchange is debilitating for the entire system."[3] The only answer is to create new demand by paying poor people more for their work. But the political authorities capable of enacting and enforcing rules to enlarge demand could not do so even if they wanted to because "globalization" has placed the matter beyond their control.

A crisis of oversupply was inevitable given the passage of time and the unwillingness of imperial America to reform its system of satellites. Even in the late 1990s, the American economy continued to serve as the consumer of last resort for the enormous manufacturing capacity of all of East Asia, although doing so produced trade deficits that cumulatively transferred trillions of dollars from the United States to Asia. This caused an actual decline in the household incomes of the bottom tenth of American families, whose real incomes fell by 13 percent between 1973 and 1995. It was only in 1997 that a weak link snapped—not, ironically, in trade, but finance—and threatened to bring the system down.

The financial systems of all the high-growth East Asian economies were based on encouraging exceptionally high domestic household savings as the main source of capital for industrial growth. Such savings were achieved by discouraging consumption through the high domestic pricing of consumer goods (which, of course, also led to charges of "dumping" of normally priced goods when they were sent abroad). To save in such a context was a patriotic act, but it was also a matter of survival in societies that provided little in the way of a social safety net for times of emergencies, and in which housing often had to be bought outright or in which interest payments on mortgages was not treated favorably as a tax deduction.

East Asian governments collected these savings in banks affiliated with industrial combines or in government savings institutions such as post offices. In organizing their economies, they had chosen not to rely primarily on stock exchanges to raise the capital their export industries needed. Instead they found it much more effective to guide the investment of the savings in these banks to the industries the governments wanted to develop. In East Asia, ostensibly private banks thus became partners in business enterprises and industrial groups, not independent creditors concerned first and foremost with the profitability of a company or the success of a loan. These banks in effect followed government orders and felt secure so long as they did so.

Superficially, corporations in most East Asian countries looked like their American or European equivalents, but in this case appearances were indeed deceptive. As the American corporate raider T. Boone Pickens discovered when he tried to buy a small Japanese company that made auto headlights, a significant block of shares was held by the Toyota Motor Company. The firm he wanted to acquire was part of the automaker's *keiretsu*, or conglomerate of cooperating firms and banks. Although Pickens acquired what in the United States would have been a controlling interest in the company, Toyota blocked his takeover and prevented him from naming his own directors and corporate officers. The fact that Pickens was able to buy the shares at all was a fluke in Japanese corporate governance, the result of a single disgruntled stockholder. Until very recently Japanese corporations were "owned" entirely by one another in elaborate cross-share-holding deals designed to keep people like Pickens out and to keep the enterprise working for the country rather than for the profits of shareholders. The sale of shares was not a way to raise capital, and the people who held them were uninterested in the risks or profits that the company's operations entailed.

This was actually a brilliant system. Oxfam, the British development and relief agency, maintains that the Cold War East Asian economies achieved "the fastest reduction in poverty for the greatest number of people in history."[4] But the stability of any East Asian economy depended on its keeping its financial system closed—that is, under national control and supervision. Once opened up to the rest of the world, the financial structures of the East Asian developmental states were extremely vulnerable to attack by foreign capital and international financial speculators. The industrial policy system produced corporations in which the burden of debt was five times greater than the value of the shareholders' investments, whereas these so-called debt-to-equity ratios for U.S. firms are less than one to one. East Asian corporations operating with such large burdens of debt were normally indifferent to the price of their equity shares. Instead, they serviced these debts at their banks with income from foreign sales. When they were unable to repay their loans, the banks themselves very quickly veered toward bankruptcy. The whole system depended on continuous growth of revenue from export sales.

East Asian bankers are no stupider or more corrupt than those elsewhere. It is just that the industrial policies of the systems within which they operate put the profitability of a loan very near the bottom of the criteria they use for making an investment decision. Instead, these bankers focus on enlarging productive capacity, achieving larger market shares, accumulating assets, and having large balance sheets. It is true that from a purely Western perspective, they should not have offered many of the loans they made. To us it seems insane to ignore commercial criteria such as profitability. But for a Korean banker, it was more important to support an affiliated company that was building cars for the U.S. market than to question whether the company was making prudent investment decisions. That was part of the logic of being a banker in a satellite country within America's hegemonic order in East Asia.

Then, without warning, that order changed. Perhaps the first important blow to the East Asian model of capitalism came in 1971, when President Nixon abolished the Bretton Woods system of fixed exchange rates, created by the United Nations Monetary and Financial Conference in the summer of 1944 at Bretton Woods, New Hampshire. The treaties that resulted from Bretton Woods were the most important efforts of the victorious Allies of World War II to create a better global financial system than the one that existed in the 1930s. The Allies intended to prevent a recurrence of the protectionism and competitive devaluations of national currencies that had deepened the Great Depression and fueled the rise of Nazism. To do these things, the Bretton Woods conference established a system of fixed exchange rates among the world's currencies. It also created the International Monetary Fund, to help countries whose economic conditions forced them to alter the value of their currencies, and the World Bank, to help finance post-war rebuilding. The value of every currency was tied to the value of the U.S. dollar, which was in turn backed by the U.S. government's guarantee that it would convert dollars into gold on demand.

Nixon decided to end the Bretton Woods system because the Vietnam War had imposed such excessive expenditures on the United States that it was hemorrhaging money. He concluded that the government could no longer afford to exchange its currency for a fixed value of gold. A more effective answer would have been to end the Vietnam War and balance the federal budget. Instead, what actually occurred was that the dollar and other currencies were allowed to "float"—that is, to be converted into other currencies at whatever rate the market determined.

The historian, business executive, and novelist John Ralston Saul described Nixon's action as "perhaps the single most destructive act of the postwar world. The West was returned to the monetary barbarism and instability of the 19th century."[5] Floating exchange rates introduced a major element of instability into the international trading system. They stimulated the growth of so-called finance capitalism—which refers to making money from trading stocks, bonds, currencies, and other forms of securities as well as lending money to companies, governments, and consumers rather than manufacturing products and selling them at prices determined by unfettered markets. Finance capitalism, as its name implies, means making money by manipulating money, not trying to achieve a balance between the producers and consumers of goods. On the contrary, finance capitalism aggravates the problems of equilibrium within and among capitalist economies in order to profit from the discrepancies. During the nineteenth century the appearance, and then dominance, of finance capitalism was widely recognized as a defect of improperly regulated capitalist systems. Theorists from Adam Smith to John Hobson observed that capitalists do not really like being capitalists. They would much rather be monopolists, rentiers, inside traders, or usurers or in some other way achieve an unfair advantage that might allow them to profit more easily from the mental and physical work of others. Smith and Hobson both believed that finance capitalism produced the pathologies of the global economy they called mercantilism and imperialism: that is, true economic exploitation of others rather than *mutually* beneficial exchanges among economic actors.

Opponents of capitalism, such as Marxists, viewed such problems as inescapable and the ultimate reason capitalist systems must sooner or later implode. Supporters of capitalism, such as Smith and Hobson, thought that its problems could be solved by imposing social controls on the monetary system, as did the Bretton Woods agreement. As they saw it, lack of such controls led to the maldistribution of purchasing power. Too few rich people and too many poor people resulted in an insufficient demand for goods and services. The "excess capital" thus generated had to find some place to go. In the maturing capitalist countries of the nineteenth century, financiers pressured their governments to create colonies in which they could invest and obtain profits of a sort no longer available to them at home. The nineteenth-century theorists believed this was the root cause of imperialism and that its specific antidote was the use of state power to raise the ability of the domestic public to consume. After the United States ended the Bretton Woods system, these kinds of problems once again returned to haunt the world.

In the 1980s, when Japanese trade with the United States began seriously to damage the American economy, the leaders of both countries chose to deal with the problem by manipulating exchange rates. This could be done by having the central banks of each country work in concert buying and selling dollars and yen. In a meeting of finance ministers at the Plaza Hotel in New York City in 1985, the United States and Japan agreed in the Plaza Accord to force down the value of the dollar and force up the value of the yen, thereby making American products cheaper on international markets and Japanese goods more expensive. The low (that is, inexpensive) dollar lasted for a decade.

The Plaza Accord was intended to ameliorate the United States' huge trade deficits with Japan, but altering exchange rates affects only prices, and price competitiveness and price advantages were not the cause of the deficits. The accord was based on good classroom economic theory, but it ignored the realities of how the Japanese economy was actually organized and its dependence on sales to the American market. The accord was, as a result, the root cause of the major catastrophes that befell East Asia's economies over the succeeding fifteen years.

Once the high yen–low dollar regime was in place, the U.S. government assumed that the trade imbalance would correct itself. The United States did nothing to end Japan's barriers against imports and still permitted Japan to export into its market anything and everything it could sell there. Japan reacted to the high yen by putting its industrial policy system into high gear in order to lower costs so it could continue its export-led growth, even at a disadvantageously high exchange rate. The Japanese Ministry of Finance also lowered domestic interest rates to make capital virtually free and encouraged industrial groups to invest more vigorously than they had ever done before. The result was fantastic industrial overcapacity and a "bubble economy," in which the prices of such things as real estate lost any relationship to underlying values. Business leaders proudly announced on American television that a square meter of the Ginza was worth more than all of Seattle. Ultimately, huge debts accumulated and the Japanese banks were stuck with at least $600 billion in "nonperforming" loans that threatened to bankrupt the entire banking system.

By 1995, the contradictions were starting to come to a head. Japan still had a huge surplus of savings, which it exported to the United States by investing in U.S. Treasury bonds, thereby helping fund America's debts and keep its domestic interest rates low. And yet Japan itself was simultaneously facing the possibility of the collapse of several of its bankrupt banks. Financial leaders said to the Americans that they needed relief from the high yen in order to increase Japan's exports. They hoped to solve their problems in the traditional way, via more export-led growth. Eisuke Sakakibara, then Japan's vice minister for international affairs in the Ministry of Finance, readily acknowledges that he intervened with Washington to lower the value of the yen and admits to his "inadvertent role in precipitating one of the 20th century's greatest economic crises."[6] The United States went along with this; facing reelection in 1996, Bill Clinton certainly did not want Japanese capital called home to prop up Japanese banks at that moment. As a result, between 1995 and 1997 the U.S. Treasury and the Bank of Japan engineered a "reverse Plaza Accord"—which led to a 60 percent fall of the yen against the dollar.

However, in the wake of the Plaza Accord, many newly developing Southeast Asian economies had by then "pegged" their currencies to the low dollar, establishing official rates at which businesses and countries around the world could exchange Southeast Asian currencies for dollars. So long as the dollar remained cheap, this gave them a price advantage over competitors, including Japan, and made the region very attractive to foreign investors because of its rapidly expanding exports. It also encouraged reckless lending by domestic banks, since pegged exchange rates seemed to protect them from the unpredictability of currency fluctuations. During the early 1990s, all of the East Asian countries other than Japan grew at explosive rates. Then the "reverse Plaza Accord" brought disaster. Suddenly, their exports became far more expensive than Japan's. Export growth in second-tier countries like South Korea, Thailand, Indonesia, Malaysia, and the Philippines went from 30 percent a year in early 1995 to zero by mid-1996.[7]

Certain developments in the advanced industrial democracies only compounded these problems. Some of their capitalists had spent the post–Plaza Accord decade developing "financial instruments" that enabled them to bet on whether global currencies would rise or fall. They had also accumulated huge pools of capital, partly because aging populations led to the exceptional growth of pension funds, which had to be invested somewhere. Mutual funds within the United States alone grew from about $1 trillion in the early 1980s to $4.5 trillion by the mid-1990s. These massive pools of capital could have catastrophic effects on the value of a foreign currency if transferred in and then suddenly out of a target country. Fast-developing computer and telecommunications technologies radically lowered transaction costs while increasing the speed and precision with which finance capitalists could transfer money and manipulate currencies on a global scale. The managers who controlled these funds began to encourage investment anywhere on earth under the rubric of "globalization," an esoteric term for what in the nineteenth century was simply called imperialism. They argued that excess capital should be allowed to flow freely in and out of any and all countries. Some economists argued that the free flow of capital was the same thing as the free flow of goods, despite mountainous evidence to the contrary.

Capital flows to developing nations in Asia and Latin America jumped from about $50 billion a year before the end of the Cold War to $300 billion a year by the mid-1990s. From 1992 to 1996, Indonesia, Malaysia, Thailand, and the Philippines experienced money and credit growth rates of 25 percent to 30 percent a year. During this same period South Korea, Thailand, and Indonesia invested nearly 40 percent of their gross domestic product in new productive capacity as well as in hotels and office buildings; the comparable figure for European nations was only 20 percent and even less for the United States. In 1996, Asia was the destination for half of all global foreign investment, European and Japanese as well as American. On the American side, by 1997 Citibank held about $22 billion in local currency loans in East Asia, about $20 billion in securities, and $8 billion in dollar loans; Morgan Bank had $19 billion in Asian securities and $6 billion in dollar loans; and Chase had $4 billion in local currency loans, $15 billion in Asian securities, and $6 billion in dollar loans.[8]

Although they did not speak out at the time, a number of famous financiers and economists have since pointed out the dangers of what is called "hot money" or "gypsy capital." George Soros, one of the world's richest financiers and head of a large "hedge fund" located in the Netherlands Antilles, asserted that "financial markets, far from tending toward equilibrium, are inherently unstable," and he warned against the folly of continuing down the path of deregulating the financial services industry.[9] Jagdish Bhagwati, one of free trade's most passionate supporters and a former adviser to the director-general of the General Agreement on Tariffs and Trade, argued that the idea of free trade had been "hijacked by the proponents of capital mobility." He claimed that there was a new

"Wall Street–Treasury complex," comparable to the military-industrial complex, which contributes little to the global economy but profits enormously from pretending that it does. The East Asian economies did not really need hot money from abroad, since in most cases they saved enough themselves to finance their own growth. Bhagwati has also pointed out that an unregulated financial system can with relative ease become divorced from the productive system it is supposed to serve and so be unnaturally predisposed to "panics and manias."[10]

There was as well a less financial ingredient in the disaster-in-the-making. Without particularly thinking about it or sponsoring any public debate on the subject, the U.S. government built its future global policies on the main military elements of its Cold War policies. It expanded NATO to include the former Soviet satellites of the Czech Republic, Hungary, and Poland; it reinforced its East Asian alliances; and it committed itself to ensuring access to Persian Gulf oil for itself and its allies. The Gulf War of 1991 was the first demonstration of this commitment. Eschewing a "peace dividend," which it might have directed toward its own industrial and social infrastructure, the United States also kept its Cold War–sized defense budgets in the $270 billion range while seeking to reorient its military focus from the possibility of war with a more or less equivalent enemy to imperial policing chores everywhere on earth.

With hegemony established on military terms and the American public more or less unaware of what its government was doing, government officials, economic theorists, and members of the Wall Street–Treasury complex launched an astonishingly ambitious, even megalomaniacal attempt to make the rest of the world adopt American economic institutions and norms. One could argue that the project reflected the last great expression of eighteenth-century Enlightenment rationalism, as idealistic and utopian as the paradise of pure communism that Marx envisioned; or one could conclude that having defeated the Fascists and the Communists, the United States now sought to defeat its last remaining rivals for global dominance: the nations of East Asia that had used the conditions of the Cold War to enrich themselves. In the latter view,

U.S. interests lay not in globalization but in bringing increasingly self-confident competitors to their knees.

In any event, buoyed by what the apologist for America Francis Fukuyama has called the "end of history"—the belief that with the end of the Cold War all alternatives to the American economic system had been discredited—American leaders became hubristic. Although there is no evidence that Washington hatched a conspiracy to extend the scope of its global hegemony, a sense of moral superiority on the part of some and of opportunism on the part of others more than sufficed to create a similar effect.

Their efforts came in two strategic phases. From about 1992 to 1997, the United States led an ideological campaign to open up the economies of the world to free trade and the free flow of capital across national borders. Concretely this meant attempting to curb governmental influence, particularly any supervisory role over commerce in all "free-market democracies." Where this effort was successful (notably in South Korea), it had the effect of softening up the former developmental states, leaving them significantly more defenseless in the international marketplace.

Beginning in July 1997, the United States then brought the massive weight of unconstrained global capital to bear on them. Whether the U.S. government did this by inadvertence or design is at present impossible to say. But at least no one can claim that America's leadership did not know about the size and strength of the hedge funds located in offshore tax havens and about the incredible profits they were making from speculative attacks on vulnerable currencies. In 1994, for example, David W. Mullins, former Harvard Business School professor and vice chairman of the Federal Reserve Board, went from being a deputy of Reserve Board chairman Alan Greenspan to a position as a director of Long-Term Capital Management (LTCM), a huge hedge fund with its headquarters in Greenwich, Connecticut, but its money safely stashed in the Cayman Islands, beyond the reach of tax authorities. In 1998, after the conditions it helped bring about had almost bankrupted the fund, the New York Federal Reserve Bank arranged a $3.65 billion cash bailout to save the company—as good an example of pure "crony capitalism" as any ever attributed to the high-growth economies of East Asia. In fact, when the bailout came to light, a number of Asian publications cynically recalled how the *New York Times* had editorialized only months earlier that in Asia "collusive practices were not only tolerated, they were encouraged" and that "the United States needs to reiterate the importance of full transparency by companies and financial institutions."[11] After the LTCM bailout, Martin Mayer, one of the most respected writers on the American financial system, observed that "the Fed [Federal Reserve Board] for all its talk of 'transparency' has made the fastest growing area of banking totally opaque, even to the supervisors themselves."[12]

In order to make it intellectually respectable for the smaller Asian economies to swallow all the money the United States, Japan, and other advanced countries were offering them, the U.S. government threw its weight behind the Asia-Pacific Economic Cooperation forum (APEC), an organization the Australians had launched at a meeting of trade ministers in Canberra in November 1989. The forum did not, however, take off until November 1993, when President Clinton decided to attend an APEC meeting in Seattle and turned it into an Asia-Pacific summit of leaders from all the major East Asian nations. The Seattle meeting also produced APEC's first "Economic Vision Statement": "The progressive development of a community of Asia-Pacific economies with free and open trade *and investment* [italics added]." Under American leadership, APEC became the leading organization promoting globalization in East Asia. At annual meetings in different Pacific Rim countries, it insistently propagandized that the Asian "tiger economies" open up to global market forces, in accordance with the most advanced (American) theorizing about capitalist economies and in order to not be left behind as mere developmental states.

The November 1994 APEC meeting in Bogor, Indonesia, committed the participants to free trade and investment in the Pacific by 2010 for developed countries and by 2020 for developing countries, such as China and Indonesia. In 1995, at Osaka, APEC members agreed to unilaterally open their economies rather than attempt to negotiate a treaty like the

North American Free Trade Agreement, which would have generated too much resistance in many of the member nations. Nothing much happened at Manila in 1996—except for a visit by the leaders to the old U.S. naval base at Subic Bay, now cleaned up of its prostitutes and turned into a free-trade and development zone. At Vancouver in November 1997, with the Asian financial crisis already under way, the United States pushed for the rapid removal of tariffs and nontariff barriers to trade in fifteen different sectors of economic activity. At Kuala Lumpur in November 1998, APEC finally came unglued. The prime minister of Malaysia, Mahathir Mohamad, had only a few months earlier reimposed capital controls over his economy to insulate it from gypsy capital, for which Vice President Al Gore openly denounced him, encouraging the people of Malaysia to overthrow him. The meeting ended in rancor, with Japan taking the lead in scuttling any further market-opening schemes for the time being. Its Ministry of Foreign Affairs declared that the United States was possessed by an "evil spirit" and accused it of endangering the region's fragile economic condition by pushing market-opening measures down the throats of countries too weak to open their borders further.[13] Malaysia and the United States did not even bother to attend the 1999 APEC meeting of trade ministers in Auckland, New Zealand.

The shock that brought this edifice crashing to the ground started in the summer of 1997, when some foreign financiers discovered that they had lent huge sums to companies in East Asia with unimaginably large debts and, by Western standards, very low levels of shareholder investment. They feared that other lenders, particularly the hedge funds, would make or had already made the same discovery. They knew that if all of them started to reduce their risks, the aggregate effect would be to force local governments to de-peg their currencies from the dollar and devalue them. Since this would raise the loan burdens of even the most expertly managed companies, they too would have to rush to buy dollars before the price went out of sight, thereby helping to drive the value of any domestic currency even lower.

The countries that had followed recent American economic advice most closely were most seriously devastated. They had opened up their economies to unrestricted capital flows without understanding the need to regulate the exposure of their own banks and firms. They did not ensure that borrowers in their countries invested the money they acquired from abroad in projects that would pay adequate returns or that actually constituted collateral for the loans. The foreign economists who advised them did not stress the institutional and legal structures needed to operate in the world of American-style laissez faire. No one warned them that if they raised their interest rates in order to slow inflation, foreign money would pour into their countries, attracted by high returns, whereas if they lowered interest rates in order to prevent a recession, it would provoke an immediate flight of foreign capital. They did not know that unrestricted capital flows had put them in an impossible position. What took place in East Asia was a clash between two forms of capitalism: the American system, disciplined by the need to produce profits, and the Asian form, disciplined by the need to produce growth through export sales.

The International Monetary Fund entered this picture and turned a financial panic into a crisis of the underlying economic systems. As already mentioned, the Bretton Woods conference of 1944 had created the IMF to service the system of fixed exchange rates that lasted until the "Nixon shocks" of 1971. It survived its loss of mission in 1971 to become, in the economist Robert Kuttner's words, "the premier instrument of deflation, as well as the most powerful unaccountable institution in the world."[14] The IMF is essentially a covert arm of the U.S. Treasury, yet beyond congressional oversight because it is formally an international organization. Its voting rules ensure that it is dominated by the United States and its allies. India and China have fewer votes in the IMF, for example, than the Netherlands. As the prominent Harvard economist Jeffrey Sachs puts its, "Not unlike the days when the British Empire placed senior officials directly into the Egyptian and Ottoman [and also the Chinese] financial ministries, the IMF is insinuated into the inner sanctums of nearly 75 developing country governments around the world—countries with a combined population of some 1.4 billion."[15]

In 1997, the IMF roared into a panic-stricken Asia, promising to supply $17 billion to Bangkok, $40 billion to Jakarta, and $57 billion to Seoul. In return, however, it demanded the imposition of austerity budgets and high interest rates, as well as fire sales of debt-ridden local businesses to foreign bargain hunters. It claimed that these measures would restore economic health to the "Asian tigers" and also turn them into "open" Anglo-American-type capitalist economies. At an earlier meeting at Manila in November 1997 called to deal with the crisis, Japan and Taiwan had offered to put up $100 billion to help their fellow Asians, but the U.S. Treasury's assistant secretary, Lawrence Summers, denounced the idea as a threat to the monopoly of the IMF over international financial crises, and it was killed. He did not want Japan taking the lead, because Japan would not have imposed the IMF's conditions on the Asian recipients and that was as important to the U.S. government as restoring them to economic health.[16]

In Indonesia, when the government ended its dollar peg and let the currency float, the rupiah fell from about 2,300 to 3,000 to the dollar but then stabilized. At that point, with almost no empirical knowledge of Indonesia itself, the IMF ordered the closure of several banks in a system that has no deposit insurance. This elicited runs on deposits at all other banks. The wealthy Chinese community began to move its money out of Indonesia to Singapore and beyond, and the country was politically destabilized, leading ultimately to the overthrow of President Suharto. All Indonesian companies with dollar liabilities rushed to sell rupiahs and buy dollars. Equities instantly lost 55 percent of their value and the currency, 60 percent. The rupiah ended up trading at 15,000 to one U.S. dollar. David Hale, chief economist of the Zurich Insurance Group, wrote at the time, "It is difficult, if not impossible, to find examples of real exchange rate depreciations comparable to the one which has overtaken the rupiah since mid-1997." He suggested that a proper comparison might be with the hyperinflation that hit the German mark in 1923.[17]

By the time the IMF was finished with Indonesia, over a thousand shopkeepers were dead (most of them Chinese), 20 percent of the population was unemployed, and a hundred million people—half the population—were living on less than one dollar a day. William Pfaff characterized the IMF's actions as "an episode in a reckless attempt to remake the world economy, with destructive cultural and social consequences that could prove as momentous as those of 19th-century colonialism."[18] Only Japan, China, and Taiwan escaped the IMF juggernaut in East Asia. Japan kept aloof even when the Americans publicly rebuked it for failing to absorb more exports from the stricken countries, for the Japanese knew that the Americans would not actually do anything as long as the marines were still comfortably housed in Okinawa. China remained largely untouched because its currency is not freely convertible and it had paid no attention to APEC calls for deregulation of capital flows. And Taiwan survived because it had been slow in removing its financial barriers. It also maintains a relatively low ratio of investment to gross domestic product, is shifting further toward a service economy whose capital needs are less, and has maintained export diversity— unlike, for example, Korea's overconcentration in products such as semiconductors destined for the American market. Foreign holdings of Taiwanese currency are negligible because its peculiar political status makes it unattractive to the hedge funds. Thus, it has been able to offer some of its own huge foreign currency holdings to help bail out countries in Southeast Asia.

After the big investors had pulled their money out of East Asia and left the area in deep recession, they turned to Russia. They calculated that there was little or no risk in buying Russian state bonds paying 12 percent interest because the Western world would not let a former superpower armed with nuclear weapons default. But the situation was further gone in Russia than these investors imagined, and so, in August 1998, the Russians defaulted on the interest payments (they still owe foreign investors perhaps $200 billion). If Russia does not repay these loans, it will be the largest default in history. These developments so scared the finance capitalists that they started pulling their money in from all over the world, threatening even well-run economies that had implemented all the economists' nostrums on how to get rich like the North

Americans. The Brazilian economy was so destabilized that in mid-November 1998 the IMF had to put together a $42 billion "precautionary package" to shore it up. Needless to say, the IMF has also helped plunge millions of poor Brazilians deeper into poverty. In order to meet the IMF's austerity requirements, the Brazilian government even had to cancel a $250 million pilot project to save the Amazon rain forest. The result was that other countries withdrew their matching funds for the Amazon, and the degradation of an area that contributes 20 percent of the globe's fresh-water supply resumed.[19]

In speeches in Russia and East Asia during the second half of 1998, President Clinton warned the peoples of these areas not to "backslide" and urged them to open their nations even further to American-style laissez-faire capitalism. But he had lost his audience. By now his listeners understood that the cause of their misery could not also be its cure. Many remembered that the Great Depression started as a financial panic then made worse by deflationary policies similar to those prescribed by the IMF in 1997 and 1998 for East Asia, Russia, and Brazil. The result in the early 1930s was a general collapse of purchasing power. That has not happened so far this time, largely because the United States went on a consumption binge and provided virtually all growth in demand for the excess output of the world. Can American "shop till we drop" be sustained indefinitely? No one knows.

The economic crisis at the end of the century had its origins in an American project to open up and make over the economies of its satellites and dependencies in East Asia. Its purpose was both to diminish them as competitors and to assert the primacy of the United States as the globe's hegemonic power. Superficially it can be said to have succeeded. The globalization campaign significantly reduced the economic power and capitalist independence of at least some of the United States' "tiger" competitors—even if, as with Russia and Brazil, the crisis could not be kept within the bounds of East Asia. This was, from a rather narrow point of view, a major American imperial success.

Despite such immediate results, however, the campaign against Asian-style capitalism (and the possibility that America's satellite states in the area might gain independent political clout as well) was ill-founded and included serious blowback consequences. The United States failed to acknowledge that East Asian success had depended to a considerable extent on preferential, Cold War–based exports to the American market. By cloaking its campaign in the rhetoric of market opening and deregulation instead of the need to reform outdated Cold War arrangements, the United States both destroyed the credibility of its economic ideology and betrayed its Cold War supporters. The impoverishment and humiliation of huge populations from Indonesia to South Korea was itself blowback enough, even if the blowback for the time being spared ordinary Americans. But if and when the stricken economies recover, they will almost certainly start to seek leadership elsewhere than from the United States. At a bare minimum, they will try to protect themselves from ever again being smothered by the American embrace. In short, by refusing to reform its Cold War structures and instead insisting that other peoples emulate the American way, the United States gave itself an unnecessary, possibly terminal case of imperial overstretch. Instead of forestalling global instability, it helped make such instability inevitable.

The triumphalist rhetoric of American leaders basking in their economy's "stellar performance" has also alarmed foreigners. When Alan Greenspan asserted to Congress that the crisis meant the world was moving toward "the Western form of free market capitalism," almost no one thought that was either true, possible, or desirable. Economics has not displaced culture and history, regardless of the self-evaluation of the economics profession. Many leaders in East Asia know that globalization and the crisis that followed actually produced only pain for their people, with almost no discernible gains.[20] Globalization seems to boil down to the spread of poverty to every country except the United States.

Clearly on the defensive, Richard N. Haass and Robert E. Litan, directors respectively of foreign policy and of economic studies at the Brookings Institution in Washington, lamented, "In some quarters [globalization] is seen as having caused the rapid flows of investment that moved in and out of countries as investor sentiment changed and were behind the Mexican [1995] and Asian financial crises." But to them this would be a wrong conclusion. To accept it would be to "abandon America's commitment to the spread of markets and democracy around the world at precisely the moment these ideas are ascendant."[21] But whether such ideas are actually ascendant is, thanks to the crisis, now in doubt, and such doubts are generating more blowback. The duties of "lone superpower" produced military overstretch; globalization led to economic overstretch; and both are contributing to an endemic crisis of blowback.

10

THE CONSEQUENCES OF EMPIRE

American officials and the media talk a great deal about "rogue states" like Iraq and North Korea, but we must ask ourselves whether the United States has itself become a rogue superpower. In November 1998, Tom Plate, a columnist on Pacific Rim affairs for the *Los Angeles Times*, described the United States as "a muscle-bound crackpot superpower with little more than cruise missiles for brains."[1] That same month a senior State Department specialist on North Korea, when asked by a right-wing journalist what it was like having to deal daily with a totally crazy regime, replied, "Which one?" Another former State Department official protested that military might does not equate with "leadership of the free world" and wrote that "Madeleine Albright is the first secretary of state in American history whose diplomatic specialty, if one can call it that, is lecturing other governments, using threatening language and tastelessly bragging of the power and virtue of her country."[2] It is possible to think of other secretaries of state who fit this description, going back to John Foster Dulles, but Albright does not even have the Cold War to justify her jingoism.

We Americans deeply believe that our role in the world is virtuous—that our actions are almost invariably for the good of others as well as ourselves. Even when our country's actions have led to disaster, we assume that the motives behind them were honorable. But the evidence is building up that in the decade following the end of the Cold War, the United States largely abandoned a reliance on diplomacy, economic aid, international law, and multilateral institutions in carrying out its foreign policies and resorted much of the time to bluster, military force, and financial manipulation.

The world is not a safer place as a result. Those who support a singular American hegemonic role in world affairs argue, as did Mark Yost, an editor of the *Wall Street Journal*, "It's all but assured that the number of nuclear powers abroad would increase significantly with the withdrawal or reduction of U.S. forces [in Asia]."[3] But in May 1998, with American forces deployed as widely as in the final days of the Cold War, the worst case of nuclear proliferation since the 1960s occurred in South Asia. Both India and Pakistan tested multiple nuclear devices, committing their countries to perfecting nuclear weapons and developing the missiles needed to deliver them—in essence, setting off a full-scale nuclear arms race in South Asia. There can be little question that a serious policy of nuclear disarmament led by the United States would have been far more effective in halting or even reversing the nuclearization of the world than the continuing policy of forward deployment of nuclear-armed troops combined with further research on ever more advanced nuclear weaponry at America's weapons laboratories.

In February 1998, Secretary of State Madeleine Albright, defending the use of cruise missiles against Iraq, declared, "If we have to use force, it is because we are America. We are the indispensable nation. We stand tall. We see farther into the future."[4] In this book I have tried to lay out some important aspects of America's role in the world that suggest precisely the opposite. I have also tried to explain how the nature and shape of this role grew out of the structural characteristics of the Cold War itself and the strategies the United States pursued, particularly in East Asia, to achieve what it considered its interests during that period and after. I have argued that the United States created satellites in East Asia for the same reasons that the former Soviet Union created satellites in Eastern Europe. For over forty years, the policies needed to maintain these client states economically, while protecting and controlling them militarily, produced serious unintended consequences, most of which Americans have yet to fully grasp. They hollowed out our domestic manufacturing and bred a military establishment that is today close to being beyond civilian control. Given that the government only attempts to shore up, not change, these anachronistic arrangements, one must ask when, not whether, our accidental empire will start to unravel.

According to a Brookings Institution study, it has cost the United States $5.5 trillion to build and maintain our nuclear arsenal.[5] It is now common knowledge that comparable costs in the former USSR led to its collapse. In 1988, just before the Berlin Wall fell, that elegant historian of imperial overextension Paul Kennedy detailed the numerous weaknesses of the Soviet economy but nonetheless concluded, "This does *not* mean that the USSR is close to collapse, any more than it should be viewed as a country of almost supernatural strength. It *does* mean that it is facing awkward choices."[6] This understandable misassessment by one of the world's authorities on imperial collapse contains an important warning for the United States. Fifteen years ago no one in Russia or elsewhere imagined that the USSR could possibly be in danger of internal disintegration. There are parallels between what happened in the former USSR after the end of the Cold War and the state of the American polity at the end of the century, even acknowledging that economically the Soviet Union had long been a shell held together by a huge underground (and technically illegal) economy, while it displayed to the external world a vast imperial army and nuclear forces.

In March 1985, Mikhail Gorbachev succeeded Konstantin Chernenko as general secretary of the Communist Party of the Soviet Union. He was no more opposed to Soviet-style socialism than his counterparts in the United States were opposed to "democracy and free markets." He was, however, keenly aware of the strains that an endless, unwinnable war in Afghanistan and the arms race with the United States were placing on an already shaky economy. A month after he came to power, Gorbachev launched a campaign of economic reform controlled from above that he called perestroika, or "restructuring." Gorbachev's relatively limited goal was to try to accelerate national economic performance by relaxing the Soviet system's centralized planning. He did not fully appreciate that weakening the vertical structure of the Soviet system without first creating horizontal (even if ideologically unacceptable) institutions, such as markets, prices, and private property, would only lead to chaos. Communist colleagues with vested interests in the old system rebelled against even his modest domestic reforms and sabotaged them. In order to counter these attacks, in 1987 Gorbachev introduced something really new—glasnost, or freedom of speech. His intent was still only to achieve a more efficient system of production and improved living standards under the established Soviet political order.

But far more than perestroika, glasnost would prove a critical miscalculation for a leader hoping to reform Soviet-style communism. Glasnost not only opened up the full horrors of the Stalinist past but also revealed the extent to which totalitarian controls had damaged all aspects of life in the USSR. Glasnost—the open discussion of the past—ended up discrediting the very institutions within which the Soviet people had worked since at least 1929, clearing the way for the abandonment of Communist ideology itself, and the subsequent loss of any form of political authority in Russia. A decade later the country was bankrupt, more or less leaderless, and riven with corruption. Russia has also become one of the world's most important breeding grounds for resentment against the Western powers. Even as the United States gloats over its "victory" in the Cold War, future Russian revanchism becomes more and more likely.

The collapse of the USSR was not foreordained. The problems in Russia came to a head when the collective costs of the Cold War finally overwhelmed its productive capacities. Gorbachev's remedies were, however, incommensurate with the problems and led to a loss of political authority, leaving the country with a crippled political system. As time ran out on the Soviet empire, Gorbachev's military restraint in dealing with Eastern Europe was admirable, but the endgame of the Soviet Union remains a cautionary tale for any overextended empire that waits too long to try to halt the drift toward crisis. In contrast to the Soviet

Union, China has thus far successfully demonstrated that it is possible to dismantle a Soviet-type economy without destroying its political arrangements.

No matter how humanely (or ineptly) Gorbachev handled the Soviet crisis of the 1980s, it was imperial overstretch that brought the Soviet Union down. Just as during the Cold War there was a symmetry between the USSR and the United States in terms of their respective empires in Eastern Europe and East Asia, so there are at least certain potential symmetries emerging in their post–Cold War fates. The United States believes that it is immune to the Soviet Union's economic problems. That may be true, although America's grossly inflated military establishment and its system of support for arms manufacturers offer parallels to the inefficiencies of the Soviet system. More significantly, unable to agree on a proper course for the country and made complacent by the wealth that flowed its way during the late 1990s, America's leaders have allowed a process to develop that might in certain ways prove analogous to political conditions in post–Cold War Russia.

On December 19, 1998, a Republican Congress voted to impeach a Democratic president—the first time in American history that an elected president had been impeached. It did so for the most partisan and flimsy of reasons: that the president had lied about sexual encounters with a subordinate in his office. In the course of trying to extricate himself from this fratricidal political battle, the president twice resorted to military strikes against other countries, a precedent for which he might well have been justifiably impeached. In August 1998, on the day impeachment evidence against him was being released to the public, Bill Clinton ordered cruise missiles fired into a Sudanese pharmaceutical plant and old mujahideen camps in Afghanistan, allegedly the assets or training bases of an international terrorist ring that had attacked U.S. embassies in East Africa; and on the eve of the House of Representatives' impeachment vote he sent cruise missiles into Iraq, allegedly once again to discipline Saddam Hussein. In neither case did the United States have United Nations or other international authority to act as it did.

The president's acquittal on February 12, 1999, superficially resolved his dispute with Congress. But much like the warfare between Gorbachev and the Communist old guard in the Soviet Union, it had the effect of further weakening the structures of political authority. Congressional willingness to resort to so untested a device as impeachment combined with a president willing to try to divert attention through warlike actions suggests a loss of prudence, even a recklessness, on the part of American elites that could be fatal to the American empire in a time of crisis.

Even though the United States at century's end appears to have the necessary firepower and economic resources to neutralize all challengers, I believe our very hubris ensures our undoing. A classic mistake of empire managers is to come to believe that there is nowhere within their domain—in our case, nowhere on earth—in which their presence is not crucial. Sooner or later, it becomes psychologically impossible not to insist on involvement everywhere, which is, of course, a definition of imperial overextension.

Already, the United States cannot afford its various and ongoing global military deployments and interventions and has begun extracting ever growing amounts of "host-nation support" from its clients, or even direct subsidies from its "allies." Japan, one of many allied nations that helped finance the massive American military effort in the Gulf War, paid up to the tune of $13 billion. (The U.S. government even claimed in the end to have made a profit on the venture.) Japan also pays more generously than any other nation for the American troops on its soil. On the economic front, the arrogance, contempt, and triumphalism with which the United States handled the East Asian financial crisis guarantees blowback for decades to come. Capitals like Jakarta and Seoul smolder with the sort of resentment that the Germans had in the 1920s, when inflation and the policies of Britain and France destabilized the Weimar regime.

In the long run, the people of the United States are neither militaristic enough nor rich enough to engage in the perpetual police actions, wars, and bailouts their government's hegemonic policies will require. Moreover, in Asia the United States now faces a renascent China, not only the world's oldest continuously existent civilization but the product of the biggest revolution among all historical cases. Today, China is both the world's most populous society and its fastest-growing economy. The United States cannot hope to "contain" China; it can only adjust to it. But our policies of global hegemony leave us unprepared and far too clumsy in even our limited attempts to arrive at such an adjustment. Meanwhile, the Chinese are very much aware of the large American expeditionary force deployed within striking distance of their borders and the naval units permanently off their coastline. It does not take a Thucydides to predict that this developing situation portends conflict.

The indispensable instrument for maintaining the American empire is its huge military establishment. Despite the money lavished on it, the endless praise for it in the media, and the overstretch and blowback it generates, the military always demands more. In the decade following the end of the Cold War, military budgets consistently gave priority to an arms race that had no other participants. For example, the Pentagon's budget for the fiscal year 2000 called for replacing the F-15, "the world's most advanced aircraft," with the F-22, also "the world's most advanced aircraft." The air force wanted 339 F-22s at $188 million each, three times the cost of the airplane it is replacing. The United States already has 1,094 F-15s, against which there is no equal or more capable aircraft on earth. The last Clinton defense budget included funds for yet more nuclear-attack submarines, for which there is no conceivable use or contingency. They merely provide work for local defense contractors and will join the fleet of America's "floating Chernobyls," along with its nuclear-powered aircraft carriers, cruising the seas waiting for an accident to occur.

The American military at the end of the century is becoming an autonomous system. We no longer have a draft army based on the obligation of citizens to serve their nation. When the Vietnam War exposed the inequities of the draft—for example, the ease with which college students could gain deferments—Congress decided to abolish conscription rather than enforce it in an equitable manner. Today, the military is an entirely mercenary force, made up of volunteers paid salaries by the Pentagon. Although the military still tries to invoke the public's support for a force made up of fellow citizens, this force is increasingly separated from civilian interests and devoted to military ones.

Equipped with the most advanced precision-guided munitions, high-performance aircraft, and intercontinental-range missiles, the American armed forces can unquestionably deliver death and destruction to any target on earth and expect little in the way of retaliation. Even so, these forces voraciously demand more and newer equipment, while the Pentagon now more or less sets its own agenda. Accustomed to life in a half-century-old, well-established empire, the corporate interests of the armed forces have begun to take precedence over the older idea that the military is only one of several means that a democratic government might employ to implement its policies. As their size and prominence grow over time, the armed forces of an empire tend to displace other instruments of foreign policy implementation. What also grows is militarism, "a vast array of customs, interests, prestige, actions, and thought associated with armies and wars and yet transcending true military purpose"—and certainly a reasonable description of the American military ethos today.[7]

"Blowback" is shorthand for saying that a nation reaps what it sows, even if it does not fully know or understand what it has sown. Given its wealth and power, the United States will be a prime recipient in the foreseeable future of all of the more expectable forms of blowback, particularly terrorist attacks against Americans in and out of the armed forces anywhere on earth, including within the United States. But it is blowback in its larger aspect—the tangible costs of empire—that truly threatens it. Empires are costly operations, and they become more costly by the year. The hollowing out of American industry, for instance, is a form of blowback—an unintended negative consequence of American policy—even though it is seldom recognized as such. The growth of militarism in a once democratic society is another example of blowback. Empire is the problem. Even though the United States has a strong sense of invulnerability and substantial military and economic tools to make such a feeling credible, the fact of its imperial pretensions means that a crisis is inevitable. More imperialist projects simply generate more blowback. If we do not begin to solve problems in more prudent and modest ways, blowback will only become more intense.

David Calleo, a professor of international politics, has observed, "The international system breaks down not only because unbalanced and aggressive new powers seek to dominate their neighbors, but also because declining powers, rather than adjusting and accommodating, try to cement their slipping preeminence into an exploitative hegemony."[8] I believe that the United States at the end of the twentieth century fits this description. The signs of such an exploitative hegemony are already with us: increasing estrangement between populations and their governments; a determination of elites to hang on to power despite a loss of moral authority; the appearance of militarism and the separation of the military from the society it is supposed to serve; fierce repression (the huge and still growing American prison population and rising enthusiasm for the death penalty may be symptomatic of this); and an economic crisis that is global in nature. History offers few examples of declining hegemons reversing their decline or giving up power peacefully, although Gorbachev's policies at the end of the Cold War may constitute one. Given that it is close to inconceivable that any American leader could have the authority and vision to act with similar restraint in dealing with our client states (for example, by withdrawing our military from the Korean peninsula), one must conclude that blowback will ultimately produce a crisis that suddenly, wrenchingly impairs or ends America's hegemonic influence. Given the almost sacred position empire bestows on the American military, it seems unlikely that the crisis will occur in that area. Thus, barring an unforeseen reform movement, it seems most probable that economic contradictions will force the unraveling of the American empire.

Marx and Lenin were mistaken about the nature of imperialism. It is not the contradictions of capitalism that lead to imperialism but imperialism that breeds some of the most important contradictions of capitalism. When these contradictions ripen, as they must, they create devastating economic crises.

Once the Cold War had ended and the United States had decided to try to convert its "slipping preeminence into an exploitative hegemony," it set out to compel every significant economy on earth to remodel itself along American lines. This ignorant project has not only failed but has brought discredit to the very idea of free trade and raised serious questions in the minds of economists in East Asia and throughout the Third World about the motives of the United States in the global economy. The world remains poised on the edge of a possible, United States–induced recession, although the United States itself has thus far been the least affected by the economic crisis. Even if a collapse of global demand is avoided, misguided American economic policies have set back thirty years of economic progress in Southeast Asia and laid the foundation for unpredictable forms of economic, political, and military retaliation by the devastated nations.

Ashok Nath, executive director of the Asialink Advertising Corporation and a strong voice in Asian business affairs, asks about the United States' push for globalization: "Is there no way to go but a generic world order in which every country is forced to have the same interpretation of democracy as the U.S.?" "Will speculators, the non-value-adding but crisis-providing segment of 'modern society,' continue their activities unbridled?" "Is the U.S., boosted by consumer spending but lacking strong savings, the next bubble economy?"[9] Such questions have become ubiquitous in East Asia in the wake of the near economic meltdown. They constitute an antiglobalization time bomb that, if it explodes, could lead to mutually destructive protectionism and a huge contraction of global economic activity.

The world economy needs leadership to re-create something comparable to the Bretton Woods agreement of 1944 to 1971, with fixed exchange rates and controls over the movement of capital. Instead of attempting to homogenize the global economy, we should be championing results-oriented trade of mutual benefit to nations that do not have identical economic systems. Foreign countries with entirely different legal, economic, and political systems do not need the International Monetary Fund to forcibly impose on them what is a dubious form of capitalism even in the United States. The IMF has already shelled out about $200 billion in a futile attempt to repair the damage that the United States' globalization schemes caused, even as its own meddling in these sick economies has often ended up making them sicker.

The need to raise incomes in the developing world in order to maintain adequate levels of global demand must also be recognized. Since this almost surely cannot (and probably should not) be done by attempting to institutionalize some version of labor rights on a global scale, the United States should establish minimum-wage levels for the manufacture of goods that are to be exported to our market. As an illustration of the need, the athletic shoe manufacturer Nike proudly announced that effective April 1, 1999, it was increasing entry-level cash wages for its workers in Indonesia by 6 percent.[10] Unfortunately, Indonesia had an 80 percent inflation rate for the years 1998 and 1999, and the World Bank projected an inflation rate of 20 percent for the year 2000.

In February 1999, at the twenty-ninth annual World Economic Forum in Davos, Switzerland, U.S. Secretary of the Treasury Robert Rubin defended finance capitalism while acknowledging that the world was in "the most serious financial crisis of the last fifty years."[11] Yet he stonewalled pleas for change from world leaders. Later that month, at a meeting of the finance ministers of the G-7 group of advanced industrial democracies in Bonn, Germany, the United States blocked all proposals for reform: it would not countenance capital controls, a "super IMF" that would act as a central bank for all nations, or anything like minimum-wage levels in poor countries. The most it would condone was cuts in interest rates by the central banks of various individual nations in order to stimulate economic activity. The United States instead advocated yet more deregulation of trade and investment.

Meanwhile, resentment is growing over American exploitation of the global economic crisis. Big American companies are buying up factories and businesses in East Asia and elsewhere at ludicrously low prices. Procter & Gamble, for instance, has picked up several state-of-the-art Korean factories for next to nothing.[12] Morgan Stanley, Bankers Trust, Salomon Brothers, and CS First Boston expect returns of around 20 percent on their purchases of real estate loans in Tokyo.[13] In Thailand, any number of American investment companies have been buying up service, steel, and energy companies at concessionary prices. In June 1998, a Washington-based merchant bank, the Carlyle Group, sent a group of its executives, led by its adviser, former president George Bush, to Bangkok to "evaluate opportunities." It plans to invest $500 million in Thailand. Asia Properties, a San Diego firm founded in April 1998, was created specifically "to take advantage of the fire-sale real estate prices along Bangkok's main thoroughfares." According to its vice president, "Asia is going through the largest transference of assets in the history of the world."[14] Many East Asians call this "vulture capitalism" and suspect that it was the true purpose of the economic advice given to them in the first place.

The Americans buying these foreclosed properties in East Asia may believe they are merely responding to the signals of normal market forces, but they would be fools to believe that the sellers agree with them. Countries like Thailand and Indonesia have long been on the receiving end of U.S. pressures to deregulate and open their countries to international investors. As a result of doing so they now find themselves destitute, selling off what they built with their own labor in the years since the Vietnam War ended. It is only a matter of time until the small nations of East Asia get tired of this American bullying and find a suitable leader to create an anti-American coalition.

In the meantime, the hollowing out of American industry continues unabated. In 1998, the primary case was steel, but the machine tools, chemical, semiconductor, and apparel industries were in the same boat. During 1998, cheap Japanese steel exports to the United States surged some sixteen times above their 1997 level. Even the most efficient American steelmakers, like Nucor of Charlotte, North Carolina, were unable to compete with Japanese cut-rate prices. In the first decade after the Cold War, the U.S. steel industry closed down thirty million tons of productive capacity. Over the past three decades, it has cut its workforce by 400,000 people. Today, it employs only 163,000 workers but pays each of them an average salary of $65,000 a year. As a result of this restructuring and major investments in the most advanced technology, the

American steel industry is today competitive with anyone in the world, yet it continues to be overwhelmed by global overcapacity.[15]

Perhaps the American policies that are burying American steel made strategic sense during the period from 1950 to 1970, when they also brought real competition to such complacent industries as automobile manufacturing. By December 1998, however, when the Japanese government decided to reinforce protection of its hopelessly inefficient farmers by imposing tariffs of 1,000 percent on imported California rice, American toleration had become purely self-destructive. In 1997, the United States supplied almost half of the 640,000 tons of rice Japan imported, virtually all of it from California's 2,500 rice farms. The new tariff was the Japanese government's way of getting around a commitment it made in 1993, in the so-called Uruguay Round of trade negotiations, to import increasing amounts of rice. There is no question that American rice farming is more efficient than Japan's and that American farmers have matched the varieties of rice favored by Japanese consumers. But the Japanese government makes its consumers pay ten times the world's price for their main food staple in order to protect the gerrymandered rural voting base of the Liberal Democratic Party.[16] Japan can get away with such policies because the United States wants to keep it as a secure staging area for the projection of military power in Asia.

What is to be done? Were awareness of an impending crisis of empire to rise among American citizens and their leaders, then it would be fairly obvious what first steps at least should be taken: adjust to and support the emergence of China on the global stage; establish diplomatic relations with North Korea and withdraw ground forces from the Korean peninsula; pay the United States' dues to the United Nations; support global economic diversity rather than globalization; extricate ourselves from our trade-for-military-bases deals with rich East Asian countries, even if they do not want to end them; reemphasize the "defense" in the Department of Defense and make its name fit its mission; unilaterally reduce our stockpile of nuclear warheads to a deterrent level and declare a no-first-use policy; sign and ratify the treaty banning land mines; and sign and ratify the treaty establishing an international criminal court.

More generally, the United States should seek to lead through diplomacy and example rather than through military force and economic bullying. Such an agenda is neither unrealistic nor revolutionary. It is appropriate for a post–Cold War world and for a United States that puts the welfare of its citizens ahead of the pretensions of its imperialists. Many U.S. leaders seem to have convinced themselves that if so much as one overseas American base is closed or one small country is allowed to manage its own economy, the world will collapse. They might better ponder the creativity and growth that would be unleashed if only the United States would relax its suffocating embrace. They should also understand that their efforts to maintain imperial hegemony inevitably generate multiple forms of blowback. Although it is impossible to say when this game will end, there is little doubt about how it will end.

World politics in the twenty-first century will in all likelihood be driven primarily by blowback from the second half of the twentieth century—that is, from the unintended consequences of the Cold War and the crucial American decision to maintain a Cold War posture in a post–Cold War world. U.S. administrations did what they thought they had to do in the Cold War years. History will record that in some places they did exemplary things; in other places, particularly in East Asia but also in Central America, they behaved no better than the Communist bureaucrats of their superpower competitor. The United States likes to think of itself as the winner of the Cold War. In all probability, to those looking back a century hence, neither side will appear to have won, particularly if the United States maintains its present imperial course.

FURTHER READING

After a lifetime spent writing academic books, I have tried to keep the notes in this one to a minimum in the hope of offering the nonexpert a provocative rather than a pedantic experience. Quotations are cited in the notes, but I believe it might be more useful with regard to general references to offer an annotated list of books, articles, and Internet sites that strike me as particularly helpful and relevant for further reading. These I have grouped under subject headings.

Arms Sales

Greider, William. *Fortress America: The American Military and the Consequences of Peace*. New York: Public Affairs, 1998.

A short but powerful introduction to the economic implications of America's massive military apparatus and the interests of the arms industry.

Shear, Jeff. *The Keys to the Kingdom: The FS-X Deal and the Selling of America's Future to Japan*. New York: Doubleday, 1994.

A brilliant exposé of "the little state department in the Pentagon" and how and why it transferred the technology of America's best fighter aircraft to Japan and got nothing in return.

Tirman, John. *Spoils of War: The Human Cost of America's Arms Trade*. New York: Free Press, 1997.

If you read no other book on America's arms trade, read this one. Tirman's treatment of the U.S. stake in Turkey's "white genocide" against the Kurds is the best available.

Aspects of American Imperialism

Arrighi, Giovanni. *The Long Twentieth Century*. London: Verso, 1994. Paperbound.

A masterful treatment of the transfer of hegemony from Britain to the United States. Brilliant on the "dialectic of market and plan" as the leitmotif of the twentieth century.

Aron, Raymond. *The Imperial Republic: The United States and the World, 1945–1973*. Englewood Cliffs, N.J.: Prentice-Hall, 1974.

A classic defense of American Cold War policy in Europe by an independent French intellectual. Aron gets it right about Europe but has not a clue to American behavior in postwar East Asia.

Cumings, Bruce. *Parallax Visions: Making Sense of American–East Asian Relations at the End of the Century*. Durham, N.C.: Duke University Press, 1999.

Important essays by the country's leading historian of modern Korea. Cumings's chapters on North Korea's nuclear program, "area studies" during and after the Cold War, and American hegemony in East Asia are indispensable.

Engelhardt, Tom. *The End of Victory Culture: Cold War America and the Disillusioning of a Generation*. New York: Basic Books, 1995. Paperbound.

The best guide to the ideology of American "good intentions" in the world, regardless of costs, and what happened to this ideology after the Vietnam War.

Greene, Graham. *The Quiet American*. New York: Bantam Books, 1957. Paperbound.

Greene is unsurpassed on Americans as imperialists, "impregnably armoured by . . . good intentions and . . . ignorance."

Hatcher, Patrick Lloyd. *The Suicide of an Elite: American Internationalists and Vietnam*. Stanford: Stanford University Press, 1990.

An insider discusses how the loss of the war in Vietnam was not an accident or the result of a conspiracy but the normal workings of the Cold War national security apparatus.

Lowen, Rebecca S. *Creating the Cold War University: The Transformation of Stanford*. Berkeley: University of California Press, 1997.

Why President Eisenhower's epithet "the military-industrial complex" must be amended to "the military-industrial-university" complex and the blowback from lost intellectual integrity that awaits American institutions of higher learning.

China

Cohen, Warren I. *America's Response to China: A History of Sino-American Relations*. New York: Columbia University Press, 1990. Paperbound.

The best short history of America's relations with China from the Opium War to the present.

http://www.huaren.org/

The Web site of Huaren, an indispensable source of information on overseas Chinese and a compilation of worldwide articles on attacks against people of Chinese ancestry.

Li, Cheng. *Rediscovering China: Dynamics and Dilemmas of Reform.* Lanham, Md.: Rowman & Littlefield, 1997. Paperbound.

The most insightful analysis available, put in personal terms, of the meaning of "reform" in China and why it is anything but threatening to the United States.

Mann, James. *About Face: A History of America's Curious Relationship with China, from Nixon to Clinton.* New York: Knopf, 1999.

A *Los Angeles Times* former Beijing correspondent offers new information and insights into official American thinking on China, from Nixon and Kissinger through the Tiananmen repression and down to Clinton's inconsistent efforts.

McBeath, Gerald A. *Wealth and Freedom: Taiwan's New Political Economy.* Aldershot, England: Ashgate, 1998.

Comprehensive analysis of Taiwan today, including its state-owned enterprises, democracy, and foreign policy after the loss in 1971 of its seat in the United Nations.

Nathan, Andrew J., and Robert S. Ross. *The Great Wall and the Empty Fortress: China's Search for Security.* New York: W. W. Norton, 1997.

An analysis by two writers who have studied China about why it is not a threat to other countries but often appears to be.

Economic Meltdown and How to Analyze It

The Asian Crisis. Special issue of *Cambridge Journal of Economics*, vol. 22, no. 6 (November 1998).

A collection of essays on the causes and consequences of the "globalization crisis" that started in East Asia in 1997. Not the usual Washington consensus.

Fingleton, Eamonn. *In Praise of Hard Industries: Why Manufacturing, Not the Information Economy, Is the Key to Future Prosperity.* Boston: Houghton Mifflin, 1999.

A seasoned observer of the Japanese economy explains why it is not in the deep trouble that American theorists and triumphalists say it is.

Gray, John. *False Dawn: The Delusions of Global Capitalism.* New York: New Press, 1999.

A historian demonstrates that global, unregulated markets are inherently unstable. America's experiment in imperial laissez-faire was the geopolitical expression of a Wall Street bubble.

Greider, William. *One World, Ready or Not: The Manic Logic of Global Capitalism.* New York: Simon & Schuster, 1997.

This is the primer for all who want to understand global capitalism and why it is coming unglued at the end of the twentieth century. Mandatory reading.

Longworth, Richard C. *Global Squeeze: The Coming Crisis for First-World Nations*. Chicago: Contemporary Books, 1998.

A veteran economics correspondent points out the many ways in which globalization could go wrong.

Weiss, Linda. *The Myth of the Powerless State*. Ithaca: Cornell University Press, 1998. Paperbound.

A powerful political rejoinder to American economic ideology. Includes chapters on economic growth in postwar Germany and on the limits of globalization.

Woo-Cumings, Meredith, ed. *The Developmental State*. Ithaca: Cornell University Press, 1999. Paperbound.

The most thorough investigation of the state-guided capitalist systems that were the vehicles for the enrichment of East Asia.

Illegal Activities of the C.I.A. and Other American Police and Intelligence Agencies

Brodeur, Paul. *Secrets: A Writer in the Cold War*. Boston and London: Faber & Faber, 1997.

Essays by a former staff writer for the *New Yorker*, focusing on environmental hazards but also on the roles of the C.I.A., the F.B.I., and the State Department in supporting capitalism over communism and in other unauthorized activities during the Cold War.

Cockburn, Alexander, and Jeffrey St. Clair. *Whiteout: The CIA, Drugs and the Press*. London: Verso, 1998.

The cover-up of the C.I.A.'s support for the Nicaraguan Contras through drug sales in the United States.

MacKenzie, Angus. *Secrets: The CIA's War at Home*. Berkeley: University of California Press, 1997.

A posthumously published classic study of numerous U.S. government campaigns to suppress controversial ideas and information within the United States.

Schlesinger, Stephen, and Stephen Kinzer. *Bitter Fruit: The Story of the American Coup in Guatemala*. Expanded ed. Cambridge, Mass.: Harvard University Press, 1999. Paperbound.

The best book on America's repression of a poor Central American country. The 1999 edition includes a foreword by Richard Nuccio, the former State Department official who sacrificed his career to help expose the cover-up of the C.I.A.'s involvement in the murder of an American citizen in Guatemala.

Japan

Arase, David. *Buying Power: The Political Economy of Japan's Foreign Aid*. Boulder, Colo.: Lynne Rienner, 1995.

This is the best analysis of Japan's foreign policy and how it uses its wealth to achieve its objectives.

Dower, John. *Embracing Defeat: Japan in the Wake of World War II*. New York: W. W. Norton, 1999.

The single most important book on the critical years of the Allied occupation, when the United States forged and Japan accepted its postwar status as America's most valuable satellite.

Hall, Ivan P. *Cartels of the Mind: Japan's Intellectual Closed Shop*. New York: W. W. Norton, 1998.

The most serious study by a genuine "Japan hand" of why the assumptions of political and economic convergence between Japan and the United States are nonsense. A graceful, well-written statement of what a foreigner must know if he or she plans to deal with Japan.

http://www.jpri.org/

Web site of the Japan Policy Research Institute. Contains over a hundred research reports, including papers on Japan's discrimination against foreigners teaching in its universities, the problems of Okinawa, and Japan's industrial policies, among many different subjects.

McVeigh, Brian J. *The Nature of the Japanese State: Rationality and Rituality*. London: Routledge, 1998.

An anthropologist analyzes the bureaucratization of Japanese life and offers an exciting essay on why Japanese politics will never resemble American politics.

Schaller, Michael. *Altered States: The United States and Japan Since the Occupation*. New York: Oxford University Press, 1997.

Diplomatic history at its best by a seasoned hand. Includes details on the decisions by Presidents Eisenhower, Kennedy, and Johnson to give secret financial help to Japan's conservative politicians.

Smith, Patrick. *Japan: A Reinterpretation*. New York: Vintage Books, 1998. Paperbound.

For readers looking for an introduction to Japan, this is the best there is. Smith takes Japanese culture seriously. A beautifully written book.

Korea

Amsden, Alice. *Asia's Next Giant: South Korea and Late Industrialization*. New York: Oxford University Press, 1989.

The classic study of how South Korea got rich and the crisis it caused for orthodox American economic theory.

Bandow, Doug. *Tripwire: Korea and U.S. Foreign Policy in a Changed World.* Washington, D.C.: Cato Institute, 1996.
A prescient analysis by a former special assistant to President Reagan on why we have stayed too long in Korea and what we ought to do about it.

Cumings, Bruce. *The Origins of the Korean War.* 2 vols. Princeton: Princeton University Press, 1981, 1990.
A tour de force on the era in Korean history that Americans know nothing about and would prefer to ignore: 1945 to 1950. Cumings's meticulous research has altered the "received wisdom" on the Korean War.

Hart-Landsberg, Martin. *Korea: Division, Reunification, and U.S. Foreign Policy.* New York: Monthly Review Press, 1998. Paperbound.
An excellent, evenhanded account of why Korea remains divided. Includes chapters on the relevance of the German experience of reunification to Korea.

http://www.kimsoft.com/korea.htm
The indispensable Web site for materials on the role of the United States in Korea, including archives on the Cheju uprising of 1948 and Tim Shorrock's U.S. government documents on the Kwangju massacre, which he obtained through the Freedom of Information Act.

Lee, Jae-eui. *Kwangju Diary: Beyond Death, Beyond the Darkness of the Age.* Los Angeles: UCLA Asian Pacific Monograph Series, 1999.
A translation into English of the most important Korean book on the Kwangju massacre, by a participant who was taken prisoner and tortured by the Republic of Korea army. With additional essays by Bruce Cumings and Tim Shorrock.

Oberdorfer, Don. *The Two Koreas: A Contemporary History.* Reading, Mass.: Addison-Wesley, 1997.
A seasoned *Washington Post* journalist on the two Koreas. Oberdorfer is outstanding on the 1994 crisis over North Korean nuclear experiments.

Shapiro, Michael. *The Shadow in the Sun.* New York: Atlantic Monthly Press, 1990.
Powerful observations of South Korea in the last years of Chun Doo-hwan, including details on the legacy of the Kwangju massacre.

Okinawa

Field, Norma. *In the Realm of a Dying Emperor.* New York: Pantheon Books, 1991.
Field's chapter on Shoichi Chibana, pp. 33–104, is the best introduction in English to the injustices inflicted on Okinawa by Japan and the United States.

Johnson, Chalmers, ed. *Okinawa: Cold War Island*. Cardiff, Calif.: Japan Policy Research Institute, 1999.

A collection of essays on Okinawa by such authorities as Masahide Ota, Kozy Amemiya, Koji Taira, Steve Rabson, Michael Millard, Patrick Smith, Carolyn Bowen Francis, Shunji Taoka, Masayuki Sasaki, and Gavan McCormack. It can be acquired on-line from http://www.nmjc.org/okinawa_cold_war_island.html.

Ota, Masahide. "The U.S. Occupation of Okinawa and Postwar Reforms in Japan Proper," in Robert E. Ward and Yoshikazu Sakamoto, eds., *Democratizing Japan: The Allied Occupation*. Honolulu: University of Hawaii Press, 1987, pp. 284–305.

An authoritative treatment of Okinawa under American rule by the scholar who became governor of Okinawa Prefecture from 1990 to 1998.

Yahara, Colonel Hiromichi. *The Battle for Okinawa*. New York: Wiley, 1995. Introduction and commentary by Frank B. Gibney.

Yahara was the highest-ranking Japanese officer to survive the Battle of Okinawa; this is the battle seen from the Japanese side. Gibney, who as a combat translator debriefed Yahara, reprints his original prisoner-of-war interrogation reports.

Overseas American Military Bases and Their Problems

Moon, Katharine H. S. *Sex Among Allies: Military Prostitution in U.S.-Korea Relations*. New York: Columbia University Press, 1997. Paperbound.

A brilliant doctoral dissertation on how the American and South Korean governments collaborate to provide prostitutes for the 37,000 American troops based in South Korea.

Sturdevant, Saundra Pollock, and Brenda Stoltzfus. *Let the Good Times Roll: Prostitution and the U.S. Military in Asia*. New York: New Press, 1992. Paperbound.

The standard work on the subject, it is extensively illustrated with photographs by the authors. Included are essays by Walden Bello, Bruce Cumings, and Cynthia Enloe.

NOTES

Prologue: A Spear-carrier for Empire

1. Stanford University Press, 1962.
2. See Chalmers Johnson, "Civilian Loyalties and Guerrilla Conflict," *World Politics* 14.4 (July 1962), pp. 646–61.
3. "Lin Piao's Army and Its Role in Chinese Society," Parts I and II, *Current Scene* (American Consulate General, Hong Kong) 4.13 and 4.14 (July 1 and 15, 1966).

1: Blowback

1. "Some Aid Canceled for Gondola Deaths," *Los Angeles Times*, May 15, 1999.
2. Department of Defense, "U.S. Military Installations" (updated to July 17, 1998), *DefenseLINK*, on-line at http://www.defenselink.mil/pubs/installations/foreignsummary.htm; and John Lindsay-Poland and Nick Morgan, "Overseas Military Bases and Environment," *Foreign Policy in Focus* 3.15 (June 1998), on-line at http://www.foreignpolicy-infocus.org/briefs/vol13/v3n15mil.html. According to one report, when the Soviet Union collapsed in 1991, the United States had 375 military bases scattered around the globe staffed by more than a half million personnel. Joel Brinkley, "U.S. Looking for a New Path as Superpower Conflict Ends," *New York Times*, February 2, 1992.
3. Charles Krauthammer, "What Caused Our Economic Boom?" *San Diego Union-Tribune*, January 5, 1998.
4. For documentary evidence, including Oliver North's notebooks, see "The Contras, Cocaine, and Covert Operations," *National Security Archive*

Electronic Briefing Book, no. 2, on-line at http://www.seas.gwu.edu/nsarchive. Also see James Risen, "C.I.A. Said to Ignore Charges of Contra Drug Dealing in '80's," *New York Times*, October 10, 1998.

5. Quoted in Ivan Eland, "Protecting the Homeland: The Best Defense Is to Give No Offense," *Policy Analysis* (Cato Institute), no. 306 (May 5, 1998), p. 3.

6. Tim Weiner, "U.S. Spied on Iraq Under U.N. Cover, Officials Now Say," *New York Times*, January 7, 1999; Philip Shenon, "C.I.A. Was with U.N. in Iraq for Years, Ex-Inspector Says," February 23, 1999; and Seymour M. Hersh, "Saddam's Best Friend," *New Yorker*, April 5, 1999.

7. Tim Weiner and James Risen, "Decision to Strike Factory in Sudan Based on Surmise," *New York Times*, September 21, 1998; and Seymour M. Hersh, "The Missiles of August," *New Yorker*, October 12, 1998.

8. Mireya Navarro, "Guatemala Study Accuses the Army and Cites U.S. Role," *New York Times*, February 26, 1999; Larry Rohter, "Searing Indictment," *New York Times*, February 27, 1999; Michael Shifter, "Can Genocide End in Forgiveness?" *Los Angeles Times*, March 7, 1999; "Coming Clean on Guatemala," editorial, *Los Angeles Times*, March 10, 1999; and Michael Stetz, "Clinton's Words on Guatemala Called 'Too Little, Too Late,'" *San Diego Union-Tribune*, March 16, 1999.

9. José Pertierra, "For Guatemala, Words Are Not Enough," *San Diego Union-Tribune*, March 5, 1999.

10. John M. Broder, "Clinton Offers His Apologies to Guatemala," *New York Times*, March 11, 1999. Also see Broder, "Clinton Visit in Honduras Dramatizes New Attitude," *New York Times*, March 10, 1999; and Francisco Goldman, "Murder Comes for the Bishop," *New Yorker*, March 15, 1999.

11. Peter W. Galbraith, "How the Turks Helped Their Enemies," *New York Times*, February 20, 1999.

12. John Tirman, *Spoils of War: The Human Cost of America's Arms Trade* (New York: Free Press, 1997), p. 236.

13. John Diamond, "CIA Thwarts Terrorists with 'Disruption'; It's Prevention by Proxy," *San Diego Union-Tribune*, March 5, 1999; and Tim Weiner, "U.S. Helped Turkey Find and Capture Kurd Rebel," *New York Times*, February 20, 1999.

14. Jon Lee Anderson, "The Dictator," *New Yorker*, October 19, 1998; Peter Kronbluth, "Chile and the United States: Declassified Documents Relating to the Military Coup," *National Security Archive Electronic Briefing Book*, no. 8, on-line at http://www.seas.gwu.edu/nsarchive; and Philip Shenon, "U.S. Releases Files on Abuses in Pinochet Era," *New York Times*, July 1, 1999.

15. Michael Ratner, "The Pinochet Precedent," *Progressive Response* 3.3 (January 28, 1999).

16. Milovan Djilas, *Conversations with Stalin* (London: Rupert Hart-Davis, 1962), p. 105.

17. Tim Golden, "C.I.A. Says It Knew of Honduran Abuses," *New York Times*, October 24, 1998. See also James Risen, "C.I.A. Said to Ignore Charges of Contra Drug Dealing in '80's," *New York Times*, October 10, 1998; National Security Archive, "Secret CIA Report Admits 'Honduran Military Committed Hundreds of Human Rights Abuses' and 'Inaccurate' Reporting to Congress," on-line at www.seas.gwu.edu/nsarchive; and Fairness & Accuracy in Reporting, "Snow Job: The Establishment's Papers Do Damage Control for the CIA," *Extra!* January–February 1997, on-line at http://www.fair.org/extra/9701/contra-crack.html.

18. Barbara Conry, "The Futility of U.S. Intervention in Regional Conflicts," *Policy Analysis* (Cato Institute), no. 209 (May 19, 1994), p. 7. Also see Barbara Conry, "U.S. 'Global Leadership': A Euphemism for World Policeman," *Policy Analysis*, no. 267, February 5, 1997.

19. Ronald Steel, *Pax Americana* (New York: Viking, 1967), p. 13.

20. Paul Kennedy, *The Rise and Fall of the Great Powers: Economic Change and Military Conflict from 1500 to 2000* (London: Unwin Hyman, 1988), pp. 514–15.

21. Giovanni Arrighi and Beverly Silver, *Chaos and Governance in the Modern World System* (Minneapolis: University of Minnesota Press, 1999), pp. 288–89.

2: Okinawa: Asia's Last Colony

1. *Los Angeles Times*, December 28, 1995.

2. Robert Burns, Associated Press, *San Diego Union-Tribune*, November 18, 1995.

3. Katharine H. S. Moon, *Sex Among Allies: Military Prostitution in U.S.-Korea Relations* (New York: Columbia University Press, 1997), p. 7.

4. *New York Times*, November 2, 1995.

5. Letter to the *San Diego Union-Tribune*, July 20, 1996.

6. *Los Angeles Times*, December 2, 1996.

7. "Proposal for a New Okinawa—the Voice of Women," *Ryukyuanist* (The International Society for Ryukyuan Studies), Newsletter no. 37, Summer 1997, p. 2.

8. *New York Times*, editorial, October 29, 1995.

9. *Time*, November 29, 1949; and Nicholas E. Sarantakes, "Keystone: The American Occupation of Okinawa and U.S.-Japanese Relations, 1945–1972," unpublished Ph.D. dissertation, University of Southern California.

10. *Japan Times*, December 8, 1995.

11. *Nikkei Weekly*, October 9, 1995.

12. The full report by Russell Carollo, Jeff Nesmith, and Carol Hernandez is

available from Investigative Reporters and Editors, Inc., 138 Neff Annex, Missouri School of Journalism, Columbia, MO 65211; $19.65, 64 pp.

13. *Nation*, July 1, 1996.

14. *Los Angeles Times*, October 8, 1995.

15. *Newsweek*, October 14, 1996.

16. *Okinawa Times*, March 9, 1996.

17. *Japan Times*, April 21, 1996.

18. *Newsweek*, October 14, 1996.

19. *Washington Post*, December 8, 1995.

20. *Okinawa Times*, April 27, 1998.

21. General Accounting Office, *Overseas Presence: Issues Involved in Reducing the Impact of the U.S. Military Presence on Okinawa: Report to the Honorable Duncan Hunter, House of Representatives* (Washington, D.C.: Government Printing Office, March 1998), p. 47.

22. See, e.g., Bill Mesler, "Pentagon Poison: The Great Radioactive Ammo Cover-up," *Nation*, May 26, 1997.

23. Bill Gertz, "U.S. Slow to Inform Japan of Accident; Hundreds of Radioactive Bullets Were Fired in Training Exercise Near Okinawa," *Washington Times*, February 10, 1997.

24. *Mainichi Shimbun*, June 25, 1997.

25. "The Okinawan Charade," Japan Policy Research Institute *Working Paper*, no. 28, January 1997.

26. *Nikkei Weekly*, May 5, 1997.

27. *Ryukyu Shimpo*, December 22, 1995, evening edition.

28. Kozy K. Amemiya, "The Bolivian Connection: U.S. Bases and Okinawan Emigration," Japan Policy Research Institute *Working Paper*, no. 25, October 1996; *Asia Times*, October 21, 22, 1996.

29. *Los Angeles Times*, October 26, 1995.

30. *Aera* (Tokyo), October 9, 1995; *Asahi Evening News*, May 6, 1997; *Asahi Shimbun*, May 17, 1997; *Japan Press Weekly*, no. 2040, May 24, 1997, p. 7; and *Nikkei Weekly*, August 11, 1997.

31. *Pacific Stars and Stripes*, July 23, 1998.

32. *Asahi Evening News*, June 28, 1998.

33. *New York Times*, April 2, 1994.

34. Morihiro Hosokawa, "Are U.S. Troops in Japan Needed?" *Foreign Affairs* 77.4 (July–August 1998), pp. 2–6.

35. Shunji Taoka, "The Japanese-American Security Treaty Without a U.S. Military Presence," Japan Policy Research Institute *Working Paper*, no. 31, March 1997; and Taoka, "The Way to Save the U.S.-Japan Alliance," *NIRA Review*, Summer 1997, pp. 3–8.

36. *Washington Post*, March 27, 1990.

37. Mary Jordan and Kevin Sullivan, *Washington Post*, March 7, 1996.

38. *Asahi Shimbun*, March 19, 1999.

39. *Asahi Shimbun*, April 18, 1996; see also Morihiro Hosokawa, "A De Facto Treaty Revision," *Japan Times International*, June 1–15, 1999.

40. "Interview with Governor Ota: Japanese Democracy on Trial," *Japan Echo*, Autumn 1996, p. 43 (from *Sekai*, July 1996).

41. Joseph S. Nye Jr., "The Case for Deep Engagement," *Foreign Affairs* 74.4 (July–August 1995), pp. 90–102.

42. *Washington Post*, December 8, 1995.

43. Department of Defense, *United States Security Strategy for the East Asia–Pacific Region* (Washington, D.C.: Department of Defense, Office of International Security Affairs, February 1995), pp. 23–24.

44. Reuters, Tokyo, March 24, 1997.

45. Reuters, Washington, July 9, 1998.

46. *Japan Times*, July 25, 1998.

47. *Defense Monitor* 19.6 (1990), p. 3.

48. Camp Foster USO, *Exploring Okinawa Travel Guide*, 4th ed. (Naha: Barclay Publishing, 1996), pp. 62, 64, 68.

3: Stealth Imperialism

1. Rudolph J. Rummel, *Death by Government* (New Brunswick, N.J.: Transaction Books, 1994).

2. Michael P. Scharf, "Results of the Rome Conference for an International Criminal Court," *American Society of International Law Insight*, August 1998, on-line at http://www.asil.org/insigh23.htm.

3. *New York Times*, October 11, 1997, and December 3, 1997.

4. See the report in the mainstream Korean newspaper *Chosun Ilbo*, November 12, 1997.

5. "Australia a Key Player in Global Landmine Removal," *Australia Report*, June 1998, p. 1.

6. *New York Times*, December 3, 1997, and October 11, 1997.

7. *Washington Post*, July 12, 1998.

8. See Dana Priest, "Free of Oversight, U.S. Military Trains Foreign Troops," *Washington Post*, July 12, 1998; Douglas Farah, "A Tutor to Every Army in Latin America," *Washington Post*, July 13, 1998; Dana Priest, "Special Forces Training Review Sought," *Washington Post*, July 15, 1998; Mary McGrory, "In Joint Training, a Singular Failure," *Washington Post*, July 26, 1998; and Lee Siew Hua, "U.S. to Review Training of Foreign Troops," *Singapore Straits Times*, August 13, 1998.

9. *Washington Post*, July 12, 1998.

10. *New York Times*, July 20, 1998.

11. *Nation*, June 15–22, 1998. See also Tim Weiner, "A Tale of Torture from an Indonesian Dissident," *New York Times*, May 8, 1998.

12. *New York Times*, November 4, 1998.

13. *New York Times*, August 1, 1998. See also David E. Sanger, "U.S. Backs Indonesian Loans but Cancels Military Exercise," *New York Times*, May 9, 1998.

14. "Indonesian Special Ops Force Praised for Protecting National Security," *Special Warfare* 10.2, Spring 1997. (This journal was formerly available on-line from http://leav-www.army.mil/fmso/lic/sfindex2.htm, but the army seems to have pulled it from the Internet.)

15. For details, see Allan Nairn's reports in the *Nation*, March 30, April 6, June 8, and June 15, 1998. On March 18, 1998, the Indonesian military expelled Nairn from the country, but he continued to file his articles from Singapore.

16. *Business Week*, Asia ed., August 3, 1998. See also David Lamb, "6 Students in Jakarta Protest Killed by Police," *Los Angeles Times*, May 13, 1998.

17. *New Republic*, July 13, 1998.

18. George Hicks, "Indonesian Mayhem and American Imperialism," unpublished manuscript dated July 26, 1998, supplied by Hicks to the author.

19. *Jakarta Post*, reprinted in the *Straits Times*, July 20, 1998.

20. *Asiaweek*, July 24, 1998, p. 30.

21. William McGurn, in *Asian Wall Street Journal*, July 10–11, 1998.

22. *Nation*, June 15–22, 1998.

23. *Washington Post*, July 25, 1998.

24. Philip Shenon (*New York Times*), "U.S. Delegation Puts Emphasis on Human Rights in Indonesia," *San Diego Union-Tribune*, August 2, 1998.

25. *International Herald Tribune*, July 21, 1998.

26. Ken Silverstein, "Privatizing War, How Affairs of State Are Outsourced to Corporations Beyond Public Control," *Nation*, July 28–August 4, 1997.

27. See the Arms Control and Disarmament's Web site at http://www.acda.gov/factshee/conwpn/wmeatfs.htm.

28. Center for Defense Information, *Weekly Defense Monitor* 2:24 (June 18, 1998), on-line at http://www.cdi.org/weekly/1998/issue24/index.html#1.

29. For details, see the SIPRI Web site at http://www.sipri.se.

30. Press release on Presidential Decision Directive (PDD) 34 of February 17, 1995.

31. Quoted by Lora Lumpe in the *Nonviolent Activist*, May–June 1995.

32. Quoted in "Clinton's Conventional Arms Export Policy: So Little Change," *Arms Control Today*, May 1995, available from the Federation of American Scientists at http://www.fas.org/asmp/library/articles/actmay95.html.

33. For details on these sales to Taiwan, see Associated Press, August 27, 1998.

34. Oscar Arias, "Stopping America's Most Lethal Export," *New York Times*, June 23, 1999.

35. Mary McGrory, in the *Washington Post*, July 26, 1998.

36. *Los Angeles Times*, June 28, 1996.

37. Jimmy Carter, "Have We Forgotten the Path to Peace?" *New York Times*, May 27, 1999.

4: South Korea: Legacy of the Cold War

1. Raymond Aron, "The Impact of Marxism in the Twentieth Century," in Milorad M. Drachkovitch, ed., *Marxism in the Modern World* (Stanford: Stanford University Press, 1965), p. 17.

2. The main sources concerning the Cheju uprising are cataloged on-line on the Korea Web Weekly at http://www.kimsoft.com/1997/cheju.htm. The most important of these are a) the memoirs of Gen. Kim Ik-ruhl, the commander of the 9th Regiment, during the early phase of the Cheju massacre; b) Wolcott Wheeler, "The 1948 Cheju-do Civil War"; c) Huh Sang-soo, "On Properly Assessing the Cheju April 3rd Popular Uprising"; d) Yang Han-kwon, "The Truth About the Cheju April 3rd Insurrection"; e) Oh Gun-sook, "Violation of Women's Rights and the Cheju April 3rd Massacre"; f) Kang Chung-ku, professor of sociology, Dong-Gook University, "The US Korea Policy, Division of Korea, and the April 3rd Insurrection"; and g) James West, "Cheju April 3rd Martial Law: Was It Legal?" Also see Bruce Cumings (history, University of Chicago), "The Question of American Responsibility for the Suppression of the Cheju-do Uprising," paper presented at the Fiftieth Anniversary Conference of the Cheju Rebellion, Tokyo, March 14, 1998, and available on-line at http://www.kimsoft.com/1997/cheju98.htm. Muccio is quoted by Cumings.

3. *Los Angeles Times*, April 16, 1996; and Lee Wha-rang, August 14, 1998, at http://www.kimsoft.com/1997/nkclinto.htm.

4. *Korea Times*, May 13, 1998.

5. United Nations General Assembly, *Report of the Special Committee on the Problem of Hungary* (New York: United Nations, 1957), p. 6.

6. *Ibid.*, p. 25.

7. *Ibid.*, p. 10.

8. *London Review of Books*, October 17, 1996.

9. *Jungang Ilbo*, September 27, 1997.

10. See *Nucleonics Week*, January 7, 1998.

11. Shorrock's analyses have been published in Korean and English primarily on the Internet. See http://www.kimsoft.com/korea/kwangju3.htm and http://www.kimsoft.com/korea/shorrok.htm. In February 1997 the Seoul High Court ordered these documents released to the Korean public despite protests from the U.S. government. See *Chosun Ilbo*, February 21, 1997. See

also Tim Shorrock, "U.S. Knew of South Korea Crackdown," *Journal of Commerce,* February 27, 1996; and "Debacle in Kwangju," *Nation,* December 9, 1996.

12. See http://www.kimsoft.com/korea/kwangju3.htm.

13. For an authoritative account, see Bruce Cumings, *Korea's Place in the Sun* (New York: W. W. Norton, 1997), p. 377.

14. Donald N. Clark, "U.S. Role in Kwangju and Beyond," *Los Angeles Times,* August 29, 1996.

15. These details are from Sam Jameson, former *Los Angeles Times* bureau chief in Tokyo and Seoul, in an unpublished paper entitled "Reflections on Kwangju," April 7, 1997.

16. *New York Times,* January 21, 1998.

17. *Asian Wall Street Journal,* October 8, 1996.

18. Tim Shorrock, "Debacle in Kwangju," *Nation,* December 9, 1996.

5: North Korea: Endgame of the Cold War

1. *U.S. News & World Report,* July 25, 1994.

2. Daniel Burstein, *Privileged Information* 1.3 (March 1995).

3. Associated Press, September 1, 1994.

4. *Tokyo Insideline,* no. 34 (November 30, 1994).

5. Agence France-Press, March 5, 1999.

6. On the seven hundred thousand Koreans in Japan, see George Hicks, *Japan's Hidden Apartheid: The Korean Minority and the Japanese* (Aldershot, England: Ashgate, 1998).

7. *Bungei Shunju* staff, eds., "Seifu naibu bunsho o nyushu, Kita Chosen wa ko ugoku" (Internal Government Document: How North Korea Will Act), *Bungei Shunju,* July 1994.

8. Bruce Cumings, *Korea's Place in the Sun* (New York: W. W. Norton, 1997), p. 476.

9. *Aviation Week and Space Technology,* September 14, 1998, p. 58f, and September 21, 1998, pp. 30–31.

10. "Successful Launch of First Satellite in DPRK [Democratic People's Republic of Korea]," http://fas.org/news/dprk/1998/980904-kcna.htm.

11. Gilman's statement at hearings of the House International Relations Committee, February 25, 1999; Tenet, *New York Times,* February 3, 1999. See also "Opening Statement from Benjamin A. Gilman, Chairman of the U.S. House of Representatives International Relations Committee, at Hearings Regarding U.S. Policy Toward the Democratic People's Republic of Korea," Northeast Asia Peace and Security "Special Report," March 24, 1999, from NAPSNet@nautilus.org.

12. *Washington Post*, August 27, 1997.

13. *New York Times*, August 28, 1997.

14. "Special State Department Briefing," U.S. Information Agency Transcript, August 26, 1997.

15. *Newsweek*, September 8, 1997.

16. *New York Times*, August 17, 1998.

17. Selig S. Harrison, "The Korean Showdown That Shouldn't Happen," *Washington Post*, November 22, 1998; *Executive Intelligence Review*, January 1, 1999, p. 46. Evidence of unauthorized disclosure of highly classified intelligence information for political purposes can be found in Bill Gertz, *Betrayal: How the Clinton Administration Undermined American Security* (Washington, D.C.: Regnery Publishing, 1999). Gertz, an avowed enemy of President Clinton, is the defense reporter for the *Washington Times*, one of the primary vehicles for disseminating leaked C.I.A. and D.I.A. documents. This book includes photocopies of highly classified documents published without U.S. government permission (pp. 219–84).

18. C. Kenneth Quinones, "North Korea's 'New' Nuclear Site—Fact or Fiction?" Northeast Asia Peace and Security Network, Special Report, Policy Forum On-Line, no. 21, October 5, 1998, available from NAPSNet@nautilus.org or on-line at http://www.nautilus.org/napsnet/fora/21A_Quinones.html.

19. *Pacific Stars and Stripes*, February 27, 1999.

20. Philip Shenon, "Suspected North Korean Atom Site Is Empty, U.S. Finds," *New York Times*, May 28, 1999.

6: China: The State of the Revolution

1. "Transcript: President Clinton's Remarks at Beijing University," June 29, 1998, at http://www.usconsulate.org.hk/uscn/wh/1998/0629e.htm.

2. *The New York Review of Books*, August 8, 1996.

3. Andrew C. Janos, "Modernization or Militarization: Germany and Russia as Great Powers," *German Politics and Society* 14.1 (Spring 1996); "What Was Communism? A Retrospective in Comparative Analysis," *Communist and Post-Communist Studies* 29.1 (March 1996).

4. See Meredith Woo-Cumings, ed., *The Developmental State* (Ithaca: Cornell University Press, 1999).

5. *Los Angeles Times*, May 28, 1994.

6. See Chalmers Johnson, "Political Institutions and Economic Performance: The Government-Business Relationship in Japan, South Korea, and Taiwan," in Frederic C. Deyo, ed., *The Political Economy of the New Asian Industrialism* (Ithaca: Cornell University Press, 1987), pp. 136–64.

7. Gerard D. Postiglione and Grace L. Mak, eds., *Asian Higher Education: An*

International Handbook and Reference Guide (Westport, Conn.: Greenwood, 1997), p. 41 (on China) and p. 349 (on Taiwan).

8. For a good description of this aspect of Taiwan's political economy, see Karl J. Fields, "KMT, Inc.: Party Capitalism in a Developmental State," Japan Policy Research Institute *Working Paper*, no. 47, June 1998.

7: China: Foreign Policy, Human Rights, and Trade

1. *Los Angeles Times*, February 11, 1999.
2. *Los Angeles Times*, February 12, 1999.
3. *Free China Journal*, March 5, 1999, p. 2.
4. *New York Times*, March 24, 1999.
5. See "The Rumsfeld Report: How Soon Might the U.S. Homeland Face a Threat from Ballistic Missile Proliferation?" Proliferation Roundtable at the Carnegie Endowment for International Peace, September 17, 1998, on-line at http://www.ceip.org/programs/npp/rumsfeld.htm.
6. *Los Angeles Times*, March 3, 1999.
7. I am indebted to participants in the Conference on International Issues in the South China Sea, sponsored by the Norwegian Institute of International Affairs, Oslo, September 20, 1995, for many of these points. See also Victor Prescott, "The Spratly Islands," *Quadrant*, October 1995, pp. 58–63.
8. Jim Mann, "CIA Gave Aid to Tibetan Exiles in '60s, Files Show," *Los Angeles Times*, September 15, 1998; Jonathan Mirsky, "The Dalai Lama on Succession and on the CIA," *New York Review of Books*, June 10, 1999. For further details on Tibet's status, see Dawa Norbu, *Red Star over Tibet* (London: Collins, 1974); *Freedom in Exile: The Autobiography of the Dalai Lama* (New York: HarperCollins, 1990); A. Tom Grunfeld, *The Making of Modern Tibet* (Armonk, N.Y.: M. E. Sharpe, 1987); John Kenneth Knaus, *Orphans of the Cold War: America and the Tibetan Struggle for Survival* (New York: Public Affairs, 1999).
9. Rone Tempest, "China Installs Its Pick for Panchen Lama," *Los Angeles Times*, December 9, 1995.
10. Foreword, in Abdul Aziz Said, ed., *Human Rights and World Order* (New Brunswick, N.J.: Transaction Books, 1978), pp. vii–viii.
11. See, e.g., Wendell L. Willkie II, "Why Does MFN Dominate America's China Policy?" *Heritage Lectures*, no. 486, March 29, 1994.
12. Lee Kuan Yew, "America's Model for Social Order Doesn't Work Anymore," *Los Angeles Times*, October 6, 1995.
13. *New York Times*, March 16, 1999.
14. See Christopher Lingle, *Singapore's Authoritarian Capitalism: Asian Values, Free Market Illusions and Political Dependency* (Fairfax, Va.: Locke Institute, 1996), pp. 117–18.

15. *New York Times*, March 16, 1999.
16. "Interview: Dalai Lama," *Los Angeles Times*, May 15, 1994.
17. November 10, 1994.
18. See Greg Mastel, *Trading with the Middle Kingdom* (Washington, D.C.: Economic Strategy Institute, 1995).

8: Japan and the Economics of the American Empire

1. Even though American archives on this period remain secret, the main details have leaked out and are discussed by Michael Schaller in *Altered States: The United States and Japan Since the Occupation* (New York: Oxford University Press, 1997); and Walter LaFeber in *The Clash: U.S.-Japanese Relations Throughout History* (New York: W. W. Norton, 1997).
2. John Hunter Boyle, *Modern Japan: The American Nexus* (Forth Worth, Tex.: Harcourt, Brace, Jovanovich, 1993), p. 352.
3. The best critique of modernization theory applied to Japan is John Dower's hundred-page introduction in Dower, ed., *Origins of the Modern Japanese State: Selected Writings of E. H. Norman* (New York: Pantheon, 1975).
4. *Business Week*, August 7, 1989.
5. *Foreign Service Journal*, December 1989.
6. *Newsweek*, October 9, 1989.
7. *Washington Post*, December 10, 1990.
8. See Chalmers Johnson, *MITI and the Japanese Miracle: The Growth of Industrial Policy, 1925–1975* (Stanford: Stanford University Press, 1982).
9. *New York Times*, August 15, 1993.
10. *Wall Street Journal*, January 8, 1986.
11. *Wall Street Journal*, January 31, 1997.

9: Meltdown

1. Rich Roesler, "Dying for Sex," *Pacific Stars and Stripes*, August 30, 1998.
2. Judith Stein, *Running Steel, Running America: Race, Economic Policy, and the Decline of Liberalism* (Chapel Hill: University of North Carolina Press, 1998), p. 4.
3. William Greider, *One World, Ready or Not: The Manic Logic of Global Capitalism* (New York: Simon & Schuster, 1997), p. 221.
4. Quoted by David Friedman, "How Wall Street's Moral Hubris Condones Social Inequality," *Los Angeles Times*, May 31, 1998. For Oxfam and its policy papers, see its Web site at http://www.oneworld.org/oxfam/index.html.
5. John Ralston Saul, "Paper Games and Monetary Chaos," *New York Times*, October 9, 1992.

6. Peter Hartcher and Andrew Cornell, "Mr. Yen, the Man Who Started the Asian Crisis," *Australian Financial Review Magazine*, July 1999, pp. 34–40. Also see Klaus Engelen, "How Bill Clinton Really Won," *European*, November 14–20, 1996.

7. Ron Bevacqua, "Whither the Japanese Model? The Asian Economic Crisis and the Continuation of Cold War Politics in the Pacific Rim," *Review of International Political Economy* 5.3 (Autumn 1998), pp. 410–23. See also Andrew Z. Szamosszegi, "How Asia Went from Boom to Gloom," *World and I*, May 1998, pp. 52–59.

8. David D. Hale, "The IMF After the Asia Crisis," Zurich Insurance Group (internal paper), February 13, 1998.

9. *San Diego Union-Tribune*, September 20, 1998. See also George Soros, *The Crisis of Global Capitalism: Open Society Endangered* (New York: Public Affairs, 1998).

10. Jagdish Bhagwati, "The Capital Myth: The Difference Between Trade in Widgets and Dollars," *Foreign Affairs* 77.3 (May–June 1998), pp. 7–12.

11. *New York Times*, editorial, November 25, 1997. See also Peter Truell, "An Alchemist Who Turned Gold into Lead," *New York Times*, September 25, 1998; "Crony Capitalism," *Nation*, October 19, 1998; Timothy L. O'Brien and Laura M. Holson, "Hedge Fund's Star Power Lulled Big Financiers into Complacency," *New York Times*, October 23, 1998; Gretchen Morgenson and Michael M. Weinstein, "Two Nobel Economists Get a Lesson in Real Economics," *New York Times*, November 14, 1998; "On Regulating Derivatives," *New York Times*, December 15, 1998; and Leon Levy and Jeff Madrick, "Hedge Fund Mysteries," *New York Review of Books*, December 17, 1998.

12. Martin Mayer, "Bailing Out the Billion-Bettors," *Los Angeles Times*, October 5, 1998.

13. Evelyn Iritani, "Trade Meeting Opens with a Spat," *Los Angeles Times*, November 14, 1998; Mark Landler, "Gore, in Malaysia, Says Its Leaders Suppress Freedom," *New York Times*, November 17, 1998; Bob Drogin, "Gore Gets Scolding from APEC, Business Leaders," *Los Angeles Times*, November 18, 1998; and Tom Plate, "Gore's Inept Criticism of the Malaysian President Has Hurt the U.S. All Over Asia," *Los Angeles Times*, November 24, 1998.

14. Robert Kuttner, "Shock Treatment for Korea Is Playing with Fire," *Boston Globe*, January 4, 1998.

15. Jeffrey Sachs, "The IMF and the Asian Flu," *American Prospect*, March–April 1998, pp. 16–21. Also see Sachs, "The 'Rescuer' Created the Crisis," *Los Angeles Times*, January 18, 1998.

16. David Holley, "Asian Nations Plan to Set Up Money Fund," *Los Angeles Times*, October 2, 1997; Edward A. Gargan, "Asian Nations Affirm I.M.F. as Primary Provider of Aid," *New York Times*, November 20, 1997; and Art

Pine, "Summers a Hot Commodity in Asian Crisis," *Los Angeles Times*, January 16, 1998.

17. David Hale, "Will Indonesia's Stock Market Track Berlin in 1923?" Zurich Insurance Group (internal paper), March 9, 1998.

18. *Los Angeles Times*, February 14, 1998.

19. "Brazil Sacrifices Rain-Forest Funds to Appease IMF on Spending Cuts," *San Diego Union-Tribune*, January 1, 1999. For details on the environmental consequences of the crisis in East Asia, see Deanna Donovan, "Strapped for Cash, Asians Plunder Their Forests and Endanger Their Future," *Analysis from the East-West Center*, no. 39 (April 1999).

20. For Greenspan's remarks, see David E. Sanger, "Greenspan Sees Asian Crisis Moving World to Western Capitalism," *New York Times*, February 13, 1998. For Asian reactions, see Takashi Kawachi, "A New Backlash Against American Influence," *Japan Echo*, April 1998, pp. 44–47; and Philip Courtenay, "Versions of Capitalism Vie for Ascendancy in Asia," *Free China Journal*, March 19, 1999, p. 7.

21. Richard N. Haass and Robert E. Litan, "Globalization and Its Discontents, Navigating the Dangers of a Tangled World," *Foreign Affairs* 77.3 (May–June 1998), pp. 2–6.

10: The Consequences of Empire

1. *Los Angeles Times*, November 24, 1998. See also Jim Mann, "Foreign Policy of the Cruise Missile," *Los Angeles Times*, December 23, 1998.

2. Charles Maechling Jr., "Erratic U.S. 'Leadership' on Display in Iraq Crisis," *International Herald Tribune*, March 23, 1998.

3. Mark Yost, "Tragedy Shouldn't Drive U.S. from Okinawa," *Asian Wall Street Journal*, December 18, 1995.

4. Quoted in Andrew J. Bacevich and Lawrence F. Kaplan, "Battle Wary," *New Republic*, May 25, 1998, p. 20.

5. *Los Angeles Times*, November 13, 1998.

6. *The Rise and Fall of the Great Powers*, 1988, p. 513.

7. Alfred Vagts, *A History of Militarism* (New York: W. W. Norton, 1937), p. 11.

8. David P. Calleo, *Beyond American Hegemony: The Future of the Western Alliance* (New York: Basic Books, 1987), p. 142.

9. Ashok K. Nath, "A Crisis That Has a Beginning, but No End," *Asia 21*, (April 1999), pp. 29–32.

10. "Nike to Raise Entry-Level Wages for Indonesian Workers," Dow Jones Newswires, March 23, 1999. See also Mark Gibney, "Treat Overseas Workers Fairly—by Law, Not Whim," *Los Angeles Times*, May 25, 1998.

11. *Los Angeles Times*, February 2, 1999.

12. *Los Angeles Times*, January 25, 1998.

13. Jacob Margolies, "Bad Loans a Great Opportunity for Investment Adviser," *Daily Yomiuri*, August 4, 1998.

14. Dean Calbreath, "Thai Buys: San Diego Investors Join Land Rush Started by Asia's Fiscal Woes," *San Diego Union-Tribune*, December 9, 1998.

15. James Flanigan, "Steel's Protest on Imports Warns of Dangers to All," *Los Angeles Times*, November 8, 1998; and Leslie Wayne, "American Steel at the Barricades," *New York Times*, December 10, 1998.

16. Mark Magnier, "Japan's Change in Rice Policy Could Hurt State's Exports," *Los Angeles Times*, December 18, 1998.

INDEX